Creating Actior Insights Using CRM Analytics

Learn how to build insightful and actionable data analytics dashboards

Mark Tossell

BIRMINGHAM—MUMBAI

Creating Actionable Insights Using CRM Analytics

Copyright © 2021 Packt Publishing

Publishing Product Manager: Reshma Raman

Senior Editor: Mohammed Yusuf Imaratwale

Content Development Editor: Nazia Shaikh, Joseph Sunil

Technical Editor: Devanshi Ayare

Copy Editor: Safis Editing

Project Coordinator: Aparna Ravikumar Nair

Proofreader: Safis Editing

Indexer: Hemangini Bari

Production Designer: Shyam Sundar Korumilli

First published: December 2021

Production reference: 2140622

Published by Packt Publishing Ltd.
Livery Place
35 Livery Street
Birmingham
B3 2PB, UK.

ISBN 978-1-80107-439-1

www.packt.com

Contributors

About the author

Mark Tossell is passionate about solving problems and improving processes using data. CRM Analytics (Einstein Analytics) and Tableau, powered by AI, are the tools of his trade. He is a proud wearer of the Salesforce Gold Hoodie and a recipient of the inaugural APAC Awesome Admin award. He is also a Trailhead learning addict, having earned over 420 badges. In addition, he is honored to be a CRM Analytics Ambassador and a Salesforce Partner solution engineer.

Mark lives in Sydney, Australia, with his wife, Christina, and son, Adam.

About the reviewers

Gayathri Shivakumar has over 23 years of experience in the IT Industry, with around 10 years' experience in Salesforce technology. She holds a double master's in computer science and is working on a doctorate in data science. A data nerd and a proud mom of two beautiful daughters, she is passionate about mentoring young minds.

I am pleased to have donned this hat for the first time as a book reviewer for this book on a subject that is very close to my heart. Thank you, Mark Tossell, for giving me this wonderful opportunity. Also, a note of thanks to my family and friends who have supported me in this endeavor.

Mustapha El Hassak is a **Salesforce Certified Technical Architect (CTA)** and 15x Salesforce Certified. He has 11+ years of experience working in IT and is currently working as a Salesforce Senior Technical Architect. He has also been a technical reviewer for the book *Talend Open Studio Cookbook*.

I thank Almighty Allah, who showers his blessings and showed me the right path, which paved the way to the successful completion of this work. I express my special thanks to my parents, Khadija and Hassan, my brother, Saïd, and my sister, Asmae, for their continued support. I also express my infinite gratitude to my wife Halima for her patience and encouragement. Finally, a big thanks to my little daughter, Sirine, and my little boy, Yahya.

Table of Contents

Section 2: Building Datasets in CRMA

3
Connecting Your Data Sources

4
Building Data Recipes

Section 3: How to Build Awesome Analytics Dashboards in CRMA

8
Building Your First CRMA Dashboard

9
Advanced Dashboard Design and Build

10

To Code or Not to Code?

11

Best Practices in Dashboard Design Using CRMA

Section 4: From Data To Insight To Action

12
Embedding and Actioning Your Insights

Other Books You May Enjoy

Index

Preface

CRM Analytics, formerly Einstein Analytics, is a powerful and versatile data analytics platform that enables organizations to extract, combine, transform, and visualize their data to create valuable business insights. Despite being a highly capable tool and in high demand in the industry, proficiency in CRM Analytics is hard to find.

Creating Actionable Insights Using CRM Analytics provides a hands-on approach to CRM Analytics implementation and associated methodologies that will have you up and running and productive in no time. The book provides you with detailed explanations of essential concepts to help you to gain confidence and become competent in using the CRM Analytics platform for data extraction, combination, transformation, visualization, and action. As you make progress, you'll understand what CRM Analytics is and where it provides business value. You'll also learn how to bring your data together in CRM Analytics, build datasets and lenses for data analysis, create effective analytics dashboards for visualization and consumption by end users, and build dashboard actions that take the user from data to insight to action with ease.

By the end of this Tableau book, you'll be able to solve business problems using CRM Analytics and design, build, test, and deploy CRM Analytics analytics dashboards efficiently.

Who this book is for

This book is for data analysts, business analysts, BI professionals, and Salesforce users who want to explore the capability and features in CRM Analytics. Basic knowledge of Salesforce and data analytics is assumed to get the most out of this book.

What this book covers

Chapter 1, What Is CRM Analytics and Where Can You Use It?, begins right at the start – what is CRMA? This is vital because it will make sure you begin on the right footing with a correct understanding of the fundamentals of CRMA. You will also evaluate your business or organization and identify how and where CRMA will provide value in terms of a business outcome. This includes reviewing business challenges, problems, and opportunities, considering how data and analytics could impact these, as well as evaluating the limitations of existing systems, processes, and people.

Chapter 2, Developing Your First OOTB Analytics App in CRMA, provides you with step-by-step instructions on how to implement and configure CRMA from scratch, including all the basic setup requirements. Once achieved, the TRCM environment will be ready for the installation, customization, and creation of CRMA Analytics apps. You will learn about the definition, makeup, and application of an OOTB Analytics app in CRMA. You will then be guided in how to install the app, configure the app via the wizard, customize it, and test the analytics. Common obstacles and questions will also be addressed.

Chapter 3, Connecting Your Data Sources, explains the various capabilities and limitations of CRMA in bringing in data from Salesforce, flat files, data warehouses, and other sources. You will learn how to connect Salesforce data objects with CRMA and create datasets. You will also learn how to bring a flat file into CRMA.

Chapter 4, Building Data Recipes, defines and explains the process of creating a data recipe in CRMA. Then, beginning with the dataset created in *Chapter 3, Connecting Your Data Sources*, you will learn to apply filters, calculations, and transformations to that data in order to create a new dataset that meets the requirements of your business use case.

Chapter 5, Advanced ETL Using CRMA Data Prep, guides you on how to use the CRMA data flow editor to its full capability. This is where the more powerful ETL work is explained and demonstrated, teaching you how to combine multiple sources of data, perform complex transformations and calculations, and create accurate, complete datasets for analytics.

Chapter 6, CRMA Lenses – Diving into Your Data One Click at a Time, shows you what a lens is (essentially a query plus a visualization), and how it is a powerful tool for understanding, testing, debugging, and showcasing data. You will also learn how lenses are the building blocks of analytics dashboards in CRMA.

Chapter 7, Security in CRM Analytics, explains in detail how to secure your CRMA data. You will be given an overview of CRMA security and then walked through each of the tools available in CRMA to determine who sees what data.

Chapter 8, Building Your First CRMA Dashboard, walks you through the essentials of building a dashboard in CRMA using the dashboard editor by gathering and assembling the required components into a complete visualization.

Chapter 9, Advanced Dashboard Design and Build, guides you in how to take advantage of the more advanced features and capabilities of CRMA – including page animations, SAQL, bindings, and more. By the end of the chapter, you will have the tools to create a complex, advanced CRMA dashboard.

Chapter 10, *To Code, or Not to Code?*, guides you in how to determine when code is required, since one of the greatest challenges faced by CRMA developers is to know when to use code (JSON, SAQL), and when not to code.

Chapter 11, *Best Practices in Dashboard Design Using CRMA*, explains great dashboard design by explaining in detail what you ought to build, the established principles of effective dashboard design, and the best practices when designing, building, and deploying CRMA dashboards.

Chapter 12, *Embedding and Actioning Your Insights*, shows you how to go from great visuals to smart decisions. This chapter will explain how record actions in CRMA dashboards enable users to action data directly in CRM.

To get the most out of this book

You will need the following to successfully execute the instructions in this book:

- The latest version of the Google Chrome browser (Chrome is the preferred browser when working with CRM Analytics)
- A working email address

This book assumes a high-level understanding of the following:

- Relevant business use cases for data analytics and business insights
- What Salesforce is and how it works
- What data sources are available in your business or organization

Software/hardware covered in the book	Operating system requirements
Salesforce and CRM Analytics	Windows, macOS, or Linux The latest version of the Google Chrome browser

Download the color images

We also provide a PDF file that has color images of the screenshots and diagrams used in this book. You can download it here: `https://static.packt-cdn.com/downloads/9781801074391_ColorImages.pdf`.

Conventions used

There are a number of text conventions used throughout this book.

`Code in text`: Indicates code words in the text, database table names, folder names, filenames, file extensions, pathnames, dummy URLs, user input, and Twitter handles. Here is an example: "Predicates can filter the data based on the `Manager` field in the `User` object."

A block of code is set as follows:

```
'Owner.Role.Roles' == "$User.UserRoleId" || 'OwnerId' ==
"$User.Id" || 'Account.OwnerId' == "$User.Id"
```

Bold: Indicates a new term, an important word, or words that you see on screen. For instance, words in menus or dialog boxes appear in **bold**. Here is an example: "In the **Setup Quick Find** box, enter `Analytics`, and then click **Settings**."

> **Tips or Important Notes**
> Appear like this.

Get in touch

Feedback from our readers is always welcome.

General feedback: If you have questions about any aspect of this book, email us at `customercare@packtpub.com` and mention the book title in the subject of your message.

Errata: Although we have taken every care to ensure the accuracy of our content, mistakes do happen. If you have found a mistake in this book, we would be grateful if you would report this to us. Please visit `www.packtpub.com/support/errata` and fill in the form.

Piracy: If you come across any illegal copies of our works in any form on the internet, we would be grateful if you would provide us with the location address or website name. Please contact us at `copyright@packt.com` with a link to the material.

If you are interested in becoming an author: If there is a topic that you have expertise in and you are interested in either writing or contributing to a book, please visit `authors.packtpub.com`.

Share Your Thoughts

Once you've read *Creating Actionable Insights Using CRM Analytics*, we'd love to hear your thoughts! Scan the QR code below to go straight to the Amazon review page for this book and share your feedback.

https://packt.link/r/1-801-07439-9

Your review is important to us and the tech community and will help us make sure we're delivering excellent quality content.

Section 1: Getting Started with CRM Analytics

This section will help you have a clear understanding of what CRMA is and what it is used for, and how to identify suitable business use cases. You will successfully implement and configure CRMA in preparation for the learning and development that follows.

This section comprises the following chapters:

- *Chapter 1, What Is CRM Analytics and Where Can You Use It?*
- *Chapter 2, Developing Your First OOTB Analytics App in CRMA*

1
What Is CRM Analytics and Where Can You Use it?

CRM Analytics (CRMA), formerly known as Einstein Analytics, is the business insights and data analytics platform that Salesforce launched in 2014. With a powerful framework to action insights directly in CRM and a variety of native connectors to ingest data from external sources, CRMA is a unique offering in the world of **Business Intelligence (BI)**.

As you can infer from the title, this chapter will introduce you to CRMA – what it is, how it works, and what it can do. We will begin by discussing data analytics from the perspective of CRMA and investigate what makes this platform different. As there are a great many BI platforms out in the digital world, you need to understand the unique place of CRMA in the data landscape and the Salesforce ecosystem.

Once you have completed this chapter, regardless of your current understanding of CRMA, you should have a good initial grasp of the platform. Whether you are a business analyst, a Salesforce administrator, or an advanced business user, this chapter will help you succinctly communicate the essentials of CRMA to your colleagues.

In this chapter, we are going to cover the following topics:

- The importance of data analytics
- What is CRMA?
- What is CRMA used for?
- How can you excel at data analytics with CRMA?

The importance of data analytics

The timing of this book could not be more appropriate – consider what Gartner recently had to say about the impact of COVID-19 upon the world around us:

"From crisis to opportunity, the role of data and analytics is expanding and becoming more strategic and mission-critical…Massive disruption, crisis, and the ensuing economic downturn are forcing companies to respond to previously unimaginable demands to resource optimize, reinvent processes and rethink products, business models, and even their very purpose. Only resilient, nimble, and creative organizations will survive and thrive."

(https://www.gartner.com/en/doc/718161-top-10-trends-in-data-and-analytics-2020)

Read that again:

"…the role of data and analytics is expanding and becoming more strategic and mission-critical…"

Businesses and organizations must become excellent at data analytics. They must excel at gathering, understanding, sharing, and actioning data. The current global pandemic has caused widespread uncertainty and unrest and has left many organizations in a precarious state. Misgivings about the global economy and fear of ongoing illness, as well as the closure of international and domestic borders, have all contributed to fragile mindsets and anxious cultures. The economic downturn, digital disruption, and growing competition have created an environment where businesses and organizations cannot ignore or minimize the value of data and insights. Data analytics has become imperative.

However, in my experience, very few organizations excel at gathering, understanding, sharing, and actioning data. Even in those organizations that create and maintain functional data analytics, it is estimated that as many as 75% of users do not use them regularly. Leaders and team members, as one of our clients once put it, are "flying blind." We certainly are not lacking information today. I think that most people will agree, though, that we are suffering from *information overload* – we are *drowning* in data! Data can be both a blessing and a curse – a help and a hindrance. After years of working in the data analytics industry and speaking with many businesses and organizations, it has become apparent to me that the subject of data insights is a frustrating one for many. What should be a great boon for the organization is, in fact, a burden.

CRMA has the power to change all this – if it's well understood, correctly implemented, and rightly used.

One such example is that of our client. 18 months ago, they were drowning in data but starving for insights. UA had terabytes of information spread across multiple systems and clouds, and actionable insights were very difficult to obtain. For a data-driven organization such as UNICEF, this was a source of great frustration. However, with the expertise of their internal team, the power of CRMA, and the help of our analytics experts and Visioneer360, the situation was drastically turned around. It can be done!

The key to going from data to insight to action is data analytics.

Data, in its raw, unprocessed form, contains the ingredients of a story – ingredients that are not of much use if they're not combined into a data "recipe" to create a story.

What do I mean by a **data story**? A data story is when information is processed and presented in such a way that it recites a narrative about a situation and draws meaningful conclusions for the reader. There are a plethora of diverse mediums and tools by which data stories can be presented, but the result of a story is actionable insight. I often express this in my three-word mantra:

Data $\longrightarrow$ Insight $\longrightarrow$ Action

Figure 1.1 – The three-word mantra

Organizations do not lack data – they lack insights into that data, and they are largely unable to obtain the true value for their data.

Every organization has data. Some organizations have insights into their data. Very few organizations action data insights.

The challenge, then, is data analytics. This is where CRMA comes in – it has the potential to *transform data*, *visualize insights*, and *enable action*.

Perhaps my story will provide some context and insight here. As a self-taught Salesforce business analyst, responsible for implementing and customizing Financial Services Cloud at a financial planning business, I was fortunate to work with a data-driven team and leadership. One of the primary drivers for implementing Salesforce was the vision for actionable business insights. This journey involved data remediation, cultural change, and analytics builds, among other things. Once the Salesforce Reports and Dashboards were up and running and were being used by the team members and leadership, the power of data insights began to be realized. However, the CEO wanted to take this to the next level and run their weekly management meetings only from Salesforce reports – no more slides and spreadsheets!

This ambitious goal required extending my skills into more advanced reporting tools, so we settled on purchasing CRMA licenses. It took some time to learn the tool and build useful dashboards, but the result was impressive. The CRMA dashboards were shared during the weekly management meetings, and the attendees were able to drill into the data and make business decisions based on live information. It was a game-changer, and I was personally hooked on the power, versatility, and actionability of CRMA.

What, then, do you need to gain value from your data, to obtain actionable business insights? Broadly speaking, there are five requirements:

- The right data, of a sufficient quality
- Clearly defined business goals
- A capable data analytics tool
- Skilled individuals to create the data stories
- Organizational commitment to consume, action, and improve the insights

As a brief aside, no one has perfect data, of course, and one advantage of data analytics is its ability to evaluate data quality and plan remediation. However, there is a point where poor data quality and completeness will hinder the usefulness of analytics dashboards to the point where time is better spent on remediation rather than analysis.

Now that we have an understanding of the importance of data analytics, we are going to dive into the subject of this book – CRMA. Why, then, was CRMA formerly known as Einstein Analytics?

What is CRMA and what is it used for?

By the end of this section, you should have a good grasp of what we are referring to when we speak of CRMA, and how it is used in the real world.

The questions *what is CRMA?* and *what is it is used for?* will be answered in the following sub-sections.

What is CRMA?

CRMA is not a Salesforce app – CRMA is a data analysis and business insights platform with integrated machine learning insights from Einstein Discovery.

To expand upon the high-level summary shown in *Figure 7.1*, CRMA is a platform that combines the following features:

- Native, two-way integration with the Salesforce CRM platform.
- On-platform data extraction, combination, and transformation in the data manager.
- External connectivity to a variety of other platforms and cloud storage providers.
- Data visualization, analysis, and exploration.
- A data action framework to enable decision-making based on insights.
- Embedded intelligence from the Salesforce Einstein platform, such as Einstein Sentiment analysis.
- Insights can be shared in various ways, such as Salesforce Chatter, URL generation, and downloads.
- On-dashboard notifications to alert users when certain criteria are met.
- A mobile TRCM Analytics App.
- CRMA/Einstein Analytics APIs and SDKs.
- Various data security tools to mask incoming data and restrict/filter outgoing insights as required.

At a technical level, as far as architecture goes, here are some details:

- In CRMA, data is searched for using an inverted index that enables fast query results – datasets containing up to a billion rows can be queried in seconds.
- CRMA data is loaded into a non-relational store via a dynamic, horizontally scalable key-value pair approach.

- The CRMA workflow engine is a software application that is designed to help users enforce a series of recurring tasks that make up a "business process" or "workflow." It applies limited transformations upon data ingestion but largely stores information in its original form.

- Data is consumed and stored in a non-relational inverted index as key-value pairs. These key-value pairs only store non-null data values, which improves efficiency and speed.

- CRMA's query engine employs techniques such as vector encoding, differential encoding, and incremental encoding to compress data and perform efficient and faster queries on compressed data.

- Quantitative data is queried in a columnar store in RAM across Salesforce's cloud.

- CRMA provides Einstein Analytics Actions, which allow you to seamlessly go from question to answer to action without logging into a separate solution – such as creating a task, updating a record, creating a case, posting to Chatter, and more!

- Heavy compression, optimization algorithms, and parallel processing fast and efficient queries on very large datasets.

- Mobile-first design – CRMA enables data creation, analysis, and action directly from mobile devices.

- Einstein Analytics is an open, scalable, and extensible platform. Being built on the secure infrastructure of Salesforce, the world's top CRM, CRMA provides easy-to-use APIs that enable deep relationships with other tools and platforms.

- Salesforce has worked with Informatica, MuleSoft, Snowflake, and other vendors to build interfaces with BI and data solutions out of the box.

- CRMA delivers fast-rendering graphics that connect the relationships between views of data by drawing SVG graphics within the browser and using an animation engine faceting and filtering. This demands fewer resources from the user's device or the server.

- The CRMA platform is built upon Salesforce's trusted, multilayered approach to data availability, privacy, and security.

Here is a visual representation of Salesforce and the CRMA architecture:

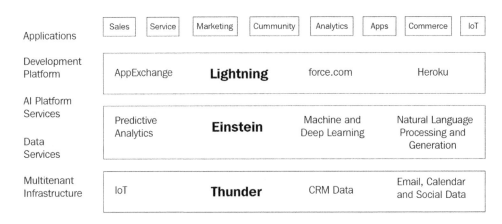

Figure 1.2 – Salesforce and the CRMA architecture

The following is a simple graphic that explains how CRMA and Einstein Discovery (referred to as **Einstein Analytics Plus**) fit within a typical data architecture that includes Salesforce:

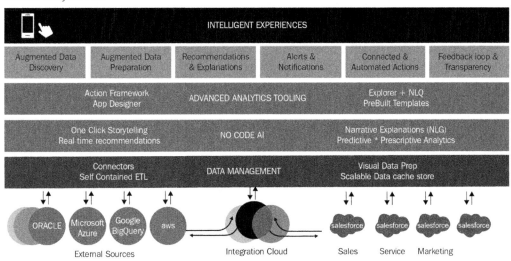

Figure 1.3 – The CRMA and Salesforce technology stack

As you can see, the business outcome of CRMA is intelligent experiences built upon the stable, secure platform of the world's #1 CRM, Salesforce.

What is CRMA used for?

CRMA is used to *extract*, *aggregate*, *transform*, and *visualize* data. That is, it is used to take raw data, process it with the aid of business acumen, and tell a story.

For example, I created the following CRMA dashboard for a business in the property development space with dummy data:

Figure 1.4 – A CRMA dashboard that visualizes property development information

What is the purpose of this dashboard? How did I use TRCM in this use case?

1. I loaded the raw data tables into CRMA.

2. I combined these tables into one dataset using CRMA.

3. I transformed the data to prepare it for visualization in CRMA.

4. I used TRCM to design, build, and share the analytics dashboard.

5. I was able to "slice and dice" the data, diving into the information to make sense of it and tell a story, with CRMA.

Now, CRMA is just one of several data analytics tools in the Salesforce ecosystem. Some others are as follows:

- **Salesforce Reports and Dashboards**
- **Einstein Analytics**
- **Tableau**
- **Datorama**
- **Pardot analytics**
- **Marketing analytics**

The main three that we are concerned about in the context of this book are **Salesforce Reports and Dashboards**, **CRMA**, and **Tableau**. How do these analytics work together? Here is a simple overview:

Salesforce Reports and Dashboards	Tableau CRM	Tableau
Salesforce Reports and Dashboards are your default tool for a quick win with real time data.	Most of your users are already in Salesforce.	Your insights will be shared among Salesforce and non-Salesforce users, or business users that are not using Salesforce
They are your "go-to" option for a quick win based upon real-time data.	You want to quickly embed and action analytics in Salesforce.	You want the option of an on-premises architecture.
Quick to configure.	You are looking for easily embedded AIs and supervised machine learning.	You require remote, federated queries.
	You want a native two-way integration with Salesforce.	You need more flexibility around how the BI platform fits in with the business tech stack.

Figure 1.5 – How do the three main Salesforce analytics tools work together?

Which analytics tool should you use for which business use case?

Here are some questions to consider (see https://marktossell.
com/2020/06/20/tableau-or-einstein-analytics-which-is-best-
for-you/ and https://marktossell.com/2020/10/31/are-you-
confused-about-einstein-tableau-and-tableaucrm-read-this/ for
more detailed information):

- Who is going to use the business insights?
- Where are they going to view and action the insights?
- How will they share those insights with others?
- How much of the data for the dashboards is stored in Salesforce?
- Where is the external data stored?
- How will external data be connected to the BI tool?
- What in-house resources will work on the analytics tool?
- What platforms are users accustomed to using?
- How many of the data consumers are Salesforce CRM users?
- What BI platform license structure suits the business best?

The following diagram shows a very simple way of looking at the comparison between
CRMA and Tableau:

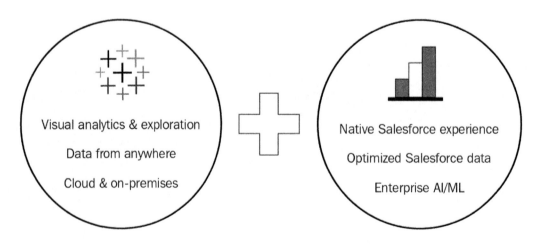

Figure 1.6 – A simple comparison of Tableau and CRMA

Now, you might be wondering, how are CRMA and Tableau different? The following tables will help you make sense of the differences between the two platforms:

Differences and Synergies in the Architecture

Architecture	Einstein Analytics	Tableau
Cloud	✔	✔
On-premises	✖	✔
Provides a persistent, dedicated data store	✔	✔
Connectors	✔	✔
Remote, federated queries	✖	✔
Action framework	✔	✖
Templated apps/templates	✔	✖
Data discovery and predictions	✔	✖
Marketing intelligence	✖	✖

Figure 1.7 – Differences and synergies in the architecture for Tableau and CRMA/Einstein Analytics

When it comes to Salesforce Reports and Dashboards, how do you know when you need to upgrade to CRMA? Here are some points to guide you:

- You need to incorporate external data.
- You want contextual record actions to action insights in CRM.
- You want to use embedded analytics.
- You require greater customizability.
- You wish to use the Analytics mobile app.
- You need predictive insights and augmented analytics.
- You want to take advantage of CRMA pages.
- You need advanced trending and waterfall charts.
- You require flexible and powerful data modeling in the data flow editor and data recipes.
- You want superior performance for up to 10 billion rows.

Real-life examples of how to use CRMA

The best way to communicate how CRMA can be used in a business is by way of four real-world case studies. The four case studies that we will go through are as follows:

- Out-of-the-box sales analytics
- Student success insights for higher education
- Property development insights
- Marketing attribution analytics

Out-of-the-box sales analytics

A very common and highly effective use case for CRMA is the suite of sales analytics standards that are available as a standard template. With some simple configuration, you can have powerful insights into your Sales Cloud data within minutes. These insights include the following dashboards:

- **Sales Analytics Home**: Provides an overview of high-level **key performance indicators (KPIs)**.
- **Leaderboard**: Gives leaders a summary of the team's and individuals' performance, including quota attainment, pipe coverage, bookings, pipe generation, closed-won business, average sales cycle time, and sales activities.
- **Trending**: Analyze pipeline changes over time, including the beginning and end values of the pipe, as well as what's moved in and out.
- **Sales Stage Analysis**: Visualizes how deals have moved through stages of the sales process, revealing bottlenecks and at-risk opportunities.
- **Whitespace Analysis**: Identifies resell and upsell opportunities.
- **Executive Overview**: Sales executives can review the pipeline's status, the projected closing, and top deals by lead source, plus high-level views of sales and service performance.

You will learn more about this app in *Chapter 3, Connecting Your Data Sources*.

Student success insights for higher education

It was exciting for my team and me to collaborate with over 20 higher education institutions in the United States, including Harvard and Cornell universities, to employ the power of Einstein and CRMA to address some of their most pressing challenges. While there are many exciting opportunities to consider in the higher education space, we initially focused on the area of student success and persistence:

- If schools could identify warning signs for students before they failed to meet the criteria for persistence, the school could act proactively to assist the student.

- If schools could predictively identify students at high risk of not persisting, based on certain key characteristics of those students, then those students could be afforded an extra level of support right from the start.

- If smart systems could suggest what actions might help a student to persist, the school would be much more effective and efficient in enabling student success.

No one has been able to solve this problem, though many have tried. However, with the power of Einstein and CRMA, we have developed a successful MVP prototype for student success, and we are engaging several colleges to build this intelligent solution for them. Here are some screenshots of the Student Success **Persistence** tab:

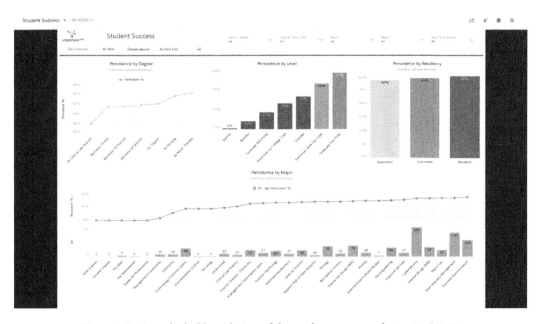

Figure 1.8 – Sample dashboard view of the student success solution in CRMA

The following is the Student Success **At Risk** tab:

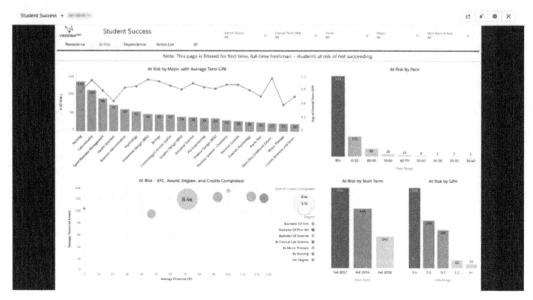

Figure 1.9 – Sample dashboard view from the student success solution in CRMA

The following is the Student Success **Action List** tab:

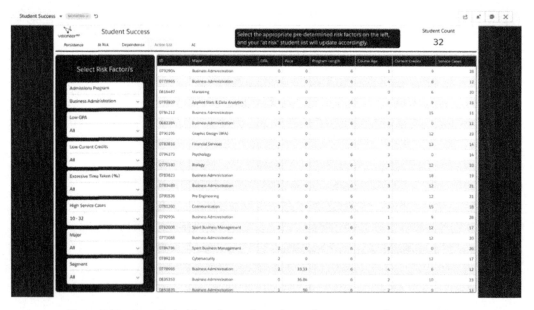

Figure 1.10 – Sample dashboard view from the student success solution in CRMA

For a video of this solution, see https://vimeo.com/329929308.

Property development insights

In this use case, the client was a Sydney apartment developer. They had a growing, thriving business, they were using Salesforce extensively, and they had bucket-loads of data, but they were unable to do the following:

- Quickly drill down into sales data using various variables.
- Perform actions from the analytics dashboard.
- Prioritize clients by the available equity and **loan to value ratio (LVR)**.
- See the total area and $ value of purchases versus target.
- See the trending total area and $ value of purchases.
- Project growth in 5 to 10 years for amounts reinvested.
- Present analytics to a client on a tablet that showed the current and projected state.

The CRMA platform, combined with their vision and our expertise, enabled us to build a solution that provided the client with insights that they had never seen before. They were finally able to go from data to insight to action.

Here are some screenshots from our property insights solution.

Here is the home page for the Property Development insights dashboard:

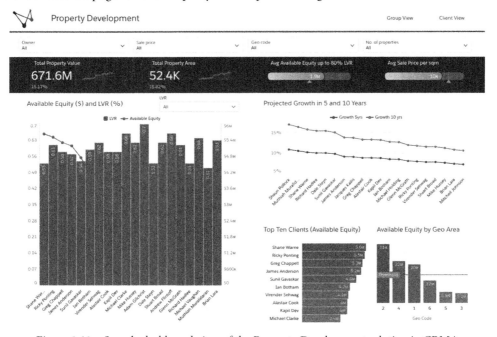

Figure 1.11 – Sample dashboard view of the Property Development solution in CRMA

This is what the view looks like for the user on the field:

Figure 1.12 – Sample dashboard view of the Property Development solution in CRMA

Marketing attribution analytics

We were asked by a marketing business in the health care space to build advanced analytics around marketing attribution, with the end goal of delivering a closed-loop attribution analytics solution. This was quite the challenge!

1. Our client was unable to show actual and projected return on marketing investment for their clients. The strategy was very hit-and-miss.

2. The client's customers had large amounts of data but were unable to utilize this data to make informed decisions around marketing channels.

3. Limited data analytics information was being manually extracted by the client on behalf of customers. These analytics did not drive intelligent business decisions.

4. Analytics was diagnostic and descriptive, but not predictive and prescriptive.

Using CRMA and Einstein, we built an innovative Analytics App that provides the following:

- Cutting-edge data analytics with integrated AI insights and predictions
- Intelligent recommendations from Einstein Discovery AI

The result enabled the client to drive channel efficiency and marketing optimization. The benefits included increased ROI on marketing investment and increased patient loyalty and enhanced patient experience. Let's check out some of the screenshots from this solution.

The following is the home page view:

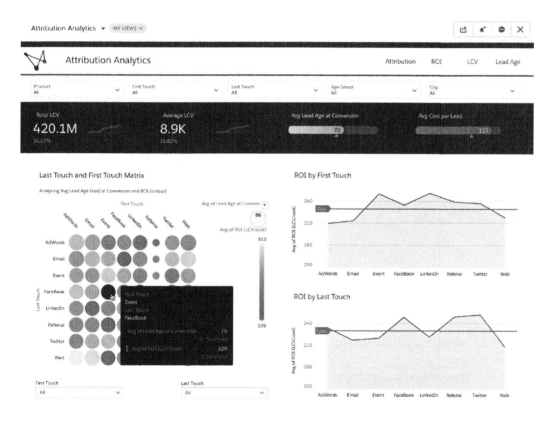

Figure 1.13 – Home page of the Attribution Analytics solution

The following is the ROI insights page view:

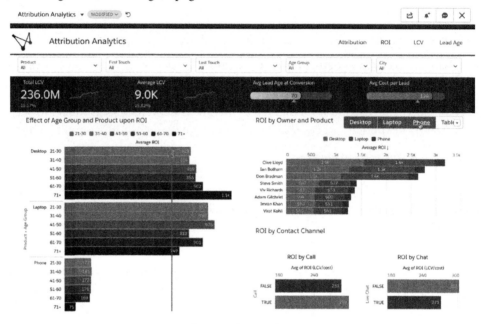

Figure 1.14 – ROI analytics in the Attribution Analytics solution

The following is the **lifetime customer value (LCV)** page view:

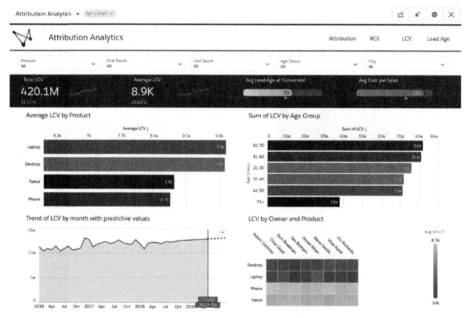

Figure 1.15 – LCV analytics in the Attribution Analytics solution

Other use cases for CRMA include insights into the following:

- Sales performance, such as actuals and forecast versus target.
- Lead conversion by lead source, region, and team member.
- ROI on marketing campaigns.
- Case management and service team performance.
- Global sales breakdown by region, territory, and country.
- Forecast sales by region and team.
- Customer attrition.
- Customer acquisition.
- Customer satisfaction.
- Supply chain performance, identifying bottlenecks, and opportunities.
- Financial services compliance with forward-looking analytics to identify clients at risk of breach.
- Higher education performance and student success.
- Opportunities for educational institutions to cross-sell and up-sell.
- White space analysis for sales organizations.
- Fundraising performance for **not-for-profit** (**NFP**) institutions.
- Donor segmentation for NFP appeals.
- Project management risks and issues.
- Resource assignment and optimization in professional services businesses.
- Geospatial data.
- Revenue, expenses, and profit, and many more!

Hopefully, this section has helped you understand how we can use CRMA to solve problems and grasp opportunities. Remember, it is all about **Data** -> **Insight** -> **Action**, as shown in *Figure 1.1*.

In the next section, we are going to examine your organization and evaluate how you are making use of data and analytics.

How can you excel at data analytics with CRMA?

As you consider what you have learned so far in this chapter, it is time to reflect on the state of data and analytics in your organization. Your data is an extremely valuable resource, one that should empower smart decision-making and guide organizational strategy. What *value* does your company data provide?

Ask yourself these questions and evaluate if your organization has any room for improvement:

- Do your leaders have accurate, current information at their fingertips to make informed decisions?

- Do you have one reliable source of information that you and your colleagues can access and depend upon? Or is information spread across multiple systems and platforms, and analyzed using a variety of tools?

- Is your team empowered and enabled by simple, actionable data analytics?

- Do you and your colleagues find yourselves gathering information from various places – such as cloud storage, CRM, spreadsheets, email, ERP, and so on – to bring it together in a spreadsheet and create the report you need to do your job?

- How do you share valuable insights and then action those insights? Is this simple and easy, or complex and difficult?

- What are your current strengths in the areas of data and analytics?

- What are your current weaknesses in the areas of data and analytics?

- What are your current opportunities in the areas of data and analytics?

- What are your current challenges in the areas of data and analytics?

- If platforms, people, and processes were not a barrier, where do you see your organization being in 12 months, in the context of using information to create actionable business insights? How likely is it that you will reach that ideal state?

I think I could summarize all of this into one simple question:

Does your organization excel at data analytics?

Honestly, in my experience across many industries and segments, most organizations do not excel. Many would not even be given a passing grade! Data analytics is a serious pain point for a typical business, whatever the size or vertical, and it is never solved by throwing money at it.

The good news is that CRMA is a powerful, comprehensive tool that can help your organization gain tremendous value from its information. How, exactly? Here are a few examples of what CRMA can do; think through these and see which ones most align with your goals and needs:

- Combine Salesforce and external data to create one trustworthy source of truth.
- Embed insights into the business process in Salesforce, empowering users to make faster, better decisions.
- Replace multiple, disconnected Salesforce reports with one cohesive and dynamic dashboard.
- Minimize or eliminate the ability to export reports from Salesforce into a tool such as Excel for aggregation, transformation, and visualization.
- Greatly simplify cross-object reporting.
- Inject real intelligence into the mix by way of the Einstein platform.
- Deliver great mobile analytics via the CRMA mobile app for iOS and Android.
- Outperform Salesforce Reports and Dashboards for large datasets.
- Enable the user to go from insight to action in just a few clicks, all on-platform and without leaving the CRMA dashboard.
- Model complex processes, combine multiple datasets, and incorporate complicated logic to create one comprehensive data source that drives real insight.

As we now move into the main content of this book, join me as we learn how CRMA can help transform your organization with the power of actionable business insights!

Summary

By now, you should have a clear understanding of the importance of data analytics and business insights in a pandemic-affected society. You have seen how CRMA, a powerful data analytics platform, integrates with Salesforce to facilitate actionable insights in any organization. You have also had the opportunity to evaluate the data analytics in your organization and see where CRMA can make a difference.

In the next chapter, we will get hands-on with CRMA and build our very first CRMA Analytics app.

Questions

Here are some questions to test your knowledge of this chapter:

- Define data analytics and what value it offers.

- Our goal is to go from data to insight to _____.

- Name five features of CRMA.

- How does CRMA differ from Tableau?

- What are five practical use cases for CRMA?

- How does CRMA provide value to your organization or clients?

- Does your organization *excel* at data analytics? If not, what is preventing it from doing so?

2
Developing Your First OOTB Analytics App in CRMA

What is a **Tableau Customer Relationship Management** (**CRMA**) analytics app? CRMA provides a variety of **out-of-the-box** (**OOTB**) analytics applications that get you started with data analytics for a variety of generic and industry-specific use cases, such as sales analytics or wealth management analytics. These apps provide prebuilt data flows and dashboards that can be configured to suit the use case and available data. OOTB apps are a great place to begin using and customizing CRMA analytics, and to get a feel for the CRMA **user interface** (**UI**), assets, and tools.

You have to walk before you can run. We are going to begin right at the start—setting up a trial CRMA **organization** (**org**), getting to know the CRMA environment, and learning basic asset definitions. We will then dive in and get our feet wet by creating and customizing our very first CRMA analytics app.

By the end of this chapter, you should have a detailed understanding of what an OOTB analytics app is in CRMA and be able to create and customize one in a **development** (**dev**) org. You should also be able to navigate the CRMA UI and use basic CRMA tools. In addition, the goal is to understand and appreciate the various CRMA assets, such as **lenses** and **stories**. We will also address some common questions and challenges in this process.

In this chapter, we will cover the following topics:

- Getting hands-on with your own CRMA environment
- What is a CRMA analytics app?
- Installing and configuring a CRMA analytics app
- Customizing a CRMA analytics app
- Common questions answered
- Troubleshooting

Technical requirements

You will need the following to successfully execute the instructions in this chapter:

- A laptop or desktop with internet access (a tablet or a phone is not sufficient)
- The latest version of the Google Chrome browser (Chrome is the preferred browser when working with CRMA)
- A working email address
- Link to CRMA dev org:

  ```
  https://developer.salesforce.com/promotions/orgs/
  analytics-de
  ```

Getting hands-on with your own CRMA environment

Let's first walk through the initial process of setting up a dev playground for CRMA so that you can use it to work along with me as we move along with the process of installing CRMA.

In order for you to get hands-on with the CRMA platform, you first need a sandbox environment that is yours to edit as you see fit—one that is already enabled for CRMA and is populated with sample data. This playground environment is known as an **Einstein Analytics-enabled Developer Edition org**. So, let's set this up.

Setting up your dev org

To sign up for and set up your dev org, follow these next steps:

1. Sign up here for your own Einstein Analytics-enabled Developer Edition org: `https://developer.salesforce.com/promotions/orgs/analytics-de`. The sign-up screen should look like this:

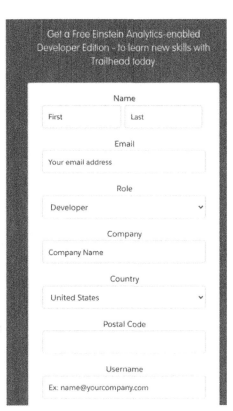

Figure 2.1 – Sign-up screen for dev org

2. Go ahead and fill out the form, and then select **Sign me up**. Note that your username will be in the form of an email address, but you will create a unique username that should not be your email address. Make something up that you can remember easily.

   Go to your email app, where you should see an email with a subject such as **Welcome to Salesforce: Verify your account**.

3. Save the **Uniform Resource Locator** (**URL**) and username somewhere safe, and click the button that says **Verify Account**. This will bring you to a page where you will create a password for the org and choose a security question. Fill this out and click on **Change Password**.

You will now arrive at the **Salesforce** home page for your dev org. It should look like this:

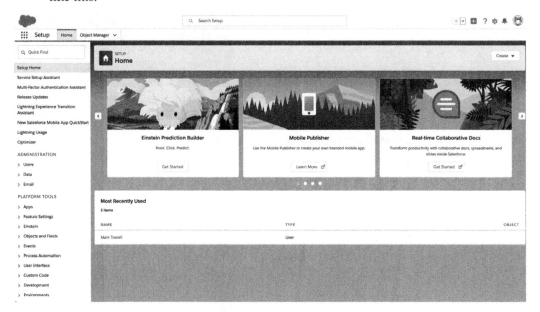

Figure 2.2 – Salesforce home page for the CRMA playground

> **Important Note**
>
> Note that this dev org is enabled for CRMA/Einstein Analytics, and is populated with enough dummy data to enable you to learn the ropes. If you are using your own environment, you'll need to make sure you have the necessary licenses, permissions, and settings. These are detailed at the end of this chapter in the *Common questions answered* section.

Let's now jump into the CRMA platform so that we can learn our way around the home page, understand the various asset and menu options, and later launch the OOTB analytics app creator.

4. Go to the **App Launcher** in the top left-hand corner and click on **Analytics Studio**, as per the following screenshot:

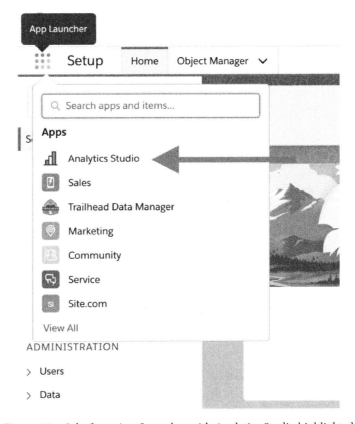

Figure 2.3 – Salesforce App Launcher with Analytics Studio highlighted

5.   You should now see your new happy place—the home page in **Einstein Analytics Studio**, as illustrated in the following screenshot:

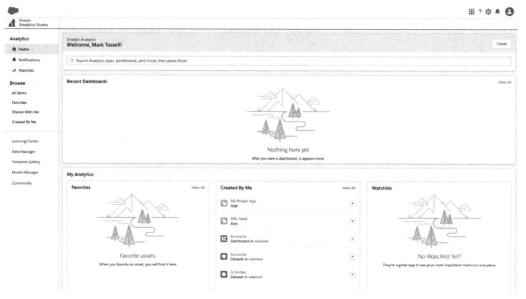

Figure 2.4 – Einstein Analytics Studio home page

Now that you have created a CRMA sandbox playground for your work, it's time to become familiar with the UI and assets that you will be using from now on.

Finding your way around the Analytics Studio home page

Now that we have successfully signed up for our happy place that is **Analytics Studio**, it will be worth exploring the **Analytics Studio** home page to get a better understanding of the different features present. So, let's go ahead and do that.

What do we have in our menu on the left-hand side? As you saw in *Figure 2.4*, there are a variety of options available on the left-hand side of the screen. Let's explore them next.

Summary of home page menu items

Here is a list of items that will be available on the home page:

- **Home**—The CRMA landing page that gives you access to your **Analytics Studio** assets.

- **Notifications**—CRMA notifications are listed here. When notifications are created in dashboards, you can manage them in this section.

- **Watchlist**—CRMA watchlist items are listed here. When watchlist items are created in dashboards, you can manage them in this section

- **All Items**—To be discussed in detail in the next section.

- **Favorites**—You can choose to make any CRMA asset a favorite, such as a dataset or a lens, and add it to this list for ease of access.

- **Shared With Me**—All items that others have shared with you are accessed here.

- **Created By Me**—All items that you create are accessed here.

- **Learning Center**—Links to various learning resources for CRMA users are listed here for ease of use.

- **Data Manager**—Data sources, datasets, and data tools are accessed here.

- **Template Gallery**—You can launch a new analytics app from a template here. This is explained in much more detail in this chapter.

- **Model Manager**—View and manage your **Einstein Discovery machine learning (ML)** models here. Note that **Einstein Discovery** ML is not covered in this book.

- **Community**—Links to the Trailblazer community, where you can collaborate with other CRMA trailblazers.

We will now look at one of these menu options in detail: **All Items**.

All Items

You will see several options and assets when you click on **All Items** under the **Browse** heading.

What are all these items on the home page? We call them CRMA assets. Let's find out a little about these now—there's much more detail to come! The following screenshot shows these assets:

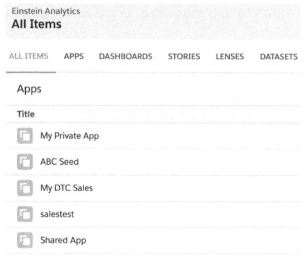

Figure 2.5 – CRMA assets as seen in a list view on the Einstein Analytics home page

Here are simple definitions of the items you see in the preceding screenshot:

- **Apps**—A container, similar to a file folder. This is used to organize and share analytics assets as required.

- **Dashboards**—A collection of data visualizations, metrics, tables, text, and other items, designed to tell a data story. You can create a new dashboard from scratch, edit an existing dashboard, or work from a template.

- **Stories**—An **Einstein Discovery** story (supervised ML insights and predictions). **Einstein Discovery** stories are used to create intelligent, predictive insights. Note that **Einstein Discovery** ML is not covered in this book.

- **Lenes**—A self-contained exploration of data; one query with a visualization or table. Lenses are created to explore data and save it for later use, share it with others, or add it to a dashboard.

- **Datasets**—A data table. Datasets are used to drive business insights. The creation and customization of datasets will be explained later in *Chapter 3, Connecting Your Data Sources*.

Search functionality

CRMA has a powerful search capability that enables users to quickly find the assets they are looking for, as seen here:

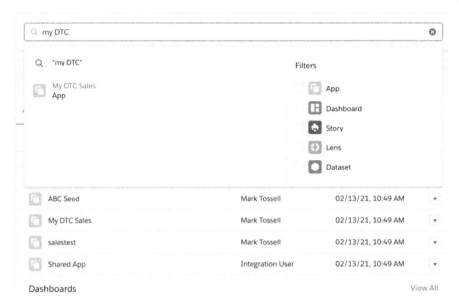

Figure 2.6 – CRMA search interface

For example, as you see in *Figure 2.6*, you can search for assets on the home page, such as the **My DTC** app, which contains datasets, lenses, and dashboards relating to **Direct to Consumer** (**DTC**) business data. If more than one asset appears in the results list, you can narrow your search using the filters on the right.

Analytics settings

You shouldn't need to make any changes to the TRCM settings yet, but should you need to at any time, you can find the settings by clicking on the settings gear icon in the top right-hand corner of the home page, as follows:

Figure 2.7 – How to reach the Settings tab

This is what the **Settings** tab for **Analytics** looks like:

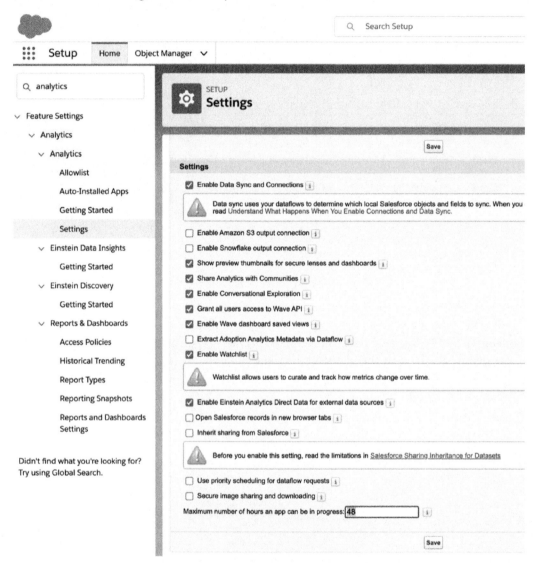

Figure 2.8 – Analytics Settings tab for CRMA

For example, you see in *Figure 2.8* that you can enable the Amazon **Simple Storage Service (S3)** output connector. This allows you to export **comma-separated values (CSV)** data from CRMA data preparation to an **Amazon** S3 bucket.

What is a CRMA analytics app?

Before we dive into the deployment and customization of a CRMA analytics app, we first need to understand what one exactly is. A CRMA application is essentially a container for four CRMA assets: **dashboards**, **stories**, **lenses**, and **datasets**. Here is a simple visual overview of a CRMA app:

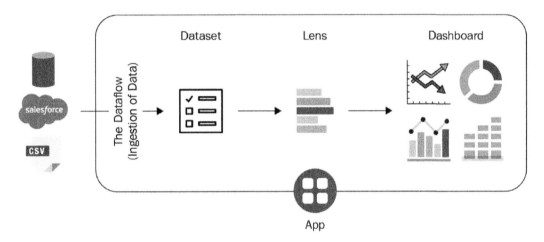

Figure 2.9 – Overview of a CRMA app

Open up the existing app, **My DTC Sales**, and you will see the previously listed assets, as well as a **Details** tab that displays system information.

As you explore the **My DTC Sales** app, and as we prepare to build our very own app, there are some basics you first need to grasp. There are three things to note about CRMA analytics apps, outlined as follows:

- **An app is secure**. That is, it can be restricted to the creator or can be opened up to other users. App-level security is one form of CRMA security.

- **An app can be shared**. There are three ways to share the contents of an app with others for collaboration, listed as follows:

  A. Give access via CRMA

  B. Post to a Chatter feed

  C. Share via the app URL

- **An app can be templated**. This is a powerful tool that enables the **Analytics** dashboard, data flow, and so on, to be packaged and deployed elsewhere.

> **Note**
>
> See here for more information about app templates: `https://`
> `developer.salesforce.com/docs/atlas.en-us.bi_`
> `dev_guide_wave_templates.meta/bi_dev_guide_wave_`
> `templates/bi_templatesdev_intro_wave_templates.htm.`

Installing and configuring a CRMA analytics app

Let's now go ahead and create our very first analytics app. We will follow the simple, intuitive OOTB process offered by CRMA, beginning with the **Create** button. The steps are listed as follows:

1. App creation
2. Basic app configuration
3. App exploration

Let's explore these steps in the following section.

App creation

Let's start by creating our app. To do so, follow these next instructions:

1. First, head up to the top right-hand corner of the page, click on **Create**, and select **App**, as illustrated in the following screenshot:

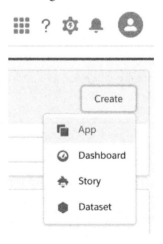

Figure 2.10 – How to begin the app creation process by using the Create button

You should now see a screen where you can select an app template. A template is a preconfigured, customizable app that is built for a particular use case.

2. Let's type `sales` in the search window and select the **Sales Analytics** app, as illustrated in the following screenshot:

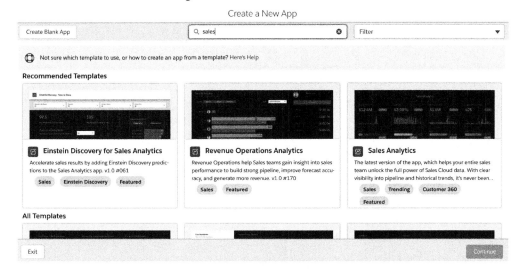

Figure 2.11 – Creating a new app

3. What then follows is a helpful synopsis of the app, along with technical details and sample dashboard screenshots. Feel free to explore them, then go ahead and click on **Continue**, which brings us to this dialog box:

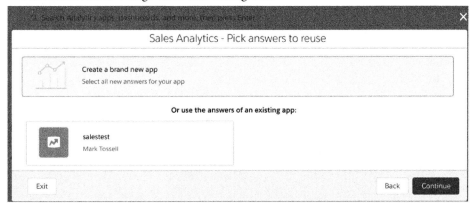

Figure 2.12 – Creating a brand new analytics app

4. Select **Create a brand new app** and click **Continue**. Einstein will then run a quick check to make sure you're ready to create an app; click on **Looks good, next**.

The app template is loaded and is ready to be configured to suit your unique requirements.

Basic app configuration

Let's begin with a basic setup; we will configure it soon. Proceed as follows:

1.   Choose **Basic** in the **Sales Analytics - Personalize** screen, as follows:

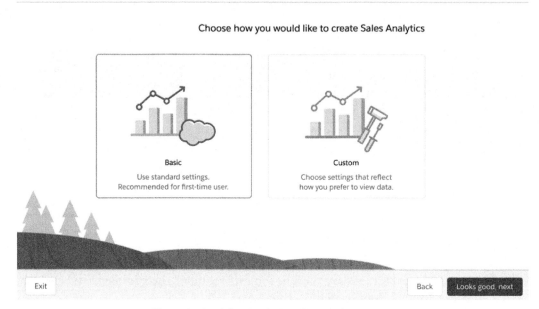

Figure 2.13 – Sales Analytics - Personalize screen

2.   Name the new analytics app, then click on **Create**.

You now have to wait a few minutes while Einstein works its magic. You should see the following screen in your browser:

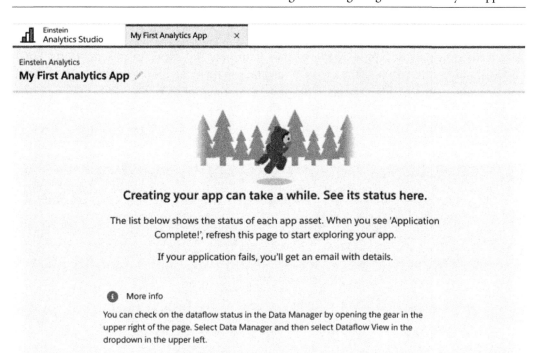

Figure 2.14 – App creation screen

Once this process is complete, your analytics app will then appear. In creating the new app, the CRMA platform has delivered an OOTB sales analytics application, complete with data flow (more about that later), prebuilt lenses and dashboards, and the datasets necessary to drive the insights.

Note that a new data flow, **My First Analytics App eltDataflow**, was implemented and run, creating 11 datasets, which you can see listed in your new app.

App exploration

Take some time now to explore the new app—your new app! Don't change anything, but click around the app, explore the assets, and get a feel for the environment. For example, try diving into the **PERFORMANCE** dashboard, which looks like this:

Figure 2.15 – OOTB PERFORMANCE dashboard

Play with the global filters at the top, click on charts to view and filter the information, watch how the table view at the bottom changes, and just get your hands dirty. You can also try creating your first lens—more about that later—by simply clicking on a dataset and experimenting, which will create something like this:

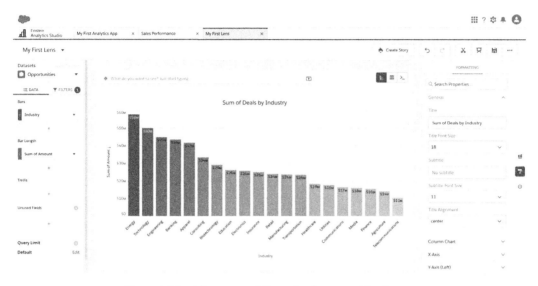

Figure 2.16 – A lens created from the Opportunities dataset

Now that you've created your first CRMA app, what if you want to change the way it is configured? What if you want to tweak the setup? Or even make sweeping changes? Read on!

Customizing a CRMA analytics app

By the end of this section, you should be able to edit the configuration of an app and thus customize it to a limited extent. These two steps are required for you to customize an app:

1. Change the app settings to custom settings.

2. Customize the detailed app settings.

Let's explore these steps in the following sections.

Changing the app settings to custom settings

Let's go into the app we created and edit the settings, as follows:

1. Click on **Reconfigure app** in the app, as per the following screenshot:

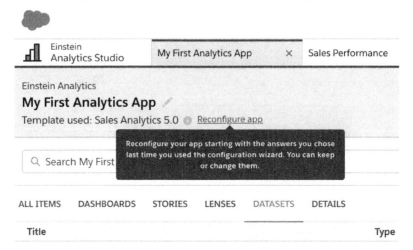

Figure 2.17 – Beginning the app reconfiguration process

2. Next, confirm that it's okay to overwrite existing settings and customizations by clicking the checkbox and hitting **Continue**. You will then see the **Sales Analytics - Personalize** screen again, so continue, and this time select custom settings when asked **Choose how you would like to create Sales Analytics**.

    You can add additional objects if desired, as illustrated in the following screenshot:

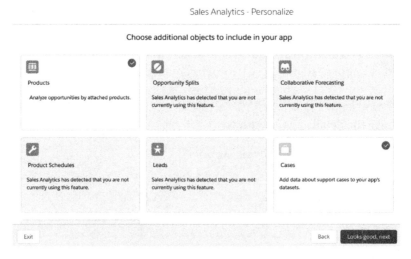

Figure 2.18 – Choosing additional objects for the analytics app

For example, if your organization uses product schedules in Salesforce, you can include that object in your analytics app by adding it here.

Customizing detailed app settings

We can now go in and start to customize the detailed settings that impact what users will see in their analytics. Let's walk through these dialog boxes and make some changes together.

The first box pertains to segmenting your customers; go ahead and edit these fields to change the app configuration, as follows:

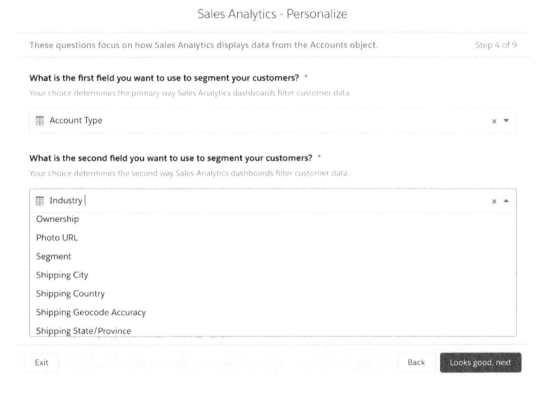

Figure 2.19 – Making changes to the customer segmentation settings

A series of dialog boxes will follow and you can make changes as you see fit, such as these:

- Customizing fields to segment geographies
- Customizing fields to segment products

- Controlling data visibility

- Adding additional fields to datasets and dashboards

Note that every OOTB analytics app has its own set of configuration options. When you get to the point where you are able to create your own app from scratch and build a custom template, you will create a new configuration wizard to suit.

Once this process of personalization is complete, you will be asked **Are you sure you want to reconfigure your app?** Absolutely! Click **OK**, then wait while your app is reconfigured.

Once the app has been rebuilt to your custom specifications, you can dive in and look around, and you will see your revised settings reflected in the assets.

Well done—you have created and customized your very first CRMA app!

However, what if the standard OOTB apps don't meet your requirements? What if you need far more bespoke analytics assets, such as a totally custom dashboard or a dashboard that brings in data from a **data warehouse**? Don't worry—CRMA is incredibly flexible, and your questions will be answered in the following chapters.

Common questions answered

As you follow along in this chapter and build your own app, you may encounter some challenges or have questions; four of the most common ones that are faced or asked are outlined next.

Which licenses do I need to build and use CRMA?

CRMA requires either **Einstein Analytics Growth** (without Discovery) or **Einstein Analytics Plus** (with Discovery) licenses. Information regarding your user licenses and **permission set licenses** (**PSLs**) can be found in **Setup**, as depicted in the following screenshot:

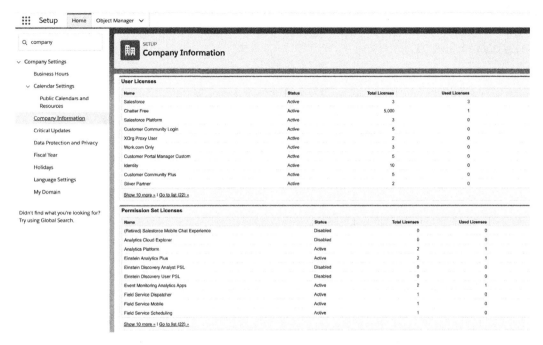

Figure 2.20 – Locating user license information in Setup

Salesforce auto-assigns an **Einstein Analytics Growth** permission set license to the user to whom you assign any CRMA permissions in your org. A PSL can also be manually assigned to users. The process of creating and assigning a permission set is detailed in the following steps:

1. In the **Setup** menu, under **Administration**, click **Users**, then **Permission Sets**, and then click **New**.

2. Associate the new permission set with a PSL. You must have purchased a CRMA license before you can select any PSL for CRMA.

3. Add permissions to the permission set from those available in the PSL.

4. Assign that permission set to users.

Which permissions do I need to access, build, and edit analytics apps?

There are two prebuilt permission sets included in the **Einstein Analytics Growth** license, detailed as follows:

- **Einstein Analytics Platform Admin**: Here, all permissions that are required to administer the CRMA platform are enabled. This includes permissions to enable the user to create CRMA templated and custom apps.

- **Einstein Analytics Platform User**: Here, all permissions that are required to use the CRMA platform and CRMA templated apps are enabled.

The basic setup involves choosing and assigning the prebuilt permission sets, via **Setup**. There are two prebuilt permission sets included in the **Einstein Analytics Plus** license, detailed as follows:

- **Einstein Analytics Platform Admin**: This set implements all the permissions that are required to administer the CRMA platform. This includes permissions to enable the user to create CRMA templated and custom apps.

- **Einstein Analytics Platform User**: This set implements all the permissions that are required to use the CRMA platform and CRMA templated apps.

Choosing and assigning the prebuilt permission sets via **Setup** is part of the basic setup, as shown in the following screenshot:

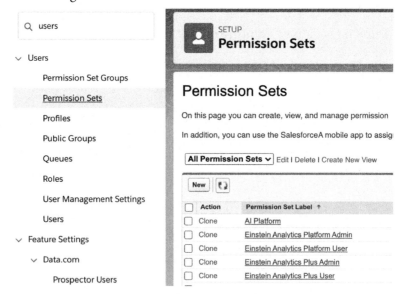

Figure 2.21 – Various CRMA permission sets, accessed via Setup/Users/Permission Sets

Under the appropriate permission set, add or remove assignments as required.

To create your own custom CRMA permission sets, employ an advanced setup by using the following link:

```
https://help.salesforce.com/articleView?id=sf.bi_help_setup_
advanced.htm&type=5
```

Highly detailed setup and configuration information can be found here:

```
https://help.salesforce.com/articleView?id=sf.bi_help_setup.
htm&type=5
```

How do I turn on CRMA in my org?

If CRMA has not been enabled, you can enable it by going to **Setup | Analytics | Getting Started**, and then switching it on.

Do AI and ML come with CRMA?

Einstein **artificial intelligence** (**AI**) in the form of supervised ML is known as **Einstein Discovery**. This comes with **Einstein Analytics Plus** licenses. However, **Einstein Discovery** is a complex tool that is often misunderstood and easily misused, and it is not covered in this book. Stay tuned!

Troubleshooting

In this section, we will quickly go over some problems that you might face when getting started with CRMA. These problems might sound simple, but they are a common occurrence for people who are getting familiar with the tool.

I can't find my CRMA app or assets

If you do not see your app on the CRMA **Analytics Studio** home page, click on the **All Items** option on the far left, under **Browse**, and you should see your app.

I can't get to the CRMA home page from the Salesforce home page

If you do not see **Analytics Studio** in the **App Launcher** in Salesforce, do the following:

1. Click on **View All**.
2. Search for **Analytics**.
3. Click on **Analytics Studio**.

You will then reach the CRMA home page.

Where is the link to reconfigure my CRMA app?

This link can easily be missed, as the font is very small. Look in the top left-hand corner of the browser page, underneath the CRMA logo, and you will see the app title. Below the title you will see **Template used: Sales Analytics 5.0**—a **Reconfigure app** link is to the right of this phrase, in blue.

You can also refer to *Figure 2.17* to understand exactly where the **Reconfigure app** link is located. The new app data flow fails during app creation.

If the data flow fails, the app creation process will not complete successfully. This failure may result in dashboard errors or other unexpected behavior. Do not edit the data-flow definition before it has run successfully at least once, or the app creation will be abandoned.

There are three possible causes for a failed data flow in this context, as outlined here:

1. **Field availability** or **org configuration**—Resolve this using the following steps:

   A. Fix the org configuration.
   B. Manually start the data flow via **Data Manager**.
   C. Click **Reset** in the app after the data flow completes.
   D. Complete the reset process without changing any of the options in the wizard.

2. **Data Sync**: If **Data Sync** is enabled, the creation of new templated apps may fail during data-flow execution because fields or objects used in the apps have not yet been replicated. This might also happen because a new version of the CRMA app includes additional default fields. Resolve this using the following steps:

   A. Open **Data Manager**.
   B. Go to the **Connect** tab.

C. Click **Run Now** under the **Sync scheduler**.

D. Click **Reset** in the app after the data flow completes.

E. Complete the reset process without changing any of the options in the wizard.

3. **App configuration**: If the app configuration is incorrect, the data flow can fail—for example, there may be incorrect field references or wrong options selected. Resolve this using one of the following steps:

A. Delete the app and create an entirely new version of the app.

B. Reset the app and choose different answers, as appropriate.

Summary

Now that we have completed the journey of creating and personalizing an OOTB CRMA analytics app, you should have a good grasp of what an analytics app is and how it works. You should have learned that CRMA app templates provide prebuilt data flows and dashboards that can be configured to suit the use case as required, and you should now be comfortable building and personalizing an app. Also, you should have gained a hands-on feel for the CRMA UI, assets, and tools, and should be confident in navigating the **Analytics Studio** home page. Finally, you have the *Troubleshooting* section as a handy reference tool, should you get stuck.

Some key takeaways that you should have gained are: first, a CRMA app is a container of CRMA assets, in the form of datasets, lenses, stories, and dashboards. Next, a TRCM app can be secured. Thirdly, a CRMA app can be shared with others in a variety of ways. Then, a CRMA app can be templated and reproduced in another environment. Lastly, you can deploy an OOTB CRMA app with standard settings or configure it to meet your personalized requirements.

In the next chapter, you will learn how to extract, connect, combine, transform, and register business data in order to create a useful dataset within CRMA.

Questions

Now try answering the following questions to test your knowledge:

- What is a CRMA asset? Give one example.

- How can a CRMA app be shared?

- What is a CRMA lens?

- True or false: A CRMA app is restricted to standard, OOTB settings.

- What is the purpose of the **Favorites** link on the side menu of the CRMA home page?

- What do you do if OOTB CRMA apps don't meet your requirements, even after you have customized them?

- How do you turn on CRMA in a Salesforce environment?

Section 2: Building Datasets in CRMA

In this section, you will learn to extract, connect, combine, transform, and register business data in order to create a useful dataset within CRMA.

This section comprises the following chapters:

- *Chapter 3, Connecting Your Data Sources*
- *Chapter 4, Building Data Recipes*
- *Chapter 5, Advanced ETL Using CRMA Data Prep*
- *Chapter 6, CRMA Lenses – Diving into Your Data, One Click at a Time*
- *Chapter 7, Security in CRM Analytics*

3
Connecting Your Data Sources

Now that you are familiar with the **CRM Analytics** (**TRCM**) user interface and have built your very first TRCM analytics app, you are ready to dive deeper into this highly capable business intelligence platform. In this chapter, you will learn how to ingest data into CRMA from various data sources. The diverse capabilities and limitations of CRMA in bringing in data from Salesforce, flat files, data warehouses, and other sources will be examined and explained, along with the frameworks and tools that enable this process. You will learn how to connect **Salesforce** data objects with CRMA and create datasets. You will also be instructed on how to bring a flat file into CRMA.

So, what will you be able to do by the end of this chapter? Well, first, you will clearly understand how to bring data into CRMA. Second, you will recognize the limitations of CRMA regarding data connections. Third, you will understand how to bring Salesforce data into CRMA. And, finally, you will be able to import flat file data into CRMA and use it to augment your Salesforce data.

In this chapter, we are going to cover the following topics:

- The capabilities of CRMA for data connections
- The limitations of CRMA for data connections
- Bringing Salesforce data into CRMA

- Augmenting your Salesforce data with flat files (CSVs)
- Common questions and challenges

Technical requirements

The following is required to successfully execute the instructions in this chapter:

- A laptop or desktop with internet access (a tablet or a phone is not sufficient).
- The latest version of the Google Chrome browser (Chrome is the preferred browser when working with CRMA).
- A working email address.
- Make sure you are logged in to your CRMA dev org, as demonstrated in *Chapter 2, Developing Your First OOTB Analytics App in CRMA*.

The capabilities of CRMA for data connections

CRMA offers you a great many options regarding the data that you can **extract**, **load**, **transform**, and **analyze**. This section will introduce you to the framework and tools that CRM Analytics provides for data ingestion and transformation. The resulting datasets will drive the lenses and dashboards that give your users the business insights they require.

In CRM Analytics, data connection and integration involve ingesting and preparing the Salesforce data and external data you want to visualize and investigate. External data is information that lives outside of the Salesforce org that is connected to your CRMA environment. This includes data from another Salesforce org, external applications, flat files, and other databases. After ingesting, connecting, and transforming the data, analytics users can analyze and explore it using CRMA lenses and dashboards.

Data preparation is the process of transforming your data into a form that is useful and helpful to the people consuming it. In order for you to understand how CRMA performs these operations, first, you must understand what datasets are, how they are designed, and how they are built. This will be explained in the following section.

Dataset definition, design, and build

First, what is a dataset? The following diagram provides a succinct definition:

What is a Dataset?

A data repository (storage) similar to file system storage but with a proprietary format and Algorithms flattening the data with inverted indexes (for volume and speed).

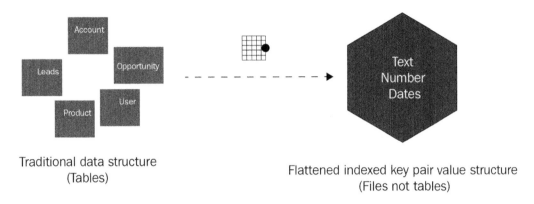

Traditional data structure
(Tables)

Flattened indexed key pair value structure
(Files not tables)

Figure 3.1 – What is a dataset?

A dataset is the building block for your analytics lenses and dashboards; it is the fountain of insights. As the old saying goes, *garbage in, garbage out*, and nowhere is this more accurate than in data analytics. As such, a great deal of your thought and effort when designing and building CRMA dashboards will be invested in the datasets that drive the metrics and visualizations.

So, how and where does CRMA extract, store, transform, and load data into datasets? The following diagram provides an overview of the CRMA data landscape and the diverse ways in which to ingest data inside the platform:

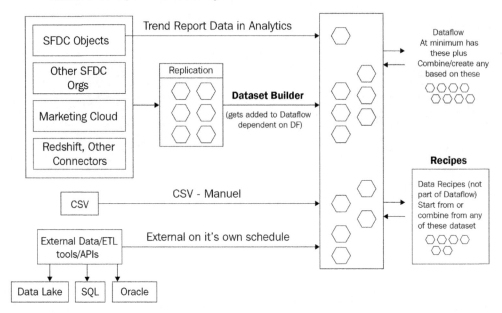

Figure 3.2 – The CRM Analytics data landscape

So, what can you learn from *Figure 3.2*? Let's consider the following points:

- Several data sources are replicated/synced (please refer to the *Data sync* section) and brought into CRMA via dataflows and recipes. These include data from the primary connected Salesforce org, other Salesforce orgs, marketing cloud, and other CRMA connectors.

- Salesforce's trend report data can be brought directly into CRMA.

- **Flat files** can be augmented to datasets by loading CSV files manually into CRMA and combining and transforming them with other data in a dataflow or recipe.

- **External Data**, **ETL tools**, and **APIs** (such as data lakes, SQL, and Oracle) augment datasets in CRMA via their own manual schedule.

- CRMA dataflows take a variety of data sources and combine and transform this data with other sources and CRMA datasets. This will be explained in much greater detail in *Chapter 4, Building Data Recipes*, and *Chapter 5, Advanced ETL Using CRMA Data Prep*.

- Recipes begin with a CRMA dataset and combine and transform this information using other data sources that have been added to CRMA. This will be explained in much greater detail in *Chapter 4, Building Data Recipes*.

So, what is meant by **data sync** or what was previously referred to as data replication? This is an important concept for you to understand, and we will explain it in the following section.

Data sync

Data sync refers to the process whereby data is staged for dataflows and recipes. Extraction occurs on a *cached free* layer for better performance and optimized extracts.

You can use data sync to separate the extraction of data from your recipes and dataflows and sync this data with CRMA on a separate schedule. By scheduling a sync from Salesforce and other systems separately and in advance, recipes and dataflows have less to do and can run faster. Additionally, CRM Analytics can sync local Salesforce data incrementally (as opposed to a complete, or full, sync) so that only records that have changed get synced.

As a result, the CRMA data sync enables dataflows to run more quickly. Otherwise, without data sync, your dataflow must perform a separate extraction every time it requires data from a Salesforce object, which is slow and wasteful.

Imagine that your organization has three CRMA dataflows, each one extracting data from Salesforce, transforming that data, and creating datasets. Every time they run, the dataflows have to extract the Salesforce data, slowing down the dataflow. In addition to this, each dataflow must perform separate, duplicate extractions from the same object.

With data sync, all of these extractions are performed as a separate process, which you can schedule to take place before running your dataflows. This synced data is then available on all of your dataflows, which, in turn, run faster because they no longer have to extract any data – just load and transform. The **extract, transform, load** (ETL) process is much faster and more efficient with data sync running.

Here are several facts to bear in mind regarding data sync:

- As your data analytics and business requirements change, the data synced to CRM Analytics must change, too. You can add, remove, and change the settings for the objects and fields included in data sync, as required.

- The data manager provides you with the ability to schedule a sync to run automatically, run a data sync manually, and monitor a sync's progress.

- By default, CRM Analytics performs incremental syncs. You can specify whether the sync extracts incremental changes or all records from each Salesforce object. As discussed earlier, incremental syncs run faster.

- If your CRMA administrator turned on CRMA before the Winter '20 release, you must enable the data sync and connections option to optimize your dataflows and connect to external data. Note that data sync is enabled by default if you turned on CRMA after Winter '20.

- You can export raw, local Salesforce data via CRM Analytics into Snowflake using the CRM Analytics output connector for Snowflake.

In the following section, you will learn how to extract and use external data in CRMA.

Ingesting and combining external data with Salesforce data

One of the main reasons for deploying and building CRM Analytics dashboards is to combine Salesforce and external data into one source of truth. So, how do you do this? Let me show you how this works by way of an example.

Log in to your CRMA dev org, navigate to the **Analytics Studio**, and perform the following steps:

1. Click on the **Create** button and select **Dataset**.
2. Select the **External Data** option, and you will be taken to **Data Manager**.
3. Click on the **Connect** link on the left-hand side.
4. Click on the **Connect to Data** button.
5. Underneath the **Input Connections** tab, click on the **Add Connection** button, which will bring you to the following window:

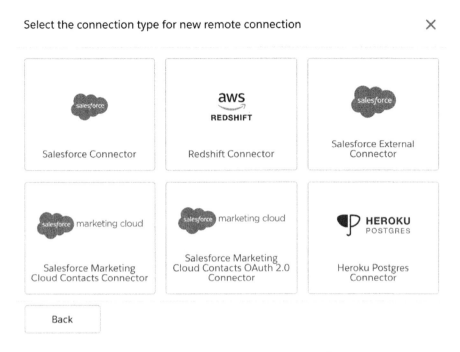

Figure 3.3 – A remote connection example

6. Scroll through the available options and you will see that there are a variety of data
    sources on offer to you here. Select the **Redshift Connector** option, and you will be
    brought to a dialog box where you need to fill in information about the connector,
    such as the following:

    (a) **Connection Name**

    (b) **Developer Name**

    (c) **Description**

    (d) **AWS Secret Access Key**

    (e) **Username**

    (f) **AWS Access Key ID**

The details that you are required to fill out vary from connector to connector. Once
you have filled in the necessary information, you need to save and test the connector.
Once correctly configured and successfully tested, the data is available for combining
and transforming in CRMA. The connector can be scheduled, edited, or deleted in the
Connect section of **Data Manager**.

Remote data connections available for CRMA

As of April 2021, the following remote data connectors are available for CRMA:

Salesforce	Applications	Databases	Analytics Mulesoft	Object Store and No SQL	Live Connections
External Salesforce org	Google Analytics	Amazon RDS (Amazon Relational Database Service)	Microsoft SQL Server	Amazon S3	Snowflake Direct
Marketing Cloud Contacts OAuth 2.0	Microsoft Dynamics	Amazon Redshift	MySQL		
Marketing Cloud Contacts	NetSuite	Google BigQuery - Legacy SQL and Standard SQL	Oracle		
Customer 360 Global Profile Data	Oracle Eloqua	Google Cloud Spanner			
	Marketo	Heroku Postgres			
		Microsoft Azure SQL Data Warehouse			
		Microsoft Azure SQL Database			
		SAP HANA			
		Snowflake			
		Amazon RDS PostgreSQL			
		Amazon RDS SQL Server			
		Amazon RDS SQL MySQL			
		Amazon RDS SQL MariaDB			
		Amazon RDS SQL Aurora			
		Amazon RDS SQL Aurora PostgreSQL			

Figure 3.4 – Remote data connections available for CRMA as of April 2021

As the CRM Analytics platform is being constantly expanded and developed, please refer to the Salesforce support documentation for the latest list of connectors:

`https://help.salesforce.com/articleView?id=sf.bi_integrate_connectors_remote.htm&type=5`

The CRMA data connection framework and tools are not without their limitations, and we are going to discuss them in the following section.

The limitations of CRMA for data connections

You have learned what can be done in CRMA as far as data integration goes. Now you will learn some limitations of data integration, as demonstrated in the following list:

- The results stored in Salesforce formula fields only update in CRMA datasets when full replication is performed for the relevant object.
- The current limit for data sync (according to the Spring '21 release) is 100 objects.
- Data sync only performs one sync per object. This is important if you need to perform multiple data syncs from one object.

> **Important Note**
> The Tableau Prep Builder can be used in cases where CRMA does not have the required ETL capability. For more information, please refer to `https://www.tableau.com/products/prep`.

Now it's time to create your first custom dataset using Salesforce data.

Bringing Salesforce data into CRMA

This section will teach you, in detail, how to ingest Salesforce data and create a dataset that is useful for analysis and exploration. Before you build your first dataset, you need to consider dataset design.

Designing a dataset

CRMA data is stored in inverted index structures. Ideally, you should start with the lowest, most granular level (that is, the child) and follow a path up to the parent table hierarchy, which constitutes a dataset answering the business case in question. You can have multiple datasets and augment to one large dataset, or you can calculate and aggregate on the fly using SAQL in the dashboard editor.

It is critical that you understand and work with the dataset as they pertain to questions of a business case nature. That is, when designing your dataset, consider the following:

- Avoid the notion of building a data warehouse in one dataset.

- At the same time, a dataset is not meant to be the substitute of one table; it is the fields from the objects (such as data tables) that pertain to the analytics use case with relevant business questions.

- Always consider multiple datasets augmenting to get the desired results or leverage different interacting charts from different datasets on the dashboard (each chart answers the business question at each lowest granule level). Datasets can be connected to the dashboard to enable faceting as required.

- **SAQL (Salesforce Analytics Query Language)** is another good option to solve certain use cases.

For example, let's imagine that your business wants to analyze the impact of products upon the win rate of opportunities. The relevant objects for analysis could be as follows:

- Account

- Contact

- Opportunity

- User

- Product

- Product family

Now, which object would provide the desired granularity for the left-hand side of your dataflow? For example, would it be the opportunity object or the product object? In this case, because you want to examine the impact of products on opportunities, with individual opportunities being the key records of interest, you would choose the opportunity object for your base granularity, then build a dataflow from there to create a dataset with the relevant information for analysis. You will understand this better once you complete the hands-on exercise later in the chapter.

One subject of debate is whether to transform data at the data layer or the designer layer (query runtime). The following table compares these two methodologies:

Data Layer	Dashboard Query Runtime
One Time	Dashboard Specific/repetitive
More Time At Start Of Implementation	Multiple Times
More Thinking/planning But Easier On The	Independent Of Data Layer
Dashboard Designer Layer	Performance Tuning Conscious
Customizing Dataflow Heavily	Less Planning/faster Jump-start
Preparing The Data And Figuring Out The Correct	Customized Saql Directly In The Dashboard Json
Grain And Pre-transformations	Can Leverage Step Editing To Create/test Query

Figure 3.5 – The data layer versus the designer layer

You must choose which method best suits your use case and data.

The simplest way to build a dataset with Salesforce data is to use the CRMA dataset builder, as demonstrated in the following section.

Dataset builder

Log in to your CRMA dev org and open up the CRM Analytics Analytics Studio. Perform the following steps in order to create a dataset from Salesforce data:

1. Navigate to the upper-right corner of the page and click on **Create**. Then, click on **Dataset**.

2. Choose the **Salesforce data** option.

3. When you arrive at the following dialog box, fill it out as you see in the following
    screenshot, with a **Dataset Name** entry of `MyFirstDataset`:

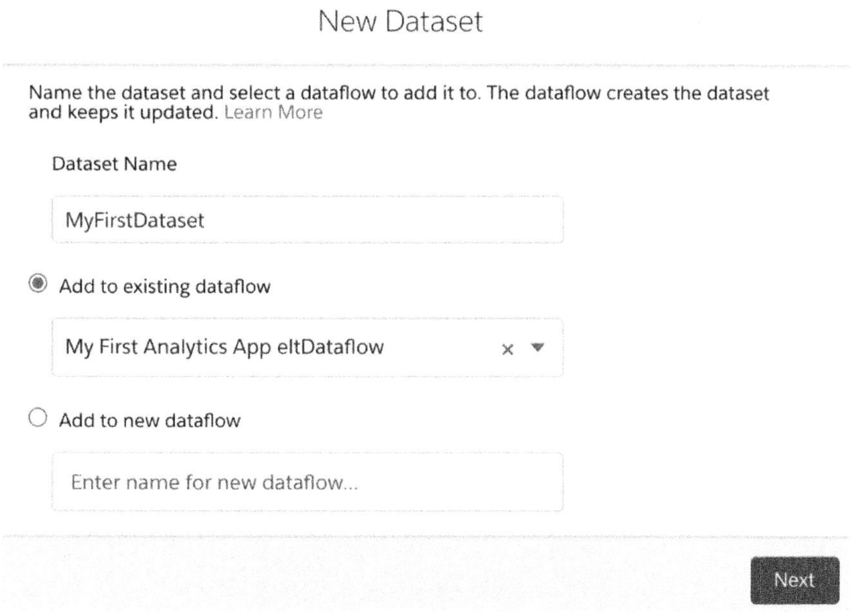

Figure 3.6 – The New Dataset dialog box filled out for this exercise

4. Click on **Next**. A new browser tab will automatically open, revealing the CRMA
    dataset builder.

Now you are going to build a simple dataset to analyze the impact of the
opportunity owner and lead source upon the win rate of opportunities. The relevant
objects that you will use for this analysis are as follows:

(a) **Account**

(b) **Contact**

(c) **Opportunity**

(d) **User**

5. Because your lowest granularity, or finest detail, is the opportunity object, you will begin there. So, type `Opportunity` into the search window to choose the first object, which will then bring you to this dialog box:

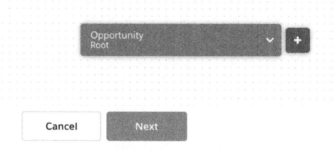

Figure 3.7 – Beginning with the dataset builder

6. Next, hover over the object and click on the **+** button – this will give you the option to add fields or related objects to the **Opportunity** object, as shown in the following screenshot:

Figure 3.8 – Adding fields and relationships to the root object

7. Go ahead and pick the following fields:

(a) **Amount**

(b) **Close Date**

(c) **Lead Source**

(d) **Name**

(e) **Opportunity ID**

(f) **Stage**

(g) **Won**

> **Note**
>
> It is important to make sure that you select any ID fields that will be required to add object relationships to the dataset; otherwise, the related objects will have no key to link to. When I add a new object related to the base object, I always add the object ID in case it is required later for relationship building.

8. Next, click on the **RELATIONSHIPS** tab and join the following objects:

(a) **Account (Account ID)**

(b) **Contact (Contact ID)**

(c) **User (Owner ID)**

You should now have an object relationship map that looks like this:

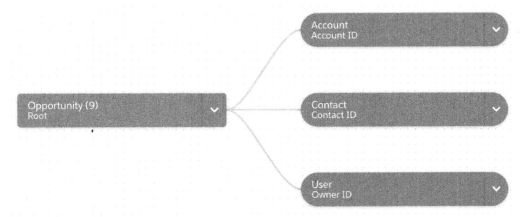

Figure 3.9 – The object relationship map

9. Follow a similar process for the **Account, Contact**, and **User** objects, and add the fields as mentioned. For **Account**, add the following fields:

    (a) **Account ID**

    (b) **Account Name**

    (c) **Industry**

    (d) **Billing Country**

    (e) **Billing City**

    (f) **Billing State/Province**

10. For **Contact**, add the following fields:

    (a) **Contact ID**

    (b) **Full Name**

    (c) **Mailing Country**

    (d) **Mailing City**

    (e) **Mailing State/Province**

11. For **User**, add the following fields:

    (a) **User ID**

    (b) **Full Name**

12. Now, what if you wanted to add information about the account owner? How would you do that? Let's consider the following options:

    (a) Finish creating the dataset in the dataset builder and then make the required changes to the data prep tool.

    (b) Add a relationship to the account object in the dataset builder.

    (c) Finish creating the dataset in the dataset builder and then use a dataset recipe to add information about the account owner.

    If you answered (b) – *Add a relationship to the account object in the dataset builder* – then you were correct. More complex changes might require you to use a recipe or the CRMA data prep tool, but adding information about the account owner can be performed easily in the dataset builder.

13. Follow a similar process to what you did so far, and add the account owner information (the **User** object).

Click on **Next**. You will see the **New Dataset** dialog box where you are given the opportunity to create the dataset. Where you are given the option to **Select an app for your dataset**, choose **My First Analytics App** in the drop-down menu (picklist), as follows:

Figure 3.10 – Creating your new dataset

14. Click on **Create Dataset**.

15. Two more steps are required before the new dataset will be created and ready to use. First, click on **Update Dataflow** and add the version description: `Added new dataset for opportunity analysis`. Click on **Update Dataflow** again.

16. Next, click on **Run Dataflow** in the upper-right corner. This message will appear: **Your dataflow is in the queue to run. Go to the data monitor to see its progress**. Navigate to **Data Monitor**, and you will be taken to the following view:

Figure 3.12 – Data Monitor showing the progress of new dataset creation

17. Click on the refresh button – highlighted in *Figure 3.12* by the red arrow – until the **My First Analytics App eltDataflow** dataflow has finished running. Ignore any error messages about the **augment_Contact** node, as this relates to missing data in the dev org regarding quota owners and is irrelevant. Your new dataset is now ready to examine, so return to the Analytics Studio.

> **Note**
>
> Often, you will need to navigate between browser tabs to switch from the Analytics Studio to the data manager.

18. Navigate to **My First Analytics App** and open your new dataset, **MyFirstDataset**. This will bring up an untitled lens where you can explore the new dataset. The initial lens view looks like this:

Figure 3.13 – MyFirstDataset, as seen in the initial lens view, ready to explore

Now that you have created your first dataset from scratch, what if you want to add more context to this dataset by augmenting a flat file (CSV file)? In the next section, we will explain how to do this, and you will be able to follow along in your CRMA dev org.

> **Note**
> Augmenting data means adding value to the base data by adding (augmenting) information from other data tables. This is similar to what you did earlier by augmenting opportunity information with account data. It is different from appending data, which simply means to increase data volume by adding more rows of data with the exact same number of columns.

Augmenting your Salesforce data with flat files

Now, you are going to use a CSV (flat) file to augment your Salesforce data by performing the following steps:

1. Go to your Analytics Studio home page, navigate to **My First Analytics App**, and click on the option to create a new dataset.

2. This time, choose the option for **CSV File**.

3. Go ahead and select a file (any CSV file will do for this exercise). Then, click on **Next**, name your CSV dataset, and click on **Next**.

4. You will arrive at the user interface for editing the dataset field attributes, which should look similar to the following screenshot:

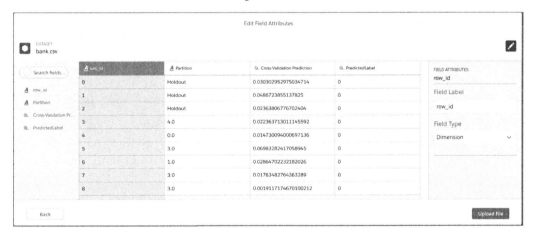

Figure 3.14 – Editing the dataset field attributes

5. Select each field/column and edit the field attributes, as required, before uploading the file to create the new dataset.

6. Once this is done, click on **Upload File** and the dataset will be created. It is now ready for exploration, transformation, and combination.

> **Note**
>
> One common error when editing dataset field attributes is incorrectly classifying dimensions as measures. For example, a zip/postal code will often be set as a measure by default, but this field is used for grouping, not mathematical calculations, so it needs to be changed to a dimension.

The process of combining CSV datasets with Salesforce and external data is performed in one of the places, all of which will be covered later in this book:

- In a data recipe – please refer to *Chapter 4, Building Data Recipes* (the *Cooking up data recipes in CRMA* section) and *Chapter 5, Advanced ETL Using CRMA Data Prep*.

- Within a lens – please refer to *Chapter 6, CRMA Lenses – Diving Into Your Data One Click At A Time* (the *Creating, editing, and cloning lenses* section).

- Within a query in the dashboard editor – please refer to *Chapter 9, Advanced Dashboard Design and Build* (SAQL).

Common questions and challenges

Here are some common questions and challenges that you might encounter when creating a dataset from Salesforce or CSV data:

- *If I make a mistake in the dataset builder, can I reopen it and make corrections?* No, you cannot reopen the dataset builder once you have chosen to create the dataset. Changes will then need to be made in the data prep tool.

- *I made an error in editing the field attributes when uploading a CSV file, and now I want to make changes – how do I do that?* You must make such changes in the CRMA data prep tool; you cannot return to the field attribute editing dialog box.

- *When augmenting a Salesforce object in the dataset builder, what if I need to make an inner or outer join, as opposed to a simple lookup or left join?* This cannot be performed in the dataset builder; it must be done in a data recipe or in the dataflow builder.

- *I have augmented CSV data to a dataset, but I need to update that CSV data. What can I do? For example, the CSV file contains sales targets, and these have changed.* The solution here is to edit the dataset, click on **Replace Data**, and upload the updated CSV. Be careful to keep the same field mappings and settings.

- *I created a dataset from Salesforce data using the dataset builder, but now the data model and structure in Salesforce have changed. What should I do?* In this case, you have two options: either recreate the dataset from scratch using the dataset builder or edit the existing dataset in the CRMA data prep tool.

Summary

In this section, you learned how to extract data from various sources and bring it into CRMA. You should now have a good understanding of the capabilities and limitations of CRMA when it comes to bringing in data from Salesforce, flat files, and other data sources, as well as the framework and tools that enable this. You have been taught how to create datasets from Salesforce data and CSV files, and you have performed hands-on exercises to do this for yourself. These lessons have formed the basis for your expertise in transforming data and building dashboards in CRMA.

In the following chapter, the process of creating a data recipe in CRMA will be defined and explained. Then, beginning with the dataset created in this chapter, you will be able to apply filters, calculations, and transformations to that data in order to create a new dataset that meets the requirements of a business use case.

Questions

Here are some questions to test your knowledge of this chapter:

- What is meant by data sync?
- Name five remote data connections available for CRMA.
- What is the dataset builder used for – to create a dataset from Salesforce data, from external data, or both?
- When working in the dataset builder, why is it important to ensure that you select any ID fields that will be required to add object relationships?
- What common error is given when editing dataset field attributes?

4
Building Data Recipes

Now that you are confident an how to create an **Out-of-the-box analytics app** template, it is time to learn how to build **custom analytics apps**, beginning with **data transformation**. In this chapter, the process of creating a data recipe in **CRMA** will be defined and explained. Beginning with the dataset created in *Chapter 3, Connecting Your Data Sources,* you will learn how to apply **filters**, **joins**, **calculations**, **transformations**, and more to that data.

So, what will you be able to do by the end of this chapter? Well, first, you will clearly understand how to create a data recipe in CRMA. Second, you will be familiar and comfortable with the data recipe UI. Third, you will be able to transform data inside recipes using functionalities such as **buckets**, **aggregation**, and **calculations**. Fourth, you will have learned how to join and append datasets, including how to use the various join types, such as **lookup** and **inner join**. And, finally, you will be confident in outputting data from recipes as a *CSV* or *CRMA* dataset.

In this chapter, we will cover the following topics:

- Cooking up data recipes in CRMA
- Transforming data in recipes

- Joining data in recipes
- A hands-on exercise in data transformation

Technical requirements

The following is required to successfully execute the instructions in this chapter:

- A laptop or desktop with internet access (a tablet or a phone is not sufficient).
- The latest version of the Google Chrome browser (Chrome is the preferred browser when working with CRMA).
- A working email address.
- Make sure you are logged in to your CRMA dev org.

Cooking up data recipes in CRMA

In this section, we will explain what a data recipe is, when and why you should use one, and how to create your first simple recipe.

What is a data recipe?

A CRMA data recipe is used to join multiple datasets into one and to prepare, clean, and transform data with *smart suggestions*, *column profiles*, and *powerful transformations*.

Recipes are perfect for Salesforce administrators and analysts with little to no data integration experience who want guidance on how to clean data, with the added benefit of previewing the transformation results. Additionally, recipes are a powerful tool for experienced data ninjas who want to create datasets using a no-code, visual interface.

A data recipe enables you to do the following:

- Preview data and see how it changes as you apply transformations.
- Remove columns or change column labels easily and quickly.
- Use column profiles to analyze the quality and makeup of your data.
- Improve and transform your data with intelligent suggestions.

- Bucket values without having to write code (**SAQL**, or **Salesforce Analytics Query Language**).

- Transform data quickly using calculated columns with the visual formula builder.

- Quickly and easily transform values to ensure data consistency with a point-and-click interface. For example, you can replace, split, and trim values without a formula.

- View the history of all the changes, and back up or move forward to replay it.

- Easily apply various joins, such as inner and outer joins, using the intuitive visual interface.

This chapter introduces you to the data recipe builder. *Chapter 5, Advanced ETL Using CRMA Data Prep*, will guide you on how to use the CRMA platform for more advanced data preparation.

> **Important Note**
> The relatively new visual data preparation tool in CRMA, known colloquially as **Data Prep 3.0**, is identical to the data recipe builder. The detailed explanations and instructions provided in this chapter also cover this new tool, referred to simply as data prep.

How do you create a data recipe?

Now, I am going to show you how to create a simple recipe. Let's begin with the dataset you created earlier, **MyFirstDataset**. Execute the following steps to get started:

1. Navigate to **Data Manager** from the Analytics Studio and select **Dataflows & Recipes** from the left-hand side menu.

2. Click on the **Recipes** tab.

3. Click on **Create Recipe**. A new browser tab will open.

4. Click on the **Select Data** button. This will open up a dialog box, called **Select Input Data**.

5. Select **MyFirstDataset** (that is, click on the checkbox), and you should view the following:

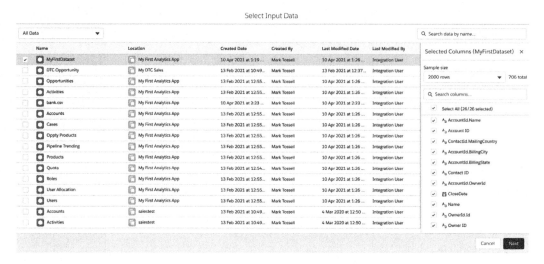

Figure 4.1 – The Select Input Data dialog box with MyFirstDataset as the data source for the recipe

6. Note that you can change the sample size used for column analysis, and you can select and deselect fields as required. Click on **Next**.

7. Click on the **MyFirstDataset** database icon.

8. On the far right-hand side of the screen, hover over the magnifying glass icon – **Open column profile** – and click on it. This will reveal the column profile as follows:

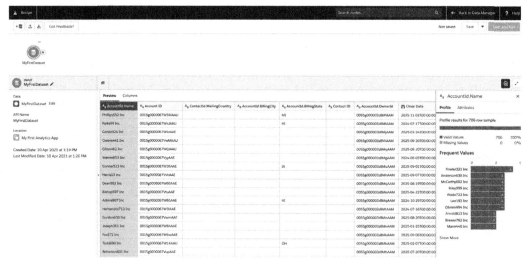

Figure 4.2 – The initial recipe screen showing MyFirstDataset with the column profile

9. Click on the + button next to the dataset icon for **MyFirstDataset** and select **Output** underneath **ADD NODE**. Please view *Figure 4.3*:

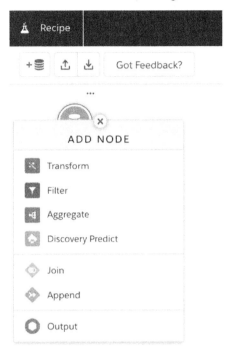

Figure 4.3 – Adding a node inside the recipe builder

10. Enter the following information as required. Then, click on **Apply**:

    (a) **Write To**: Dataset

    (b) **Dataset Display Label**: MyFirstRecipe

    (c) **Dataset API Name**: MyFirstRecipe

    (d) **App Location**: My First Analytics App

11. Click on **Save and Run**.

12. Name the recipe MyFirstRecipe.

13. Click on **Save**. You will observe a message that reads **Recipe has been queued to run**.

14. Click on **Back to Data Manager** in the upper-right corner of your screen. You should see that your recipe has run successfully.

15. Return to the Analytics Studio and click on **DATASETS** underneath **All Items**. You should find your new MyFirstRecipe dataset there, as defined by the recipe you ran.

This was a very simple example, purely designed to show you how to create a recipe. Following the detailed explanations to come, you will work through a comprehensive, hands-on exercise to hone your skills.

Now, let's take a look at how recipes can be used to transform data in your datasets.

Transforming data in recipes

A data recipe is a fast, intuitive, and powerful tool for data combination, aggregation, and transformation. The following sections will walk you through the various tools at your disposal in these recipes:

- Adding data
- Appending data
- Filtering data
- Aggregating data
- Transforming data

At the end of these explanatory sections, you will work through a hands-on exercise to hone your data recipe skills.

Adding data

Even though you will likely choose input data when you create a recipe, you can add more data to an existing recipe as required. The recipe builder canvas will show a separate input node for each set of data that you add.

In order to add more data to an existing recipe, simply click on **Select Data** in the upper-left corner of the recipe builder canvas, which is represented by the standard dataset icon with a + button next to it. Follow similar steps to those that you used to add the source dataset when creating your recipe. All of the columns are included by default.

> **Important Note**
>
> You cannot use a trending dataset as input data for a recipe. To include data from a trending dataset, you will need to use a dataflow.

Appending data

Simply put, appending data means adding rows from one dataset, or multiple datasets, to another. For example, use the **Append** node to combine service records from two different Salesforce environments, each containing case records from a certain region.

To append, as shown in *Figure 4.3*, add a new node to your recipe and select **Append**. Alternatively, to append data from an existing dataset in the recipe, select the + button next to the data node to be appended and drag over the existing dataset, as shown in the following screenshot:

Figure 4.4 – Appending an existing dataset to your recipe

Once you have added the **Append** node, you should see something similar to the following screenshot. Here, you will be able to review the default column (field) mapping assigned by the recipe builder based on the column names:

Figure 4.5 – Matching fields in preparation to append data

The following steps must be performed in order to append data:

1. Adjust the mappings, map any unmapped columns manually, or leave the columns unmapped.

2. To map two columns, simply enter the column name from the appended rows next to the corresponding recipe column.

3. If you wish to add a column from the appended rows that do not exist in the recipe, click on the + button below the mapped columns – **Add Mapping** – and select the column. Then, leave the recipe column blank.

4. Click on **Apply** to add the appended node to the recipe.

5. Save the recipe.

Important Note

If a column is mapped for one source and not the other, the **Append** node will insert null values for all source rows to which the column does not apply.

If a recipe column contains unique IDs that identify each row, you must ensure that the appended data does not duplicate the row IDs. The **Append** node does not identify and remove duplicate records, nor does it validate the uniqueness of the columns.

Filtering data

The filter node in data recipes enables you to quickly filter your data to suit the use case. That is, you can remove rows of data that you want to exclude from your output dataset(s).

To filter your data, follow these steps:

1. Add a new node (as shown in *Figure 4.3*) to your recipe and select **Filter**.

2. Add filter conditions, as shown in *Figure 4.6*. If you choose to define a filter condition on a dimension column, you can select a filter value from the list.

3. Click on **Apply**.

4. Save the recipe.

The following screenshot shows what the **user interface** (**UI**) looks like when adding filter conditions:

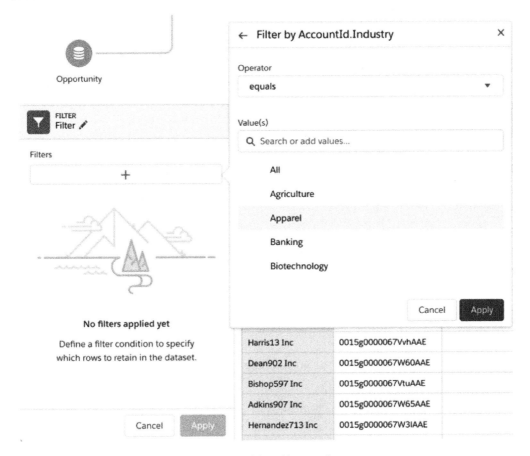

Figure 4.6 – Adding filter conditions

The list of available dimension values only comes from the sampled rows, not all of the rows in the dataset. If a value does not appear in the list, you can either change your sample size or manually enter the value in the filter condition and click on **Add new value**.

Aggregating data

An aggregate node is used when you need to roll data up to a higher level of granularity. You can aggregate data using any of the following functions:

- **UniqueCounts**: This only refers to unique values in the selected column.

- **Sum**: This calculates the total by adding all values in the selected column.

- **Average**: This calculates the average value of the selected column.

- **Count**: This counts all values in the selected column.

- **Maximum**: This calculates the maximum value of the selected column.

- **Minimum**: This calculates the minimum value of the selected column.

- **Stddevp**: This calculates the population standard deviation, which measures the spread of data distribution.

- **Stddev**: This calculates the sample standard deviation, which measures the spread of data distribution for a given sample.

- **Varp**: This calculates the population variance, which indicates how spread out the data points are in a specific population.

- **Var**: This calculates the sample variance, which indicates how spread out the data points are for a given sample.

You can group by any dimension or date column, and you can also pivot dimensions as columns. For example, you can group opportunities by account to get account-level details, such as the *total opportunity amount*, the *average number of cases*, and the *average number of days to close an opportunity* for each account. Then, you can pivot on account type to analyze each combination of account and account type.

To aggregate your data, follow these steps:

1. Add a new node (as shown in *Figure 4.3*) to your recipe and select **Aggregate**.

2. Add one or more aggregates.

3. Add one or more dimensions or date columns in the **Group Rows** field in order to group rows.

4. You can pivot dimensions as columns by adding up to two-dimension columns in the **Group Columns** field, selecting the values for each column, and clicking on **Apply**.

5. Once your aggregations have been configured, click on **Apply**.

6. Save the recipe.

This is what the UI looks like when you add an aggregate node:

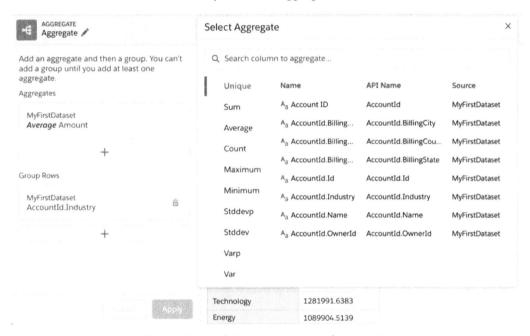

Figure 4.7 – Applying an aggregate node to a recipe

Note Regarding Aggregation And Data Granularity

When you use the aggregate node, lower (source) data granularity is lost in that stream of the data recipe. However, the recent release enables you to bring back the granularity with joins after aggregation.

Next, you will learn how to use the powerful transformation tools that are at your disposal in CRMA.

Transforming data

A data recipe can contain transformations that enable you to *prepare*, *clean*, and *transform* your data. These transformations are contained in a **Transform node**, and you can join multiple transformations together to shape data sequentially.

The transformation node provides a great deal of flexibility and functionality – the UI looks like this:

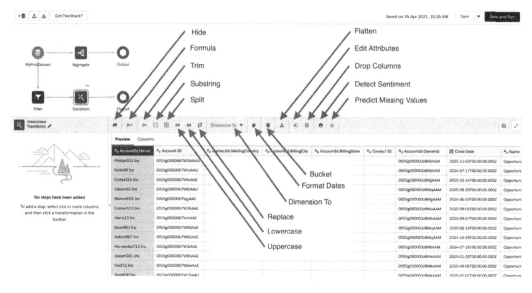

Figure 4.8 – Adding a transformation node

In this section, the following transformations will be covered:

- **Apply formulae**
- **Trim**
- **Substring**
- **Split**
- **Uppercase and lowercase**
- **Replace**
- **Dimension to measure**
- **Dimension to date**
- **Format dates**
- **Bucket**
- **Flatten**
- **Edit attributes**
- **Drop columns**

- **Detect sentiment**
- **Predict missing values**
- **Discovery predict**

So, let's get started with the first one!

Apply formulae

This creates a column in the recipe that displays values based on a formula calculation. This calculation will pull in data from other fields in the same row or across rows. You need to enter formulas in **EA-SQL format** – a collection of standard and custom functions for *numeric*, *string*, and *date* data.

The formula dialog box looks like this:

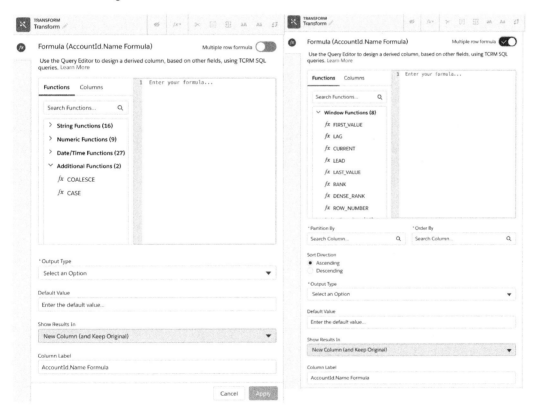

Figure 4.9 – Custom formula dialog box without (left-hand side) and with (right-hand side) the multiple row formula option enabled

In order to add a formula to your recipe, follow these steps:

1. Select a column in the **Preview** tab.

2. To add the formula for the calculated column, select the **Formula** button in the **Transform** toolbar and select **Custom Formula**. The formula editor will then appear.

3. In the formula editor, type in the formula and add the necessary parameters using the correct syntax.

4. For formulas with window functions, select the **Multiple row formula** option. Choose the column used to partition the rows in **Partition By**, the column used to sort the data in **Order By**, and the sort direction in **Sort Direction**.

5. Identify each column in the formula by its API name by either typing in the API name or selecting the column from the **Columns** tab.

6. In **Output Type**, choose between text, numeric, date, or datetime.

7. Depending on the output type, you can assign these attributes: **Precision** (the maximum number of digits in a numeric column), **Scale** (the number of digits to the right of the decimal point in a numeric column), **Length** (the maximum number of characters in a text column), and **Date Format**.

8. In **Default Value**, set a value to show whether the expression returns no results.

9. You can change the label of the calculated column as required.

10. To add the formula as a step in the **Transform node**, click on **Apply**. The calculated column will then appear in the recipe preview.

11. **Save** the recipe.

> **Tip**
> Common calculations have their own function buttons in the **Transform** toolbar – these fill in the formula with the correct column and syntax for you. The toolbar displays appropriate functions based on the number and type of columns selected. To use a function, just click on the **Function** button in the **Transform** toolbar.

There are the five types of functions available:

- **Date and time functions**: These are used to adjust or calculate values from dates in your recipe.

- **Numeric operators and functions**: These are used to calculate values from measures in your recipe.

- **String functions**: These are used to create values based on other strings.

- **Window functions**: These are used to perform calculations across rows. The **Multiple Row Formula** option must be selected to use window functions.

- **Additional functions**: These are used with the `text`, `number`, `date_only`, and `datetime` data types to add logic to formulae.

Trim

This transformation removes leading and trailing spaces from a string. You can choose to show the results in one of three places:

- The original column (overwrite).

- A new column – keep the original (the new column needs to be given a label).

- A new column – drop the original (the new column needs to be given a label).

Substring

This starts at the character position in a value and extracts the number of characters in length into a new field. The formula editor will appear, and the following text will be prefilled:

```
substr([target column], position, length)
```

The inputs required for the substring function can be found in the dialog box, as follows:

- **Output Type**
- **Length**
- **Default Value**
- **Show Results In**
- **Column Label**

Split

This transformation divides a column value into two new values at the specified delimiter. The inputs required are as follows:

- **Delimiter**
- **Show Results In**
- **Column 1 Label**
- **Column 2 Label**

> **Note**
> Split transformation always creates two new columns.

Uppercase and lowercase

This option converts values in the selected field into uppercase or lowercase.

Replace

This transformation finds a specific value in a field and replaces it with a new value. Note that a new field is created, which contains both the replaced values and the unchanged values. You can also use the replace transformation to replace nulls with a value.

The inputs required are as follows:

- **Find** or **Search** for null (in the search window)
- **Replace** (in the search window)
- **Show Results In**
- **Column Label**

Dimension to measure

This transformation converts the `Dimension` column type into `Measure`, which allows mathematical calculations on its values. You can choose whether to show the results in the original column, in a new column and keep the original, or in a new column and drop the original.

Dimension to date

This transformation converts the `Dimension` column type into `Date`, which allows you to group and filter by date components, such as the year and the month. You can choose whether to show the results in the original column, in a new column and keep the original, or in a new column and drop the original.

Format dates

This transformation converts dates in the selected `Dimension` column into the specified format. Optionally, you can convert the column type into `Date`. A consistent format allows you to correctly filter and group records by date, including filtering by the date component, such as `Day`. A consistent date format also ensures that you can convert the column type from a dimension into a date.

The inputs required are as follows:

- **Original Formats** (such as `yyyy-MM-dd'T'HH:mm:ss.SSS'Z'`)
- **Change To** (select the destination format)
- **Convert column type to Date** (checkbox)
- **Show Results In**
- **Column Label**

> **Warning**
> Values with unrecognizable formats will be replaced with null values.

Bucket

The bucket transformation is a quick and easy way in which to group and organize data by bucketing your measure, dimension, and date fields. Buckets are added by clicking on the + button within the bucket window and defining ranges. Here is an example of what this can look like:

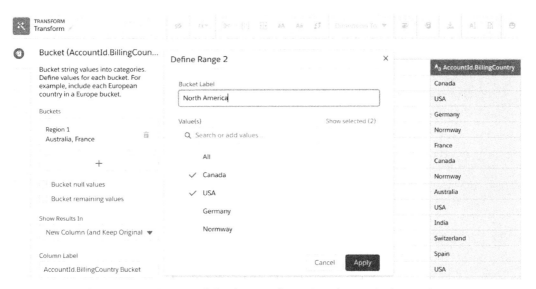

Figure 4.10 – An example bucket transformation of countries into regions

Buckets are a useful tool when you want to create a heat map from two measures, for example, or create a derived dimension for deeper analysis and machine learning.

Flatten

This option will flatten ranked data for a hierarchy into two columns. The hierarchy nodes column lists all of the ancestors for each node. The hierarchy path column contains a string that details the hierarchy path. Please refer to *Figure 4.11* for an example.

In order to configure the flatten transformation, you must specify the field that contains the corresponding parent based on the hierarchy and the field that contains every node in the hierarchy. This will then generate one record for each hierarchy node, referred to as the child node. Every record contains two generated columns that store the hierarchy for each child node. One column contains the ancestors for each node in the hierarchy, and the other column contains the hierarchy path.

The steps required to flatten data are as follows:

1. Select the dimension column that contains all of the child nodes in the hierarchy.
2. Click on the **Flatten** button.
3. Enter the **Parent Column** property details.
4. Choose whether or not to **Include child node** in the generated hierarchy nodes and path columns.
5. Enter the **Hierarchy Nodes Column Label** property – this is the name of the multi-value output column that contains a list of all ancestors in the hierarchy, in order from the lowest level to the highest level.
6. Enter the **Hierarchy Path Column Label** property – this is the hierarchical path of all ancestors in the hierarchy, in order from the lowest level to the highest level, where nodes are separated by forward slashes.
7. Preview the results to ensure that the flattened hierarchy is correct.
8. Click on **Apply** to add the flatten transformation to the recipe.

Here is an example of a flattened dataset showing how ancestors are stored:

ROLE ID (CHILD NODE)	ROLE NAME	PARENT ROLE ID	ROLES	ROLE PATH
1	Salesperson 1	10	10, 20, 30	/ 10/20/30
2	Salesperson 2	10	10, 20, 30	/ 10/20/30
3	Salesperson 3	11	11, 20, 30	/ 11/20/30
10	Regional Manager 1	20	20, 30	/ 20/30
11	Regional Manager 2	20	20, 30	/ 20/30
20	Vice President 1	30	30	/ 30
21	Vice President 2	30	30	/ 30
30	CEO	Not applicable	Not applicable	Not applicable

Figure 4.11 – An example of a flattened dataset showing how ancestors are stored

More details on how the flatten transformation is used will follow in *Chapter 5, Advanced ETL Using CRMA Data Prep*.

Edit attributes

Use this transformation to change the column names and value formats. For example, you can edit the following:

- **Label**
- **API Name**
- **Length**
- **Precision**
- **Scale**

Drop columns

Drop unwanted input columns from the recipe. This will leave you with a subset of columns to use in transformations and include in the final dataset. For example, you can drop input columns used for a calculated column.

Detect sentiment

This transformation is used to determine the sentiment of text, whether positive, negative, or neutral, and adds those values to the specified column.

If Einstein cannot determine the sentiment of a field, the sentiment is set to null.

Predict missing values

CRM Analytics intelligently replaces any missing values in the selected column with predictions based on values in other strongly correlated columns in your data.

Discovery prediction

This populates your datasets with predictive and prescriptive intelligence, as Einstein calculates and saves predicted outcomes on a row-by-row basis. Additionally, you can store descriptions of top predictors and improvements. The discovery prediction node enables you to evaluate predictions across your data, assess multiple models before deploying to production, and visualize aggregated prediction information in a dashboard.

As this book does not cover the machine learning models and predictions of Einstein Discovery, the discovery prediction transformation is not covered here in detail.

Joining data in recipes

Use the **Join node** to add columns of data from related objects to existing data in a recipe. You might use one of the following join methods, depending on how you want to combine your data: *lookup*, *left join*, *right join*, *inner join*, or *full outer join*.

The following screenshot shows an example of how to create an outer join:

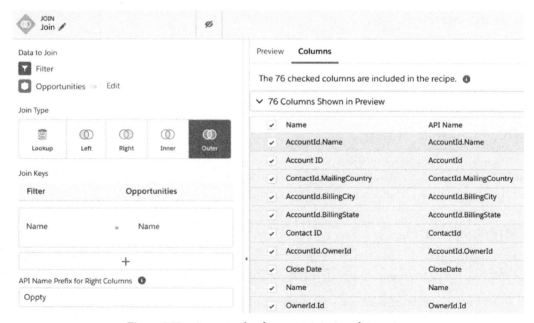

Figure 4.12 – An example of an outer join in a data recipe

Perform the following steps to join data in a recipe:

1. Select the **Add Node** button (+) between two nodes or at the end of a recipe with at least one input node.

2. Select **Join**.

3. Choose which data to join and select which columns to include.

4. Click on **Next**.

5. Select the desired **Join Type**.

6. Change the **Join Keys** setting as required. Note that the recipe will add suggested keys from both sets of input data. You can use multiple keys (a maximum of five) to match records if required.

7. Enter a prefix (**API Name Prefix for Right Columns**) for the columns coming from the right data source. This will prevent API name conflicts between columns in the left and right data sources.

8. Select the columns in the **Columns** tab in the right-hand side panel to include in the recipe.

9. Click on **Preview** to preview all of the included columns and their data.

10. If you need to hide columns from the preview, click on the **Hide** button (Æ).

11. Click on **Apply** to add the node to the recipe.

12. **Save** the recipe.

> **Types of data joins**
>
> I have assumed that you have an understanding of the various types of data joins. Note that this subject is explained, in detail, in *Chapter 5, Advanced ETL Using CRMA Data Prep*.

Outputting data from recipes

The output node writes recipe results to a CRMA dataset or an external system. The inputs required are as follows:

- **Write To**: Either to a dataset or a CSV file.

- **Dataset Display Label**.

- **Dataset API Name**.

- **App Location**.

- **Sharing Source**: This option is required if sharing inheritance is turned on.

- **Security Predicate**: This option adds row-level security with a predicate filter.

> **Warning**
>
> Setting the **Dataset API Name** option to be the same as an existing CRMA dataset will overwrite that dataset.

Soon, you will have more output options to choose from, as the following are currently in development:

- Amazon S3 output connection

- Salesforce output connection

- Snowflake output connection

- Tableau Online output connection

A hands-on exercise in data transformation

In this hands-on exercise, we want to create a new dataset to analyze the service cases that belong to accounts with open opportunities.

Perform the following steps to modify your existing `MyFirstRecipe` recipe using various transformations; it is critical that these steps are executed carefully in order:

1. Open the `MyFirstRecipe` recipe from **Data Manager**.

2. Create a second branch inside the dataflow directly after the input node.

3. Add a **Filter** node to this new branch in order to include all opportunity stages, except for **Closed Lost** and **Closed Won**.

4. To the right-hand side of the **Filter** node, add a **Join** node to augment the opportunity data with case information. Select only these **Case** fields: **Account ID**, **Case Number**, **Status**, **Subject**, and **Case Type**. Use a **Left join** node, match it by **Account ID**, and add the API name prefix of **Case**.

5. To the right-hand side of the **Join** node, add an **Aggregate** node. You want to calculate the number of cases, the number of open deals, and the average open opportunity size for each account.

6. Add a **Transform node** to the **Aggregate** node so that you can bucket by the deal size, as follows:

   (a) Small is less than 500,000.

   (b) Medium is between 500,000 and 1,000,000.

   (c) Large is greater than 1,000,000.

   (d) Show results in a new column – **Avg Deal Size** – and keep the original column.

7. In the same **Transform node**, truncate the average deal size to remove the decimal place; then, remove the source column and rename the truncated column to **Avg Deal Amount**.

8. In the same **Transform node**, rename Unique Case Number to # of cases and rename Unique Opportunity ID to # of open deals.

9. Add an output node (OpptysCases), as follows:

   (a) **Display Label**: Cases for Accounts with Open Deals

   (b) **API name**: Cases_Accounts_Open_Deals

   (c) **App Location**: My First Analytics App

10. Save and run the recipe.

> **Note**
>
> It is a best practice to save your recipe using the **Download recipe JSON** button before modifying it.

Your finished recipe should look like this:

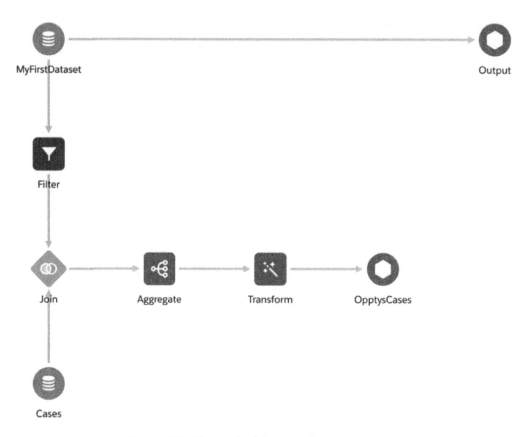

Figure 4.13 – The result of the recipe from the exercise

Explore your resulting dataset to test your work and determine whether the results look correct. You should end up with something that looks like the following:

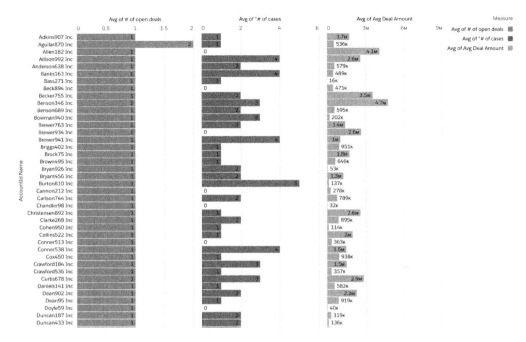

Figure 4.14 – The resulting dataset from the exercise

Now that you have completed the hands-on data transformation exercise, it's time to review what you have learned in this chapter.

Summary

In this chapter, you learned how to create and modify a data recipe in CRMA, becoming intimately familiar and comfortable with the data recipe visual UI. Now, you should be able to transform the data in recipes using a variety of functions such as *buckets*, *aggregation*, and *calculations*. Additionally, you learned how to join and append datasets using various types of joins such as *lookup* and *outer join*. Finally, you should now be confident in outputting data from recipes as a CSV or CRMA dataset.

In the following chapter, you will be introduced to the full capability of the CRM Analytics dataflow editor. This is where, traditionally, the more powerful **ETL (extract, transfer, and load)** work is performed. You will be instructed on how to combine many sources of data, perform complex transformations and calculations, and create multiple datasets.

Questions

Here are some questions to test your knowledge of this chapter:

- What is a data recipe, and when should you use it?

- When would you need to append data in a recipe?

- What types of dataset joins are available in the recipe editor?

- Where can you find common calculations?

- What is one real-world use case for the bucket transformation?

- Explain the **Detect Sentiment** transformation.

- Fill in the blanks:

  You must indicate the field that contains every _____ in the data hierarchy and also the field that contains the analogous _____based on the hierarchy in order to compose the flatten transformation. This will create one record for every hierarchy node, which is referred to as the _____ node.

- The **Split** transformation always creates _____ new columns.

5
Advanced ETL Using CRMA Data Prep

This chapter will demonstrate how to use the **CRM Analytics (CRMA)** Data Prep tool to its full capability. This is where the more powerful **extract, transform, and load** (**ETL**) work will be explained and demonstrated, instructing you in how to combine many sources of data, perform complex transformations and calculations, and create accurate, complete datasets for analytics.

Understanding and applying your data prep and dataflow skills are critical as a foundation for building accurate and useful data analytics in CRMA.

By the end of this chapter, you will have a much deeper understanding of how to join Salesforce and external data. You should be able to apply advanced use cases of the **Aggregate** node. You will develop an understanding of how to apply complex formula transformations to your data. Going ahead, you will be proficient in working with dates in CRMA Data Prep. You will know the reasoning behind flattening datasets and how to best perform that function. You will understand the use of the **Predict Missing Values** node and you will be proficient with sentiment detection. You will understand how to use nested recipes. Finally, you will have completed a complex, hands-on exercise in data transformation using the **CRMA Data Prep** tool.

In this chapter, we will cover the following topics:

- Advanced use of the Data Prep tool

- Advanced hands-on exercise

Notes Regarding the Data Recipe Builder, Data Prep, and Dataflow

1. The visual **graphical user interface (GUI)** tool for building and editing recipes is synonymous with the new Data Prep tool in CRMA. Salesforce is looking to consolidate data development on Data Prep recipes and is seeing organic adoption of the Data Prep recipe editor. However, there is a significant portion of the ETL workload that's still on dataflows. The CRMA engineering team is still working on parity items for recipes such as fiscal calendar offsets and update nodes.

2. A very useful blog post about moving from the legacy Dataflow Editor tool to Data Prep can be found here: `https://www.salesforceblogger.com/2021/02/22/from-dataflow-to-data-prep/`.

Technical requirements

You will need the following tools/software to successfully execute the instructions in this chapter:

- The latest version of the Google Chrome browser (Chrome is the preferred browser when working with CRMA)

- A working email address

Be sure to be logged in to your CRMA dev org.

Advanced use of the Data Prep tool

As you dive into more complex and powerful usage of the Data Prep tool, you will begin with one of the most common requirements for the ETL process—**data joins**.

The ETL Process

ETL is a data integration process that encompasses three distinct but interrelated steps (extract, transform and load) and is used to synthesize data from multiple sources many times to build a dataset that reflects business rules and meets analysis requirements.

Diving into data joins

We looked briefly at joining and augmenting your data in *Chapter 4, Building Data Recipes*. In this section, we will dive much deeper into this important area of data transformation. First, let's begin by understanding the various types of data joins.

Understanding the various types of joins

There are four common ways to join your data, as seen in the following diagram:

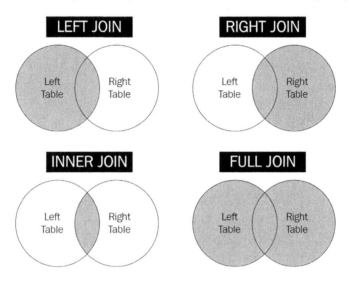

Figure 5.1 – The four types of Structured Query Language (SQL) data joins

The four types of joins can be understood as follows:

- **Left join**: A left join includes all rows from the left (recipe) data stream and only adds matching rows from the right data stream.

- **Right join**: A right join includes all rows from the right data stream and only adds matching rows from the left (recipe) data stream.

- **Inner join**: An inner join only includes matching rows from the left (recipe) data stream and right data stream.

- **Full (outer) join**: A full outer join includes all rows from the left (recipe) data stream and right data stream, regardless of whether or not they have matches.

> **Note**
> These joins include all matched rows in the target table when multiple rows match.

When it comes to the **Join** node in CRMA, there are **five** types of joins, as seen in the following screenshot:

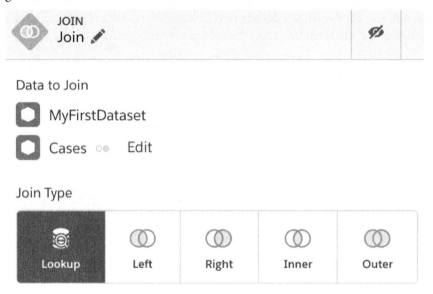

Figure 5.2 – The five types of joins in the Join node

The fifth join type added in CRMA is **Lookup**. A **Lookup** join returns all rows from the left data stream (recipe data) and only includes matching rows from the right data stream (lookup source). If multiple matches are found in the lookup source, the lookup join will return either a single row or all matching rows, depending upon how you have configured it. The lookup join outputs only one row for each row in the left data stream in order to ensure that the grain of the results does not change.

> **Considerations when using joins**
>
> Unlike a lookup, a join creates a separate record for each match in the target dataset when multiple rows match. Before using a join, ensure that you understand the implications of duplicate rows.

The type of join used will depend upon the use case involved. Let's consider a practical example for each type of join, as follows.

Lookup join

A lookup join is perhaps the most common of all CRMA joins. It is used, for example, when a dataset contains the **identifier** (**ID**) of opportunity owners and the dataset needs to include relevant details about those individuals, as contained in the Salesforce **User** object. The lookup source on the right is the **User** object, and the left data stream is the recipe dataset. Any user record that matches the user ID in the recipe dataset will return information around the user and augment it to the recipe dataset without adding any rows.

Left join

An example of a left join would be when multiple opportunities are associated with an account in Salesforce, and the goal is to add a row for each opportunity, changing the granularity of the dataset from one row per account to one row per opportunity. The left data stream in this case would be the Salesforce **Account** object, and the target stream would be the **Opportunity** object.

Right join

A right join can be used, for example, to create a dataset that begins with the Salesforce product object and creates a dataset that includes all product family records and excludes products that have no parent product family. The left stream is the product object, and the target (right) data stream is the product family object. This is a "parents without children" use case whereby "orphan" records are excluded.

Inner join

An inner join is used to create an intersection or overlap of two data sources, where only rows that match both data streams are included. For example, looking at the preceding "parents without children" example, an inner join would create a dataset that only includes product records with a parent product family and product family records with child products. Both parents without children and children without parents are excluded. The left stream is the product object, and the target (right) data stream is the product family object.

Full outer join

One example of a way in which a full outer join can be used is when you want to combine products and product families and include a record for every possible combination. You would have a record for each of the following:

- Product records with no parent product family
- Product family records with no child product

- Product records with a parent product family
- Product family records with child products

As you may have guessed, the left stream is the product object, and the target (right) data stream is the product family object.

Now, we will look in more detail at joining Salesforce objects.

Joining Salesforce objects – deep dive and practical example

Please build a fresh new recipe in your demo CRMA environment, as follows:

a. First, we will join the account data to the opportunity data, like this:

1. Create a recipe from the **Opportunity** object using SFDC_LOCAL with all columns selected.
2. Create a **Join** node.
3. Under **Select Input Data to Join**, select the **Account** object using SFDC_LOCAL with all columns selected.
4. Under **Join Type**, choose **Lookup**.
5. Under **Join Keys**, select the **Account ID** value for both keys.
6. Under **API Name Prefix for Right Columns**, leave **Account** as the default.
7. For the target lookup fields (with the prefix of **Account**), select only these five fields:

- **Account ID**
- **Account Name**
- **Industry**
- **Owner ID**
- **Segment**

8. Click on **Apply**.
9. Save the recipe as **Joining Exercise**.

b. Next, you will augment this dataset with user information for the account owner, as follows:

1. Create a **Join** node at the end of the data stream created so far.

2. Under **Select Input Data to Join**, select the **User** object using SFDC_LOCAL with all columns selected.

3. Under **Join Type**, choose **Lookup**.

4. Under **Join Keys**, select the account **Owner ID** value for **Join** and the **User ID** value for the user.

5. Under **API Name Prefix for Right Columns**, leave **User** as the default.

6. For the target lookup fields (with the prefix of **User**), select only these fields:

    • **User ID**

    • **Username**

    • **Full Name**

7. Click on **Apply**.

8. Save the recipe as **Joining Exercise**.

c. Lastly, you will use an inner join to create a table only of opportunities where the account has associated events, where events not related to the opportunity accounts are excluded. Proceed as follows:

1. Create a **Join** node at the end of the data stream created so far.

2. Under **Select Input Data to Join**, select the **Event** object using SFDC_LOCAL with all columns selected.

3. Under **Join Type**, choose **Inner**.

4. Under **Join Keys**, select the **Account ID** value for both keys.

5. Under **API Name Prefix for Right Columns**, leave **Event** as the default.

6. Keep all target lookup fields.

7. Click on **Apply**.

8. Add an **Output** node to create a dataset called **Joining Exercise**.

9. Save and run the recipe as **Joining Exercise**.

Your recipe/data prep flow should look like this:

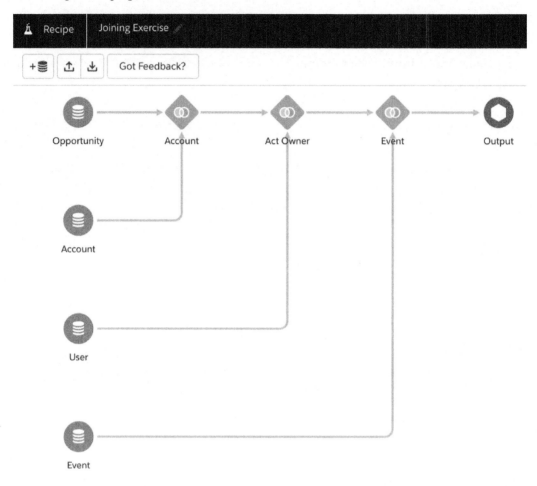

Figure 5.3 – Data prep flow for the joining exercise

Look at the resulting dataset in CRMA using a simple lens (lenses will be explained in detail in *Chapter 6, CRMA Lenses – Diving into Your Data One Click at a Time*). Do you see how the joins are reflected in your data? The data should look like this:

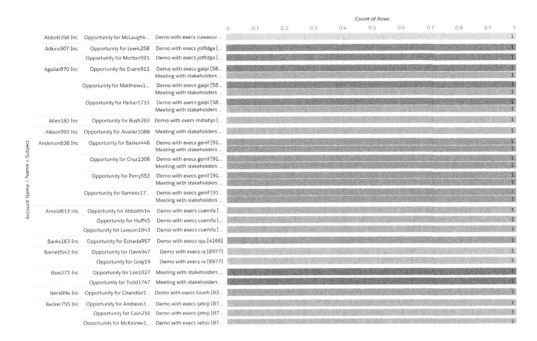

Figure 5.4 – The Joining Exercise dataset

Bringing connected data together by joining

When it comes to external data, CRMA provides a great deal of flexibility with a variety of data connectors, and these can be used to join external data with Salesforce data. Real-world examples of this include the following:

- Connect order data from external **enterprise resource planning** (**ERP**) and join it with sales data in Salesforce so that you can compare pipelines, won deals, and actuals.

- Connect target data from a **comma-separated values** (**CSV**) file stored in an **Amazon Web Services** (**AWS**) **Simple Storage Service** (**S3**) bucket so that up-to-date sales targets can be used to create a target line in sales charts for comparison.

- Connect data from other Salesforce orgs so that the data from all Salesforce environments (databases) can be combined and viewed on a page in CRMA.

- Connect service data from a business legacy platform via a MuleSoft connector and combine this with Salesforce case data for a comprehensive view of customer service.

- Connect near-live inventory data, exported from an ERP platform and stored in Snowflake, via the Snowflake Direct Connector.

- Connect sales opportunity data from an external spreadsheet via AWS S3 and append this data to Salesforce pipeline data for a complete list of opportunities.

The following walkthrough shows you how to perform the last example, where we will append external sales data to Salesforce pipeline data for a complete list of opportunities, using AWS S3 and the CRMA connector. If you wish, you can create your own AWS S3 bucket using a free AWS account, add a CSV file with opportunity data, and follow along in your CRMA dev org. The following steps must be carried out in order:

1. Go to **Data Manager** and select the **Connect** menu item on the left.

2. Click on **Connect to Data**.

3. Select **Input Connections** from a choice of three types of connections (input connections, MuleSoft connections, and live connections).

4. Select **Amazon S3 Connector**.

5. Under the **Set up your connection** dialog box, enter data as required, based upon your AWS S3 bucket details, noting that names must have no gaps.

6. Click on **Save and Test**.

7. When instructed **Select an object**, choose the **Opportunity** object, and hit **Continue**.

8. When instructed **Select fields**, select **All**, and click on **Continue**.

9. Review the **Preview Source Data** dialog box and press **Save**.

10. You will then see the new connector in your list of active connections.

11. Click on the dropdown to the right of your AWS S3 connector and click on **Run Data Sync**. This will bring in data from the S3 bucket and also enable data preview in the data prep window.

12. Create a new dataset using Data Prep and begin with the **Opportunities** dataset.

13. Click on the **Add Input Data** button (top left-hand side of the screen) and add the S3 opportunity data.

14. Drag the + icon next to the S3 data node across to the **Salesforce Opportunity data** node, creating a **Join** node, and select **Append**.

15. Under the **Append** node, in the **Data to Append** dialog box, map columns (fields) as required in order to join the new rows of data from your S3 bucket.

16. Add an **Output** node to set up your new hybrid dataset that includes both Salesforce and external opportunity data.

17. Click **Save and Run** to create the dataset.

The following screenshot shows what your connector should look like after successful setup and prior to data sync:

Figure 5.5 – The AWS S3 connector successfully set up in Data Manager, prior to sync

In the following screenshot, you can see how things should look when the S3 dataset has been added to the data prep flow:

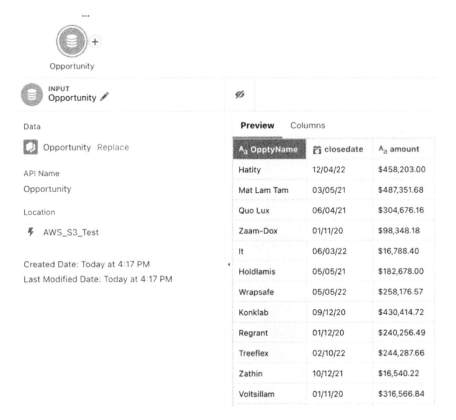

Figure 5.6 – The S3 dataset added to the data prep flow

The following screenshot shows what you see when opportunity data is appended to Salesforce data using the **Join** node:

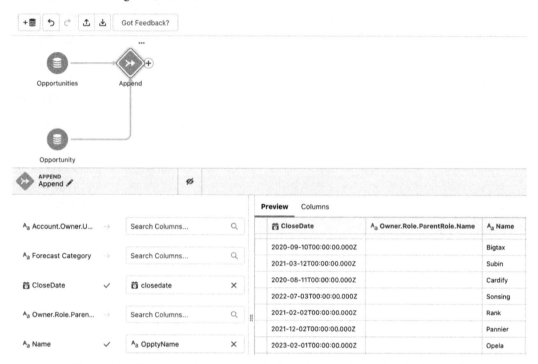

Figure 5.7 – S3 opportunity data appended to Salesforce data using the Join node

There are many other examples of how to bring connected data together by joining; perhaps the only limit is your imagination and the ever-growing list of CRMA connectors!

Advanced use of the aggregation node

You already learned about the basic use of the aggregation node, but there are a number of ways in which this node can be used to a whole other level. Here are three examples:

- You can create a number of data streams in the data prep flow, perform aggregation and rollup in each stream as required, then rejoin these streams and augment the granular data using a **Join** node.

- Create two datasets, based upon the same data, that have different levels of base granularity for two different use cases: data visualization and analysis, and **machine learning** (**ML**) model building.

- Join multiple Salesforce objects (such as **Account**, **Opportunity**, and **Product**), split the resulting dataset into several data streams, then use the **Aggregate** node to create roll-up summary datasets as required.

You can see an example in the following screenshot of what it looks like when you create multiple data streams using aggregation nodes; this example uses only one Salesforce object, but the permutations and options are endless:

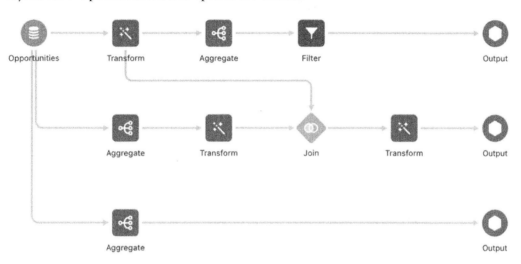

Figure 5.8 – A simple example of multiple data streams using aggregation nodes

Using unique and basic arithmetic functions

As seen in *Chapter 4, Building Data Recipes*, a number of options are available when aggregating data. Let's look at these in more detail.

Using the Unique aggregation

The **Unique** aggregation is useful when you do not want to generate a total count of rows, but you do want to count the number of unique occurrences of a certain value.

For example, if you have a dataset that has a granularity of product-line items, you could count the number of occurrences of unique values of opportunities by record ID, and create a dataset that shows how many opportunities are associated with a certain product.

Using basic arithmetic functions

Basic arithmetic functions provide great flexibility to group and aggregate your data. The **Select Aggregate** dialog box for the **Aggregate** node is seen in the following screenshot:

Select Aggregate			✕

Q Search column to aggregate...			

Unique	**Name**	**API Name**	**Source**
Sum	⌕ Amount	Amount	opportunity1
Average	⌕ Opportunity Age	OpportunityAge	opportunity1
Count	⌕ Probability (%)	Probability	opportunity1
Maximum			
Minimum			
Stddevp			
Stddev			
Varp			
Var			

Figure 5.9 – Basic arithmetic operations in the Aggregate node

Here are some examples of use cases for basic arithmetic operations in the **Aggregate** node:

- Use **Average** to calculate the average age of closed/won opportunities to determine how long it takes to close deals, and group by industry to compare and benchmark.

- Use **Maximum** to determine the longest time that it takes to resolve service cases, compare it to the business **service-level agreement** (**SLA**) metrics, and group by type of case to understand the "worst-case" scenarios for the business.

- Use **Minimum** to understand and identify the lower ceiling of values for a grouping, such as minimum deal size or shortest time to close service cases.

- Use **Stddevp** to calculate the spread of data distribution, such as a financial analyst using the Stddevp function to calculate deviations in revenue.

The following screenshot shows an example of basic arithmetic operations being used for an opportunities dataset; note how the values vary by lead source:

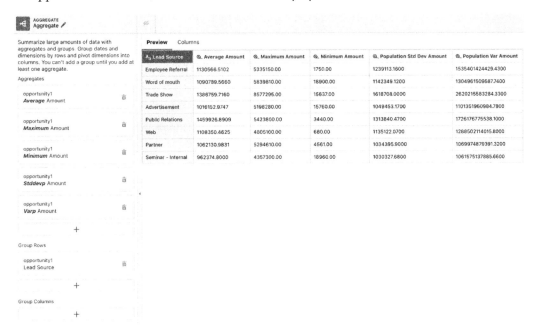

Figure 5.10 – Example of basic arithmetic operations being used for an opportunities dataset

The following lens shows what this data looks like in visual form:

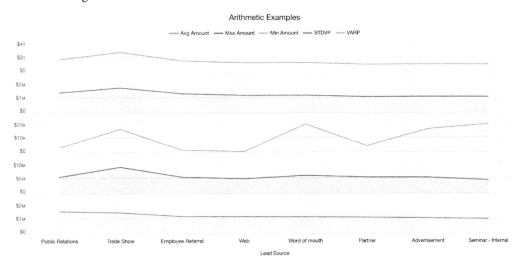

Figure 5.11 – Data from Figure 5.10 in visual form

Aggregation and grouping

The **Aggregate** node is a powerful tool that can be used to calculate aggregations and augment them to your granular dataset, generate pivot tables, and more.

For example, imagine that you want to compare average deal sizes by industry for your sales team members with the industry averages across the whole team. How would you do that? Here's how:

1. First, you would create your baseline values for average deal size and maximum deal size by industry, using an aggregation node, as seen in the following screenshot:

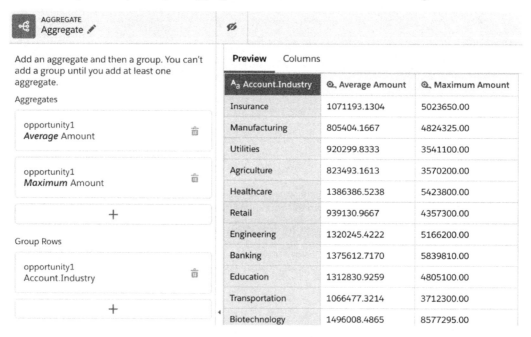

Figure 5.12 – Aggregated (baseline) numbers for industries

2. Now that you have calculated baseline values by industry, you need to join the aggregated data stream with the granular data stream, as seen in the recipe shown here:

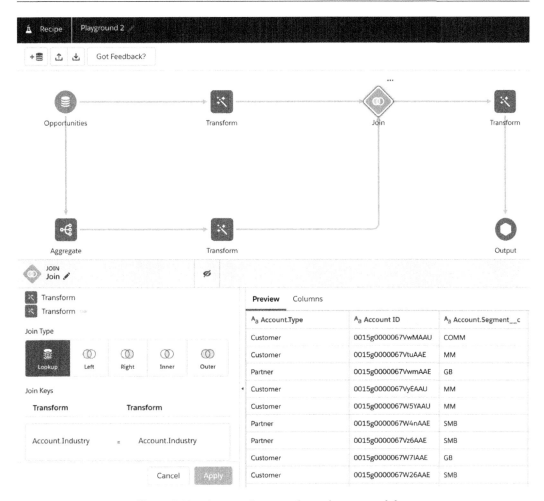

Figure 5.13 – Augmenting granular and aggregated data

Notice in *Figure 5.13* that the original dataset you ingested, Opportunities, was split into two streams, one for the aggregation and one for the granular data, and these are then combined into the dataset that drives the industry study insights.

A **Transform** node was added to the combined stream (see the top-right corner of *Figure 5.13*) to calculate the difference between the average deal size by industry for each sales team member with the average deal size by industry across the whole team.

Example results of this aggregation and augmentation are seen in the lens displayed in the following screenshot, where the results were filtered to narrow them down into one sales team member:

Figure 5.14 – Industry average study based upon baseline comparison

Why, when, and how to use complex formula transformations

In preparing your datasets for analysis, visualization, or modeling, you will need to incorporate logic and calculations that reflect business rules and requirements, and this often becomes complex. In that case, buckets and other simple functions are no longer up to the task, and you need to employ complex formula transformations.

You will now be given a walkthrough of explanations and use cases for these complex transformations.

Custom formulas

Custom formulas enable you to create a derived value or column in a Data Prep recipe that displays values based on a calculation that can include input from fields in the same row or across rows—for example, you can create a **Profit** column based on input from **Revenue** and **Cost** columns. Formulas must be entered in **Enterprise Architect** (**EA**)-SQL format, a collection of standard and custom functions for numeric, string, and date data.

When you add a function in the formula window, the necessary parameters will be added for you. You can see an example of this here:

```
months_between(timestamp2, timestamp1, roundOff(optional))
```

Date functions

As you may have guessed, you use date functions to calculate values from dates in your recipe. The date functions available are listed here:

- `add_months`—Returns the date with a specified number of months after the start date
- `current_date`—Returns the current date
- `current_timestamp`—Returns the current date and time
- `datediff`—Returns the number of days between the start date and the end date
- `date_add`—Returns the date with a specified number of days after the start date
- `date_format`—Converts the timestamp to a specified date format
- `date_sub`—Removes a specified number of days from the start date
- `day`—Returns the day component of the date/timestamp
- `dayofmonth`—Returns the day-of-the-month component of the date/timestamp
- `dayofweek`—Returns the day-of-the-week component of the date/timestamp, where 1 = Sunday, 2 = Monday, and so on
- `dayofyear`—Returns the day-of-the-year component of the date/timestamp
- `months_between`—Returns the number of months between two timestamps
- `now`—Returns the current date and time in a specified format
- `to_date`—Converts the date string to a specified date format

- `to_timestamp`—Converts the timestamp string to a specified timestamp format

- `to_unix_timestamp`—Returns the Unix timestamp of a specified time

- `trunc`—Replaces a specified portion of the timestamp, and all portions after, with zeros

The following **Transform** node example shows how to calculate the week of the year of an opportunity close date:

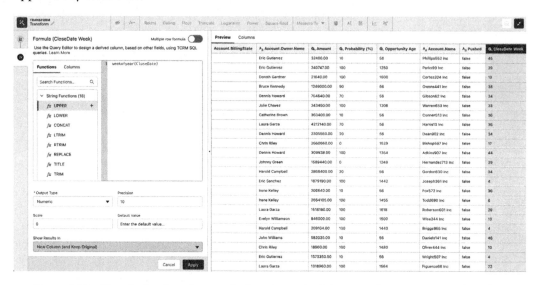

Figure 5.15 – Use of a date function to calculate the week of the year of an opportunity close date

Numeric operators and functions

Numeric functions calculate values from measures in your recipe. Be sure to use the **application programming interface (API)** name of the column in the expression, not the label, when entering a formula.

The following math operators can be used:

- + for the sum of two values

- − for the difference between two values

- * for the multiple of two values

- / for dividing the first value by the second

- ( ) for evaluating expressions within parentheses first

The following numeric functions are available for use in an expression:

- abs—Calculates the absolute value of a number

- cell—Rounds a number up to the nearest integer

- exp—Returns a value for *e* raised to the power of a specified number

- floor—Returns a number rounded down to the nearest integer

- format_number—Formats a number by rounding to a specified number of decimal places or by applying a certain format

- log—Returns the logarithm of the number in a specified base

- power—Raises a number to the power of another number

- round—Returns the nearest number to a number you specify, limiting (rounding) the new number by a specified number of digits

- sqrt—Returns the square root of a given number

- truncNumber—Truncates a specified number of decimal values from the number, or converts to an integer

The following example shows how numeric functions and operators are combined to create a custom formula:

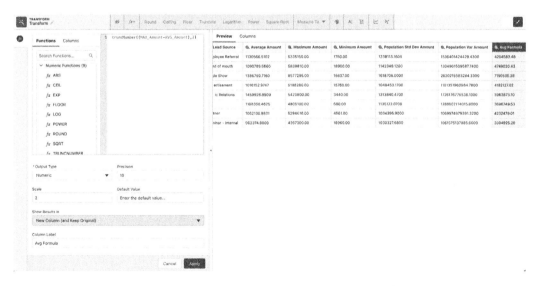

Figure 5.16 – Example formula using numeric functions and operators

String functions

String functions are used to create values based on other strings, as in text strings or dimension fields.

You can use the following string functions in a formula expression:

- `char_length`—Returns the number of characters in a specified string
- `concat`—Returns a string by merging the values of specified columns and input strings
- `endsWith`—Returns `true` if a specified string is found at the end of the column value
- `instr`—Returns the first location of the `searchString` value in a specified `field` column
- `lower`—Returns a string with all characters in lowercase
- `ltrim`—Removes a specified substring from the beginning of a string
- `replace`—Replaces a substring with another string
- `rtrim`—Removes a specified substring from the end of a string
- `startsWith`—Returns `true` if a specified string is found at the beginning of the column value
- `string`—Converts a date or number value to a string data type
- `substr`—Returns characters from a string, starting at a specified position and of a specified length
- `title`—Returns a string with the initial character of every word in uppercase and the remaining characters in lowercase
- `trim`—Removes a specified substring from the beginning and end of a string
- `upper`—Returns a string with all characters in uppercase

Here is an example of using the `concat` function to combine account and account owner information into a new column:

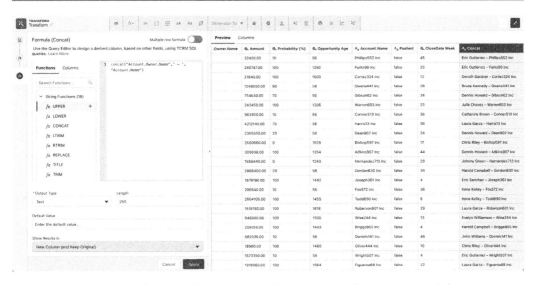

Figure 5.17 – Using the concat function to combine account and account owner information into a new column

Window functions

Window functions are employed in a Data Prep recipe to perform calculations across rows, as opposed to across columns. For each row of input data, these functions perform a calculation on a selection (window) of related rows and return a result for each row (unlike aggregation, which groups rows). For example, you can calculate the change in opportunity amount over time using the lag function based upon a snapshot date. The **Multiple row formula** option must be selected to perform window functions.

You can use the following window functions in a formula expression:

- current—Returns a value from the current record in the window (partition)

- dense_rank—Returns the rank of each record in the window based on order (where ranks are consecutive; they don't repeat when the values match)

- first_value—Returns a value from the first record in the window

- lag—Returns a value from the previous record in the window

- last_value —Returns a value from the last record in the window

- lead—Returns a value from the next record in the window

- rank—Returns the rank of each record in the window based on order, while repeating the rank when the values are the same, and skips as many on the next non-match

- row_number—Returns the row number in the window, incrementing by 1 for every row in the window

- sum—Returns the cumulative sum from groups of value

An example of a window function would be to rank the deals per salesperson by the deal amount, as seen in the following screenshot:

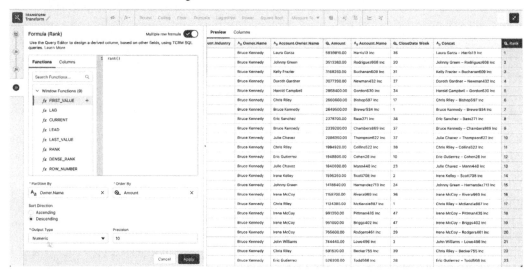

Figure 5.18 – Using a window function to rank deals per salesperson by the deal amount

Additional functions

Two additional functions are available—the case function and the coalesce function.

The case function

The case function handles if/then/else logic for formulas. This function can be used with TEXT, NUMBER, DATE_ONLY, and DATETIME data. The syntax for the case function is shown here:

```
case primary_expr(optional)
when condition
then result_expr
...
```

```
else
default_expr
end
```

For example, you could use the `case` function to handle null values where missing values are replaced with the word `Null`. The `case` function can also be used to bucket data, although this is often better handled using the standard `bucket` function.

The coalesce function

The `coalesce` function can do the following:

- Join two or more things or groups or dimensions to form a larger entity.
- Replace nulls with the first non-null value in the expression.

This function can be used with TEXT, NUMBER, DATE_ONLY, and DATETIME data. The syntax is shown here:

```
coalesce(expr1,expr2)
```

For example, you can use the `coalesce` function to take two datasets or two streams from the same dataset (usually by filtering), and merge them into one.

Common Functions

Common functions have their own buttons in the **Transform** toolbar—when used, these will automatically fill in the formula with the column name and predefined syntax to save time.

Working with dates in the Data Prep tool

One of the more challenging areas of data preparation and transformation in CRMA has historically been working with dates. As the engineering team at Salesforce has continued to develop the new Data Prep ETL tool of CRMA, this is now easier than ever before.

Date fields are the key to understanding trends over time. Dates are critical for keeping teams aware of upcoming milestones and deadlines. You can now use **Date and Time** transformations in CRMA Data Prep to perform calculations based on dates, all in the GUI with *no code*.

Two common ways in which you may need to work with dates in CRMA is to add or subtract days or months and calculate a date difference.

Add or Subtract Days or Months

You can use the **Add or Subtract Days or Months** function to add or subtract days or months from a date column by following these simple steps:

1. Select the target date column while in the **Transform** node.
2. Select the **Add or Subtract Days or Months** function from the toolbar.
3. Enter the function attributes as follows:

- **Start Date Column**
- **Days or Months**
- **Number of Months Before or After**
- **Date Format**
- **Show Results In**
- **Column Label**

The following screenshot shows how to quickly select the **Add or Subtract Days or Months** function from the **Transform** node toolbar:

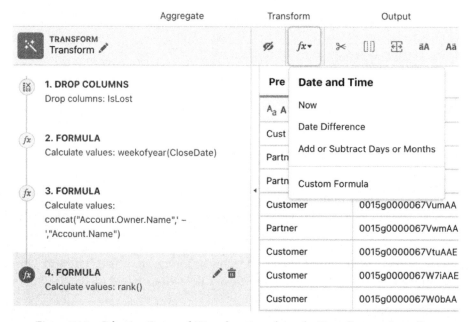

Figure 5.19 – Selecting Date and Time functions from the Transform node toolbar

Here is an example use of the **Add or Subtract Days or Months** transformation where 1 month was added to the close date of opportunities and the date format was simplified:

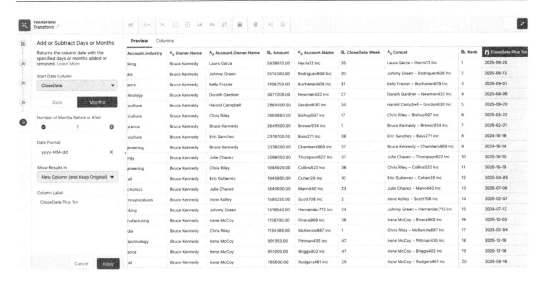

Figure 5.20 – Example use of Add or Subtract Days or Months

Date Difference

Use **Date Difference** to calculate the duration between two selected date columns as days, months, or years.

For example, you might want to calculate the number of months until deals are expected to close. Using the **Now** and **Date Difference** functions makes this easy! The following screenshot shows how this can be done simply and quickly, with no code:

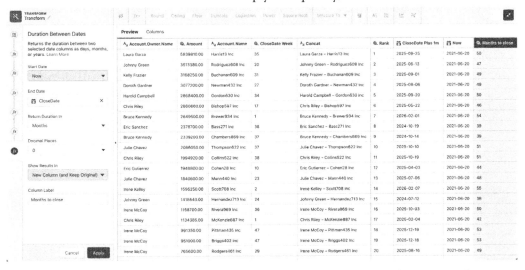

Figure 5.21 – Calculating the number of months until deals are expected to close by using the Date Difference function

A deeper understanding of how and why to flatten your data

One of the most common use cases for flattening your data is to prepare data for use in security predicates—that is, data concerning role hierarchy is used to decide who sees what in a dataset or dashboard, based upon hierarchy data pertaining to the logged-in user.

See *Chapter 7, Security in CRM Analytics*, for more information about security predicates.

You will now learn about the hierarchy data type and how it can be used with a flatten transformation to prepare data for CRMA security purposes.

Role hierarchy data type in Salesforce

The role hierarchy data type is associated with the standard Salesforce **User** object. It relates users to each other in a different hierarchy as an alternative to the standard manager user field.

The characteristics of the role hierarchy data type are outlined here:

- It is only allowed on the **User** object.
- It is a specialized version of the lookup relationship, in that it automatically self-references back to the **User** object, and it is similar to the standard lookup in that you can only create up to 40.
- In the **user interface** (**UI**), a hierarchical field includes a dropdown of user types (for example, **User**, **Partner User**, **Customer Portal User**) that limits the lookup field to those users.
- Hierarchical fields support filters.
- Users selected in the hierarchy cannot be any users below that user in the hierarchy or the same user on the current record.
- It is supported in approval processes. Salesforce allows us to select from the standard user manager field or any hierarchical fields when configuring an approval process and determining the next approver. Also, you can create a new hierarchical field on the fly while configuring the approval process, without having to build it in advance.

A role hierarchy is created and configured via Salesforce **Setup**, as you can see in the following example:

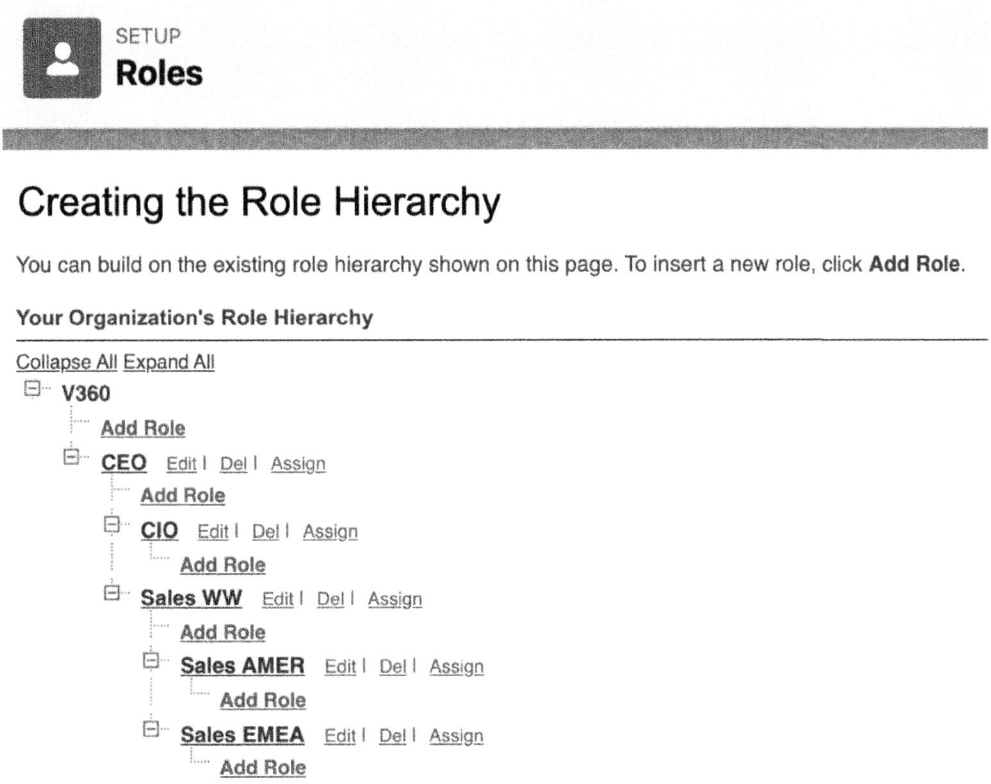

Creating the Role Hierarchy

You can build on the existing role hierarchy shown on this page. To insert a new role, click **Add Role**.

Your Organization's Role Hierarchy

Collapse All Expand All

⊟ **V360**
    ├── Add Role
    ⊟ **CEO** Edit I Del I Assign
        ├── **Add Role**
        ⊟ **CIO** Edit I Del I Assign
            └── **Add Role**
        ⊟ **Sales WW** Edit I Del I Assign
            ├── **Add Role**
            ⊟ **Sales AMER** Edit I Del I Assign
                └── **Add Role**
            ⊟ **Sales EMEA** Edit I Del I Assign
                └── **Add Role**

Figure 5.22 – Creating a role hierarchy in Setup

Flatten transformation

Detailed instructions on how to use a flatten transformation were given in *Chapter 4, Building Data Recipes*. In this section, we will look at how to flatten data in preparation for use in security predicates. This will enable you to add row-level security to a dashboard and dataset with the help of role hierarchy data.

Salesforce has provided a very powerful feature in **Flatten Transformation** to configure the data security in a **customer relationship management** (**CRM**) system to be incorporated in native CRMA.

Consider the use-case scenario of access to opportunity records for a sales organization configured using their role hierarchy in their Salesforce CRM. Let's walk through this example. The role hierarchy of the org is depicted here:

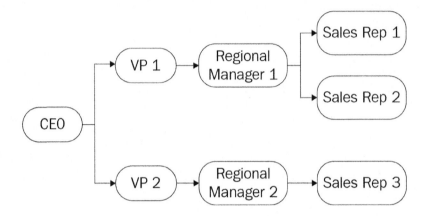

Figure 5.23 – Role hierarchy of the org in this example

In the preceding diagram, we have three sales reps, where **Sales Rep 1** and **Sales Rep 2** report to the **Regional Manager 1** role, and **Sales Rep 3** reports to the **Regional Manager 2** role. Access in this scenario works as follows:

- Opportunity records owned by **Sales Rep 1** and **Sales Rep 2** are accessible by **Regional Manager 1** and the roles shown in the preceding diagram.

- Opportunity records owned by **Sales Rep 3** are accessible to **Regional Manager 2** and the roles shown in the preceding diagram.

- **Regional Manager 2** should not be able to access the opportunities of **Sales Rep 1** and **Sales Rep 2** unless shared manually or by a sharing rule.

- **Regional Manager 1** should not be able to access the opportunities of **Sales Rep 3** unless shared manually or by a sharing rule.

The flatten transformation builds the table seen in the following screenshot to enable configuration of these access levels in CRMA:

ROLE ID (SELF ID)	ROLE NAME	PARENT ROLE ID	ROLES	ROLEPATH
1	Salesperson 1	10	10, 20, 30	\10\20\30
2	Salesperson 2	10	10, 20, 30	\10\20\30
3	Salesperson 3	11	11, 20, 30	\11\20\30
10	Regional Manager 1	20	20, 30	\20\30
11	Regional Manager 2	20	20, 30	\20\30
20	Vice President 1	30	30	\30
21	Vice President 2	30	30	\30
30	CEO	Not applicable	Not applicable	Not applicable

Figure 5.24 – Flatten transformation table

How is this facilitated by the **Flatten Transformation** node? The `UserRole` object in Salesforce holds all the information on role hierarchy, and this object is used in **Flatten Transformation** as follows:

1. Select **Add Input Data in the Recipe**.
2. Select the `UserRole` object.
3. Add a **Transformation** node.
4. Select the **Role ID** column.
5. Select **Flatten**.

The **Transformation** node looks like this:

Figure 5.25 – The Transformation node in CRMA, prior to configuration

Now, let's look at the options to configure **Flatten Transformation**, as follows:

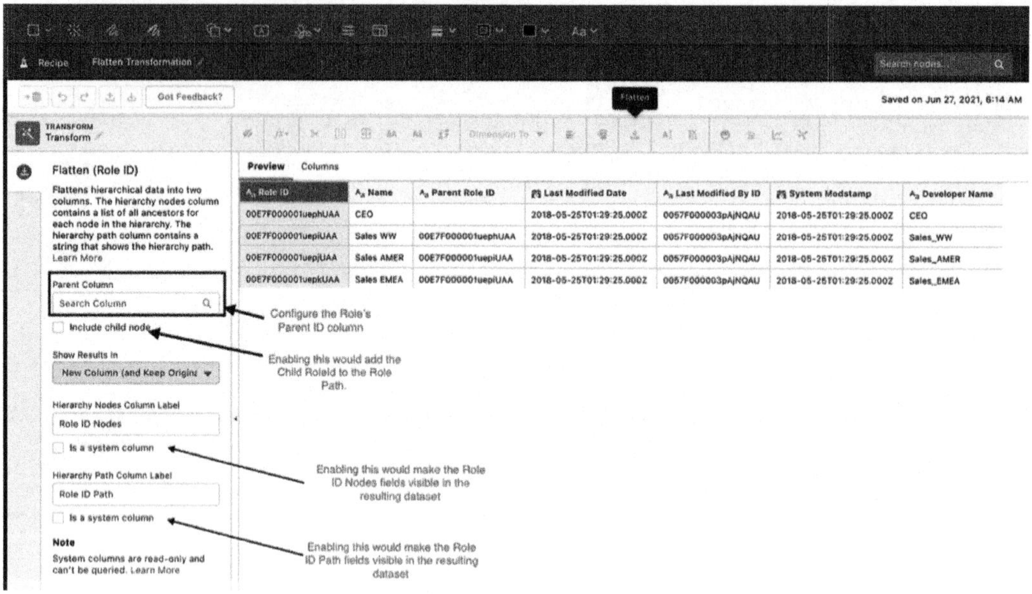

Figure 5.26 – Options to configure Flatten Transformation

Including the child node option will enable the role ID of the row to be part of the role ID path. The following screenshot presents a **Flatten** table with the **Include child node** option enabled:

ROLE ID (SELF ID)	ROLE NAME	PARENT ROLE ID	ROLES	ROLEPATH
1	Salesperson 1	10	1, 10, 20, 30	\1\10\20\30
2	Salesperson 2	10	2,10, 20, 30	\2\10\20\30
3	Salesperson 3	11	3,11, 20, 30	\3\11\20\30
10	Regional Manager 1	20	10,20, 30	\10\20\30
11	Regional Manager 2	20	11,20, 30	\11\20\30
20	Vice President 1	30	20,30	\20\30
21	Vice President 2	30	21,30	\21\30
30	CEO	Not applicable	30	30

Figure 5.27 – Flatten table with the Include child node option enabled

Flatten Transformation, once configured, adds the following two fields to the dataset:

- **Role ID Nodes**
- **Role ID Path**

These fields can also be renamed in the **Transform** node, as illustrated in the following screenshot:

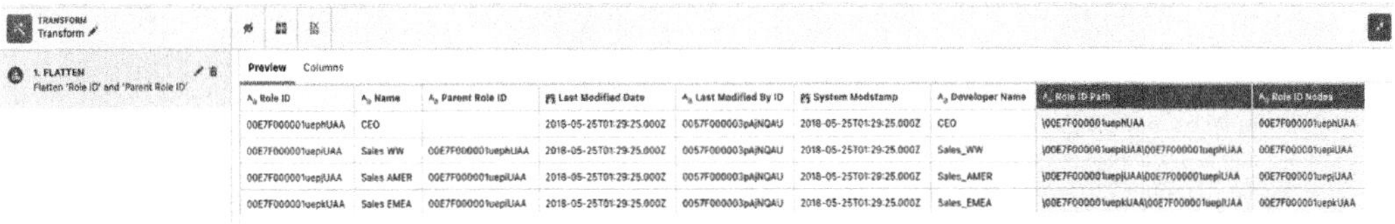

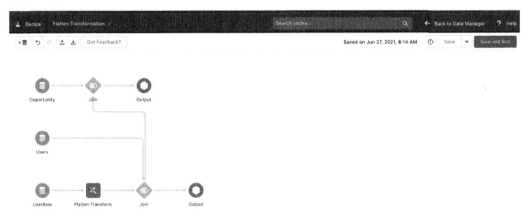

Figure 5.28 – Renaming fields in the Transform node

Regarding the two highlighted columns, the following applies:

- **Role ID Path**: This column has all the role IDs that are above the role ID in the row listed, separated by a backslash. If **Include child node** is enabled, it lists the role ID of the row as well in the path (self).

- **Role ID Nodes**: This column has all the role IDs in the hierarchy of the role ID in the row listed as a multi-value.

The **Transform** node can then be used in the join to map the owner ID of the opportunity record and the user ID from the user role to determine the accessibility of each record, as seen here:

Figure 5.29 – Use of the Transform node in the join to map the owner ID of the opportunity record and the user ID from the user role

This **Role ID Path** field or **Role ID Nodes** field is then used in the security predicate to determine the accessibility of a row in the dataset. See *Chapter 7, Security in CRM Analytics*, for more information about security predicates.

Predict Missing Values – how and when to use

When can you use the **Predict Missing Values** transform to fill in missing values in a dimension column? First, in order to make an accurate prediction, each column must have fewer than 200 unique values. Also, you must verify that these predictive columns contain clean, high-quality data, or the predicted values will be misleading.

How can you use the **Predict Missing Values** transform? Note the following:

- When you click **Apply** to add a transformation to the **Transform** node, the preview pane will show the original column with the missing values and the new column with **Predict** at the end of the header.

- You will see **Prediction TBD** for predicted values in the new column.

- The predicted values will not appear until after you run the recipe.

- Run the recipe to generate the predictions—you can then view the dataset as a values table to see the predictions.

- Add the **Drop Columns** transformation after the **Predict Missing Values** transformation to drop the original column from the dataset, as required.

> **Limitations to Keep in Mind**
>
> Firstly, if there are not enough rows to make accurate predictions, CRMA will not insert any predicted values. Secondly, you cannot apply any transformations on predicted columns. Finally, recipes that predict values can sometimes take longer to run.

Sentiment detection explained

Using **natural language processing (NLP)** and ML, sentiment detection can extract valuable information from text fields, such as reviews, case comments, and social media posts. Use the **Detect Sentiment** transformation in a Data Prep recipe to categorize that information into one of the following three sentiments:

- **Positive**
- **Negative**
- **Neutral**

In other words, you don't need a new ML project, an ML system, new infrastructure, or a separate data pipeline to detect sentiments from your unstructured data. The **Detect Sentiment** transformation in CRMA Data Prep does it all!

Some potential use cases for the **Detect Sentiment** transformation include the following:

- Customer service/**customer satisfaction (CSAT)** based upon survey responses
- Sales coaching and trend identification
- Social media brand management

The **Detect Sentiment** transformation supports English text only and works on a single-dimension column. It processes non-English text as English and ignores all images. The transformation returns `null` when the input value is `null` and returns `neutral` when the input value is an empty string (`''`).

Advanced hands-on exercise

The purpose of this exercise is to create a single dataset that contains a summary of every account that meets all of the following conditions: has open opportunities, at least one activity, and an open case attached to the account.

The resulting dataset should allow the user to determine the following via direct exploration of the lens based on the dataset:

- Account name
- Age of account
- Owner name
- No. of open opportunities
- No. of open cases
- Average case duration
- No. of activities
- Total amount
- Total expected amount
- Total amount (opportunity with line items)
- Total amount (opportunity without line items)

Resources required

Data sources that are available in your CRMA environment will be used for the purpose of this exercise. Please use the datasets found under the **My First Analytics App** app so that the results will be consistent with the following steps:

- **Opportunities**
- **Cases**
- **Activities**
- **Accounts**
- **Users**

Steps to follow

Build a new recipe in your demo CRMA environment and follow these steps:

1. Select **Opportunities**, **Accounts**, **Activities**, **Cases**, and **Users** for your recipe input data. The panel on the right allows the selection of columns, and although you can proceed by selecting all columns, ideally you would only want to work with the columns required.

2. Add filters that are required as per the exercise objectives.

3. Add some aggregation nodes as you know that **Opportunities**, **Cases**, and **Activities** have a lower granularity than **Accounts**. As such, you will need to aggregate all of them to the same granularity (**Accounts**) so that you are able to perform joins in the later steps to meet the objectives.

4. Your aggregation on the **Opportunities** data input will split the opportunity and expected amounts into two columns—with line items and without, as that was a requirement. However, this also means that you do not have a field that has the total amount and total expected amount. Create a **Transform** node that helps you bring the totals back into the dataset build.

5. Make the necessary joins so that you can work toward your final dataset.

6. As you have already aggregated the open opportunities to the account level and also made activities and cases summarized at the same granularity, you need to add a couple of inner joins to merge them, maintaining the **Accounts**-level granularity that we require in the final dataset.

7. Add lookup joins to bring in the names as per the requirement. It is important that at every step, you select the correct fields that need to be carried through (per the exercise requirements).

8. Add one final transformation where a custom formula is added to calculate the age of the account.

9. Run the dataflow to create your dataset.

10. Explore via a lens.

Solution

The completed data recipe should look like this:

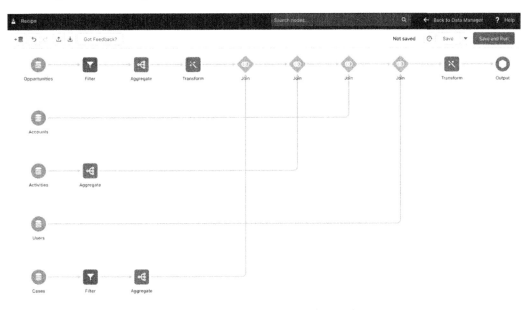

Figure 5.30 – Completed data recipe for the hands-on exercise

When you open the completed dataset as a lens, it will look like this:

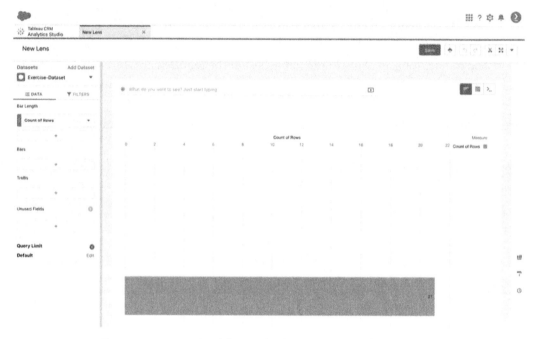

Figure 5.31 – Completed dataset for the hands-on exercise: bar view

Looking at the dataset as a values table, it will look like this:

Figure 5.32 – Completed dataset for the hands-on exercise: values table view

For more information about using lenses to explore data, see *Chapter 6, CRMA Lenses – Diving into Your Data One Click at a Time.*

Summary

In this chapter, you learned how to use the more advanced ETL tools available in Data Prep and CRMA recipes. You should now be able to join, aggregate, flatten, and transform your data with confidence using the CRMA data preparation GUI. This includes the use of complex and custom transformations using formulas.

In the following chapter, you will learn how to use the data exploration tool known as a CRMA lens, and you will understand how lenses are the building blocks of CRMA dashboards.

Questions

Here is a list of questions to test your knowledge:

- What is the difference between a lookup join, an inner join, and a full join?

- Give one real-world example of how to use a full join.

- Why would you need to connect data from external sources with Salesforce objects? Give one practical example.

- Explain how to combine aggregation and grouping using two data streams in one recipe.

- The **Multiple Row Formula** option must be selected to perform window functions. What are window functions, and when might you use them?

- What is a flatten transformation, and what is a use case for this?

6

CRMA Lenses – Diving into Your Data One Click at a Time

Lenses are the investigative journalists of CRM Analytics (CRMA). In this chapter, you will learn what a lens is and how it is a powerful tool to understand, test, debug, and showcase data. You will also be taught how lenses act as the building blocks of analytics dashboards in CRMA.

The ability to build and deploy CRMA lenses is crucial for your ability to create, edit, test, and deploy CRMA dashboards. Lenses are a critical building block of CRMA data analytics.

By the end of this chapter, you will have a good grasp of what lenses are and how they work. You will also be intimately familiar with the lens UI and be skilled in creating, editing, and cloning lenses. Finally, you will understand how lenses are the building blocks of CRMA dashboards and will be competent in using them as such.

In this chapter, we will cover the following topics:

- Lenses – the investigative journalists of CRMA
- Creating, editing, and cloning lenses
- Using lenses to create a CRMA analytics dashboard
- Tips and hints

Technical requirements

You will need the following to successfully execute the instructions in this chapter:

- A laptop or desktop with internet access (a tablet or phone is not sufficient)
- The latest version of the Google Chrome browser (Chrome is the preferred browser when working with CRMA)
- A working email address

Ensure that you're logged into your CRMA dev org.

Lenses – the investigative journalists of CRMA

What exactly is a lens? Think of a lens as your data exploration tool in CRM Analytics, combining a data query with a visualization in a simple, powerful, and dynamic interface.

A lens enables you to perform the following tasks:

- Explore the various characteristics of your dataset, including dimensions, measures, field labels, and names.
- Slice and dice data using various measures, dimensions, filters, and formulas.
- Create visualizations and tables that can be clipped to a dashboard.
- Create visualizations and tables that can be shared with other users.

In the next section, you are going to get your hands dirty in CRMA and work with lenses.

Creating, editing, and cloning lenses

Now that you understand what a lens is and what it is used for, you are going to build and edit a lens in CRMA. Before you get started, here is what the lens UI looks like, with a few key components labeled for reference:

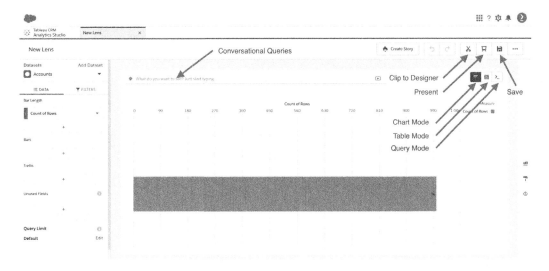

Figure 6.1 – The CRMA lens UI

You will now learn how to work with lenses in Chart Mode.

Working with Chart Mode

Open Analytics Studio and follow these steps:

1. Select **MyFirstDataset** from the **All Items** list. This will bring you to the lens UI, which will open in the default Chart Mode.

2. On the left-hand side of your screen, use the drop-down list to choose **Sum of Amount** for **Bar Length**.

3. Choose **OwnerId.Name** for **Bars**.

4. Click on the drop-down arrow next to **Sum of Amount** and select **Sort Descending**.

5. On the far right-hand side of your screen, click on the **Formatting** icon, which looks like a paintbrush.

6. Add a title in the **Title** box called **My First Lens**.

7. Save your lens by clicking on the **Save** button, name it **My First Lens**, and save it as **My First Analytics App**.

Congratulations! You have created your first lens in CRMA. The result should look like this:

Figure 6.2 – MyFirstDataset viewed as a lens

Before you begin working with this lens and exploring the CRMA len's functionality, you need to understand the admin tools, as shown in the following screenshot:

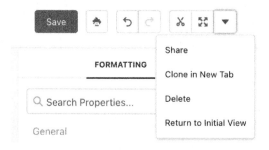

Figure 6.3 – Lens admin tools

The lens admin tools are as follows:

- **Save**: Save the lens to a CRMA app for future use.

- **Create Story**: Create an Einstein Discovery story from the lens.

- **Undo/Redo**: Undoes or redoes the latest action.

- **Clip to Designer**: If a dashboard is open in the dashboard editor, the lens is clipped, or exported, to the dashboard as a widget.

- **Present**: Enables full-screen mode for presenting.
- **Share**: Shares the lens with other users; more details will be provided shortly.
- **Clone in New Tab**: Creates a new lens from the current lens by cloning it and creating a new tab.
- **Delete**: Deletes the lens.
- **Return to Initial View**: Undoes all the changes and returns to the very first lens view.

The options that are available under the **Share** menu are as follows:

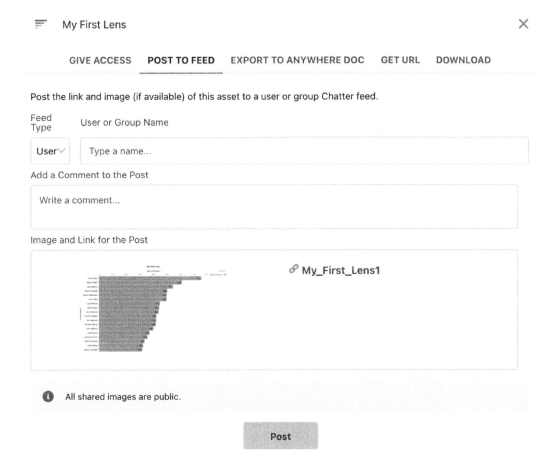

Figure 6.4 – Options available under the Share menu

Let's look at the five options available for a lens under the **Share** menu:

- **GIVE ACCESS**: Invites others to view, edit, or manage the lens via the Analytics app.
- **POST TO FEED**: Posts the link and image of the lens via Chatter.
- **EXPORT TO ANYWHERE DOC**: Salesforce Anywhere (previously known as Quip) users can see the current view of your data once the lens has been published.
- **GET URL**: Users with CRMA access to the lens can access it directly using the URL link.
- **DOWNLOAD**: The data can be downloaded as an image, Excel spreadsheet, or as a `.csv` file.

Now that you have created a simple lens, let's explore the data and learn how to take advantage of the powerful lens functionality. Begin with your lens, **My First Lens**, and follow these steps:

1. Click on **Clone In New Tab** and save this new lens as **Top Ten Sales Reps**.
2. Add a second measure to the lens by clicking the + symbol under **Bar Length** and choosing **Count of Rows**.
3. Under **Query Limit**, click on **Edit**, enter 10, and hit **Apply**.
4. Change the lens's title to **Top Ten Sales Reps**.
5. Increase the lens's title to 18.
6. Add a filter by selecting the **Filters** tab, clicking on the + button, typing stage in the search bar, selecting **Stage**, choosing **Closed Won** as the value, and clicking on **Apply**. Note that the order changes when the filter is applied.
7. **Save** your lens.

At this stage, the lens should look like this:

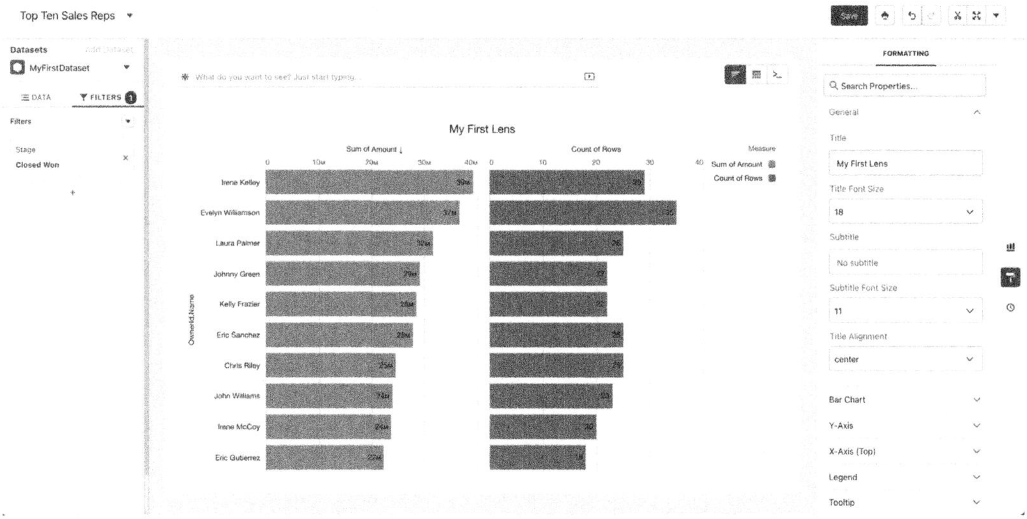

Figure 6.5 – Lens's progress once the filter has been applied

Continue to edit your lens as follows:

1. On the far right-hand side, click on the **Charts** button, which looks like a column chart, then select the **Combo** chart under **LINES**.

2. Click on **Formatting** (the paintbrush icon), then click the drop-down arrow next to **Combo Chart**. Click on the **Axis Mode** dropdown and select **Dual Axis**.

3. Scroll down the right-hand menu until you see the **Legend** dropdown. Click on it and deselect the **Show legend header** check box.

4. Under the **Position** dropdown, select **top-center**.

5. Scroll down the right-hand menu until you see the **Conditional Formatting** drop-down arrow. Click the arrow, click on the drop-down list for **Apply Conditional Formatting To**, and select **Measure**.

6. Pick a new color for both **Sum of Amount** and **Count of Rows**.

7. Scroll up (close the expanded sections if you want to) and expand **X-Axis** by clicking on the arrow.

8.   Add a custom title of **Sales Rep** for **X-Axis**.

9.   Scroll up and add a **subtitle** for the **Ranked in descending order by value of deals won** lens.

10.   Change **Subtitle Font Size** to **14**.

11.   **Save** your lens.

12.   Click on the **Present** button to go into full-screen presentation mode.

By now, your lens should look like this:

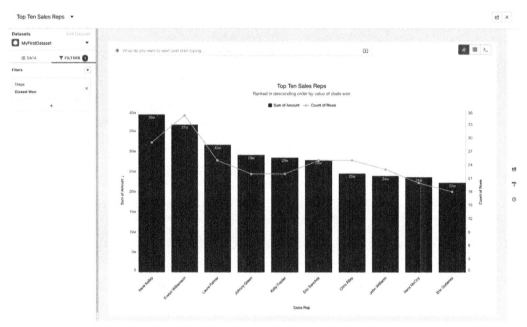

Figure 6.6 – Lens progress as a combo chart with conditional formatting and subtitles added

Next, you must create a visual that will also show how each sales rep is doing compared to their target:

1.   Click the **Exit Full Screen** button at the top right-hand side of the screen, which looks like an **x**.

2.   Change the chart type to **Polar Gauge**. Notice that when you do so, the **Count of Rows** measure moves to **Unused Fields**.

3.   Click on the **Formatting** tab and expand **Range Values** by clicking on the arrow.

4.   Change the value of **Max** to **40000000**.

5. Expand the **Trellis** section and change **Type** to **Matrix** and **Size Ratio** to **Square**. Notice how much easier the lens is to read.

6. Apply conditional formatting to **Sum of Amount**, change the value of the top bin to **30000000**, and select red for the top bin and green for the bottom bin.

7. Expand the **Polar Gauge** section and change **Center Size** to **70%**.

8. Change the subtitle to **Performance to Target ($30M)**.

9. **Save** the lens.

The matrix of polar gauges should look like this:

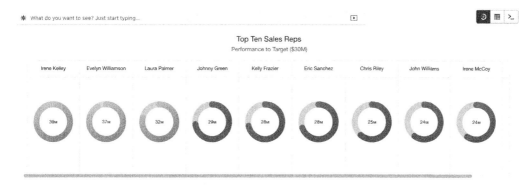

Figure 6.7 – Matrix of polar gauges

Now, let's learn how to drill down into the lens data. Open **My First Lens** and follow these steps:

1. Select the bar for **Johnny Green** by clicking on it.

2. When you do so, a new button will appear next to the **Chart Mode** button. Hover over this new button to view its **Drill down to group selections by the chosen dimension** function. Click on the **Drill down** button.

3. You can either select an industry or view a data table for Johnny Green's records. Select **AccountId.Industry**.

4. What you can see now has been filtered by **OwnerId.Name = Johnny Green**. You could drill down even further if you wish to, look at the values table for individual records, and so on.

5. Close the lens without saving it.

The drill-down functionality in a lens looks like this:

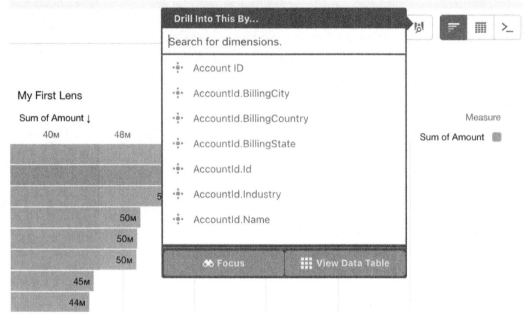

Figure 6.8 – Drill-down functionality in a lens

Now, let's create a new lens to compare measures and understand correlations and comparisons using a scatter plot. Follow these steps:

1. Open the **Opportunities** dataset in **My First Analytics App**.

2. Add a filter for **Closed** set to **Open**.

3. Create a scatter plot chart where **X-Axis** is **Sum of Amount**, **Y-Axis** is **Count of Rows**, **Bubble Size** is **Avg of Amount**, and **Bubbles** is **Industry**.

4. Save this as **Oppty Scatter Plot** in **My First Analytics App**.

The lens should look like this:

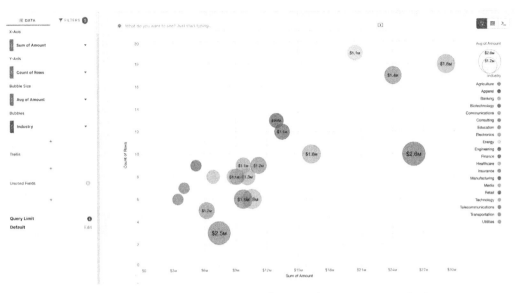

Figure 6.9 – Measure comparison, as shown in the Oppty Scatter Plot lens

How is this kind of visualization useful? A scatter plot can be used for the following purposes:

- Demonstrating the relationship between two variables – positive or negative, non-linear or linear, and/or strong or weak

- Identifying correlational relationships

- Identifying data patterns, such as clustering

One powerful feature of lenses is the ability to add or join a second dataset to your visualization. Let's go ahead and try this by performing the following steps:

1. Open the **Opportunities** dataset in **My First Analytics App**.

2. In the top left-hand corner, click on **Add Dataset**.

3. The datasets are joined as a **left blend** by default, but this can be changed. Leave this set to **Left Blend**.

4. For **Bar Length**, select **Sum of Amount** for the **Opportunities** dataset.

5. Sort this measure in descending order.

6. For the second **Bar Length**, select **Count of Rows** for the **Cases** dataset.

7. For bars, choose **Account Name** for both the **Opportunities** and **Cases** datasets.

8. Choose the **Pyramid** chart type and format it as necessary.

9. Change **Query Limit** to **10,000**.

10. Save the lens as **Blended Datasets** in **My First Analytics App**.

This lens, which contains two datasets, shows both the sum of deals and the total number of cases, by account name, for all accounts with opportunities. It should look something like the following, depending on your customizations:

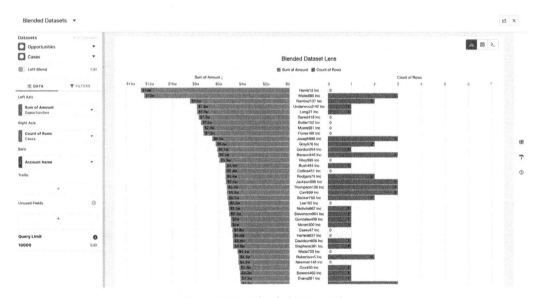

Figure 6.10 – Blended Datasets lens

The ability to add a second dataset to a lens is very powerful as it saves the need to create a new dataset using a recipe, or co-grouping data streams in SAQL, to combine data from two datasets into one visualization. For example, this makes it quick and easy to combine opportunity data and target data into one chart. There are many other use cases for this feature.

Using the Show Fields panel

On the left-hand side of the lens UI, next to the dataset's name, is a drop-down arrow. Click on this to reveal the **Show Fields** panel. Click on this to reveal the **Fields** panel, which looks like this:

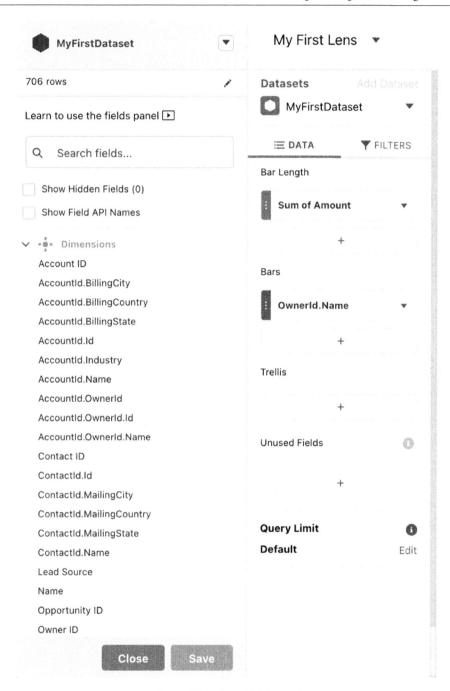

Figure 6.11 – The Fields panel

The options that are available for each field are as follows:

- **Rename**: To rename the field label.
- **Hide**: To hide the field.
- **Edit Values** (dimensions or dates only): A field label can be edited here, and a default color can be added for each value.
- **Format Numbers** (measures only): Numbers can be formatted to suit your requirements, such as currency rounded or percent.
- **Copy API Name**: Copies the field API name to your clipboard.

> **Note Regarding Changes Made in the Fields Panel**
>
> It is important to note that any changes that are made here will apply to the dataset wherever it is used – these are global changes.

With the knowledge you've gained thus far, it's time to get your hands dirty with a practical exercise.

Hands-on exercise

Follow these steps in your CRMA Analytics Studio:

1. In the CRMA Analytics Studio, open **My First Analytics App** and click on the **Cases** dataset to create a new lens.

2. Save the lens as **Service Data Analysis** in **My First Analytics App**.

3. To begin with, create a time combo chart with **Avg of Case Duration** and **Count of Rows** trended over **Closed Date (Year-Month)**.

4. **Save** your lens.

The lens should look something like this:

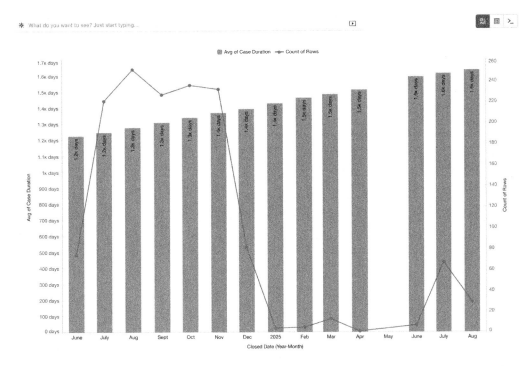

Figure 6.12 – Hands-on exercise starting point (case data)

Change the chart type to combo (instead of time combo), then modify your data so that the x axis is the industry and answer these questions:

- What account industry has the most cases?

- What account industry has the highest average case duration?

- Set some custom colors and modify the value names for some **Account.Industry** fields.

- Use the drill-down button to slice and dice several industries by other dimensions, such as **Billing Country**, **Priority**, and **Status**.

- Experiment with the following chart types and understand where each is useful: Line, Combo, Timeline, Flat Gauge, Polar Gauge, Donut, Matrix, Waterfall, and Scatter Plot.

- What is the best chart for looking at the correlation of case priority and status? Build this lens and save it as a copy (cloned lens).

- Use the trellis functionality and think where it could best be used.

What did you learn about by diving into your data with lenses? The following are some example questions:

- What limitations did you hit while working only with clicks, not code?

- Are there any chart types that you are unsure of using, or think are not of much use in the real world?

- Can you create charts of exactly the right look and feel, or is customization limited in lenses?

Now that you're confident with Chart Mode, it's time to use a flexible, no-code analysis tool in TRCM lenses called Table Mode.

Analyzing your data using Table Mode

In this section, you will learn how to use one of the more flexible and powerful tools in CRMA – tables.

First, let's look at the values table.

Values table

The values table is used to look at record values. Open **My First Lens** and change to **Table Mode – Values Table**. The lens will change to a table view, like this:

Figure 6.13 – Initial values table view

Follow these steps to create a new table view:

- Select **Clone in New Tab** and save as **My First Table View**.
- Filter the data by **Stage = Closed Won**.
- Filter the data by **Close Date = 1/1/2025 – 30/6/2025**.
- Change **Query Limit** to **1,000**.
- Edit your columns as you see fit – see the following screenshot.
- Select the **Formatting** tab and choose a new table **theme**.
- Change the table's **spacing**. Select **Fit To Widget** under **Column Width**.
- Modify the **Header** details.
- Add a table background color.
- Remove the row index column.
- Click on the **Column** tab and add **Conditional Formatting** to a measure column – see **Figures 6.15 and 6.16**.
- Experiment with the other settings under the **Column** tab.
- **Save** your lens.

Your edited table columns should look as follows:

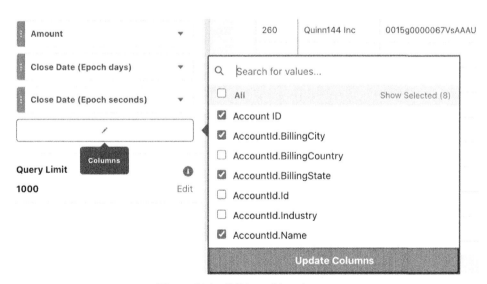

Figure 6.14 – Editing table columns

The conditional formatting for the table columns should look like this:

Figure 6.15 – Conditional Formatting

The following screenshot shows the continuation of the conditional formatting for table columns:

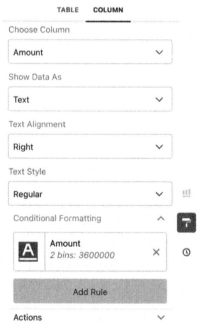

Figure 6.16 – Adding conditional formatting to a measure column

Your modified table might look something like this:

AccountId.Name	OwnerId.Name	Name	AccountId.Industry	Amount ↓	Close Date
Carr889 Inc	Johnny Green	Opportunity for Norman1354	Communications	5,294,610	2025-01-11
Stevenson954 Inc	Eric Gutierrez	Opportunity for Daniel875	Insurance	5,023,650	2025-05-08
Nichols662 Inc	Catherine Brown	Opportunity for Alvarado1597	Manufacturing	4,824,325	2025-04-28
Flores188 Inc	Kelly Frazier	Opportunity for Cunningham175	Retail	4,357,300	2025-02-16
Torres548 Inc	Evelyn Williamson	Opportunity for Watson580	Biotechnology	4,090,880	2025-05-23
Watts685 Inc	John Williams	Opportunity for Rogers1242	Biotechnology	3,907,275	2025-04-01
Rios830 Inc	Johnny Green	Opportunity for McDonald1503	Apparel	3,851,250	2025-02-03
Doyle498 Inc	Chris Riley	Opportunity for Martin1417	Transportation	3,712,300	2025-03-31
Fleming816 Inc	Laura Palmer	Opportunity for Smith309	Insurance	3,709,600	2025-02-09
Wood74 Inc	Johnny Green	Opportunity for Jackson1400	Engineering	3,555,960	2025-01-13
Rodriguez608 Inc	Bruce Kennedy	Opportunity for Houston1041	Media	3,513,380	2025-05-13
Joseph988 Inc	Dennis Howard	Opportunity for Weber619	Energy	3,474,950	2025-06-19
Dawson161 Inc	Evelyn Williamson	Opportunity for Dennis1374	Education	3,463,920	2025-05-05
Byrd23 Inc	Evelyn Williamson	Opportunity for Bates1547	Education	3,426,450	2025-06-05
Rodgers79 Inc	Eric Gutierrez	Opportunity for Dennis524	Banking	3,390,620	2025-02-06

Figure 6.17 – Sample of a customized values table

Values tables are extremely useful for preparing tables for dashboards or diving into your data one row at a time for detailed analysis. You can also add subtotals and totals using the summary button with the Σ symbol.

Now, it's time to look at the compare table tool for diving into your data.

Compare table

Compare table is one of the most powerful declarative tools for analyzing your data. The column editor can be used to perform the following tasks:

- Add calculations and filters to your table.
- Perform arithmetic across the columns and rows.
- Create labels by manipulating string values.
- View measures side by side.
- Concatenate dimension values.
- Create simple buckets.
- Add image URLs.

In the following exercise, we will perform the following steps with a compare table:

1. Calculate a running total for the number of won deals.

2. Rank sales reps by the sum of won deals.

3. Calculate the share of total for each rep.

4. Calculate a deal win % for all reps, calculated by deal count (now amount).

Let's begin by creating our first compare table:

1. Open **My First Lens**.

2. Clone **My First Lens** in a new tab and save it as **My First Compare Table**.

3. Change to **Compare Table** mode.

4. Add **Count of Rows** as a second column/measure.

Now, go into column editing mode, as shown in the following screenshot, by clicking on **Edit this Column**:

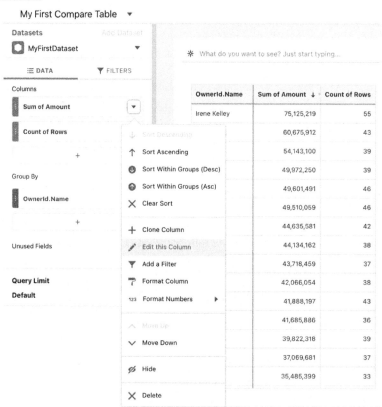

Figure 6.18 – Column editing mode

To obtain the answers that you are seeking, follow these steps:

1. Rename column A – **Column Header** – **Sum of Deals**, format it as **Currency**, and click **Apply**.

2. Next to **EDITING COLUMN**, you will see an arrow called **Edit right column**. Click on it to edit column B.

3. Rename column B **Deal Count** and click **Apply**.

4. Next to **EDITING COLUMN**, you will see a + sign – **Add column**. Click on it to create column C.

5. Rename column C **Cumulative Deal Sum**.

6. Add a standard function (see the following screenshot) to calculate the **running total** and format it as **currency**.

7. Click **Close** and **Save**.

Adding a standard function looks like this:

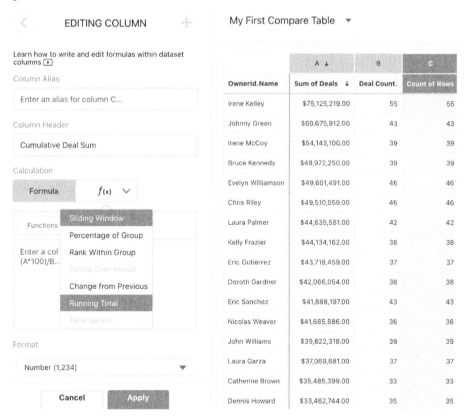

Figure 6.19 – Using a standard function to calculate the running total

So far, your progress should look like this:

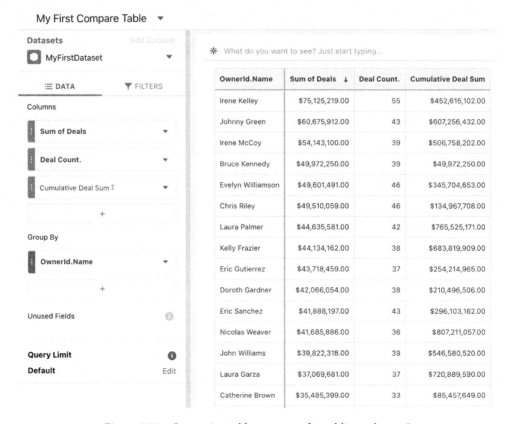

Figure 6.20 – Comparing table progress after adding column C

Now, we need to rank sales reps by the sum of won deals. Edit column C and continue as follows:

1. Click **Add column** and rename this new column, column D, **Ranking**.

2. Add the **Rank Within Group** function – using $f(x)$ – and rank descending using **Sum of Deals**.

3. Add a fifth column and name it **Share of Total**.

4. Use the **Percentage of Group** function to calculate **Share of Total** for each rep.

5. Click **Apply**, then **Close**, and then **Save**.

Your progress should match what's shown in the following screenshot:

My First Compare Table ▾

Datasets
⬤ MyFirstDataset   ▾

≣ DATA   ▼ FILTERS

Columns

▌ Sum of Deals   ▾

▌ Deal Count.   ▾

▌ Cumulative Deal Sum Σ   ▾

▌ Ranking Σ   ▾

▌ Share of Total Σ   ▾

                    +

Group By

▌ OwnerId.Name   ▾

                    +

Unused Fields   ⓘ

Query Limit   ⓘ
Default   Edit

✳ What do you want to see? Just start typing...

OwnerId.Name	Sum of Deals ↓	Deal Count.	Cumulative Deal Sum	Ranking	Share of Total
Irene Kelley	$75,125,219.00	55	$452,615,102.00	1	9.31%
Johnny Green	$60,675,912.00	43	$607,256,432.00	2	7.52%
Irene McCoy	$54,143,100.00	39	$506,758,202.00	3	6.71%
Bruce Kennedy	$49,972,250.00	39	$49,972,250.00	4	6.19%
Evelyn Williamson	$49,601,491.00	46	$345,704,653.00	5	6.14%
Chris Riley	$49,510,059.00	46	$134,967,708.00	6	6.13%
Laura Palmer	$44,635,581.00	42	$765,525,171.00	7	5.53%
Kelly Frazier	$44,134,162.00	38	$683,819,909.00	8	5.47%
Eric Gutierrez	$43,718,459.00	37	$254,214,965.00	9	5.42%
Doroth Gardner	$42,066,054.00	38	$210,496,506.00	10	5.21%
Eric Sanchez	$41,888,197.00	43	$296,103,162.00	11	5.19%
Nicolas Weaver	$41,685,886.00	36	$807,211,057.00	12	5.16%
John Williams	$39,822,318.00	39	$546,580,520.00	13	4.93%
Laura Garza	$37,069,681.00	37	$720,889,590.00	14	4.59%
Catherine Brown	$35,485,399.00	33	$85,457,649.00	15	4.4%

Figure 6.21 – Comparing the table's progress after adding Share of Total

Finally, you must calculate the deal win rate for each rep, calculated by deal count (now amount):

1. Add a sixth column based on the count of rows, naming it **Won**.

2. Add a filter to this column where **Won** = **True**.

3. Add one last column and rename it **Win Rate**.

4. Add a simple formula for calculating the win rate, truncated to two digits, as per the following code snippet.

5. Set **Format** to **Percent**.

6. Click **Apply** and then **Close**.

7. Sort **Win Rate** in descending order.

8. Click on **Save**.

This is the formula for calculating the win rate, truncated to two digits:

```
trunc (F/B,2)
```

The preceding formula will return the following result:

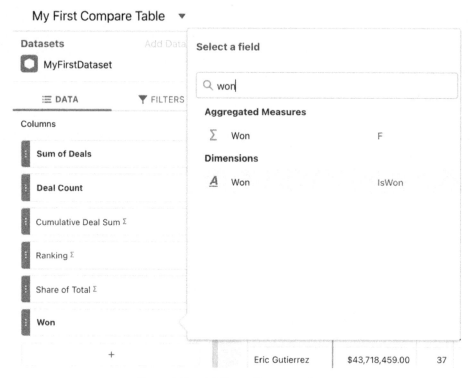

Figure 6.22 – Adding a filter to a column

Your completed table should look like this:

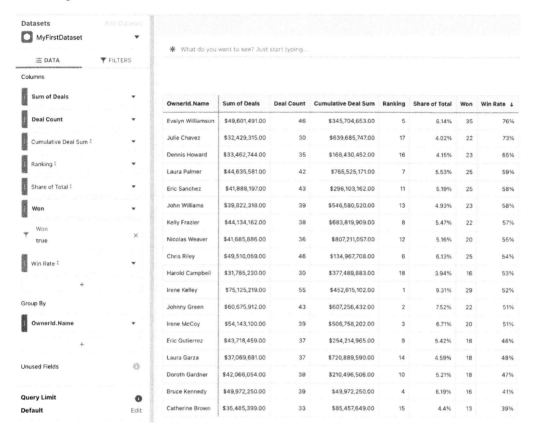

Figure 6.23 – Completed My First Compare Table

Now, create a combo chart that shows the sum of deals and win rate. Clone it in a new tab and save it as **Win Rate and Sum of Deals by Sales Rep**. The finished chart should look like this:

Figure 6.24 – Win Rate and Sum of Deals by Sales Rep

There is a great deal more that can be done with compare tables – dive into your dev org and find out for yourself!

Pivot table

You are most likely familiar with pivot tables; they are a common feature in tools such as spreadsheets. A pivot table is an interactive way to summarize data and analyze numerical data in detail. A pivot table is useful for doing the following:

- Subtotaling and aggregating numeric data, summarizing data by categories and subcategories.

- Expanding and collapsing different levels of data to focus on the results and drill down into the details at the summary level.

- Moving rows to columns or columns to rows (known as pivoting) to see varying summaries of your data.

- Filtering, sorting, grouping, and conditionally formatting the most useful and relevant subsets of data, enabling you to focus on the information you need.

By opening **My First Lens** and creating a pivot table with the second grouping of industry, we will see something like this after filtering the results:

Figure 6.25 – Pivot table example

Now, it's time to move on from Table Mode to Query Mode.

Query Mode

Now that you're confident with the Chart and Table Modes, the only mode left to understand is the powerful code-based analysis tool in TRCM lenses known as Query Mode. Query Mode utilizes **Salesforce Advanced Query Language (SAQL)** to query your data, as opposed to the declarative and low-code approaches we've examined so far.

Query Mode looks like this:

Figure 6.26 – Query Mode example

We are not going to dive into the details of Query Mode here because SAQL will be studied in detail in *Chapter 9, Advanced Dashboard Design and Build*. For a detailed reference on writing SAQL, see the CRMA SAQL Developer Guide here:

https://developer.salesforce.com/docs/atlas.en-us.232.0.bi_dev_guide_saql.meta/bi_dev_guide_saql/bi_saql_intro.htm

Now that you are confident in using CRMA lenses, you need to understand how you can clip lenses to a dashboard.

Using lenses to create a CRMA analytics dashboard

Lenses can be used to create a dashboard, or added to an existing dashboard, using the **Clip** function. While we are going to look at dashboard building in detail later in *Chapter 8, Building Your First CRMA Dashboard*, we will quickly look at how to create a simple dashboard and add the two lenses we created earlier. Follow these steps:

1. Open the **My First Lens**, **My First Table View**, and **Service Data Analysis** lenses.

2. From the CRMA Analytics Studio home page, click on **Create** and select **Dashboard**.

3. Select **Blank Dashboard**.

4. For each lens, go to the lens, click on the **Clip to Designer** button that has a scissors icon, ensure the lens will be exported as a widget, and click on **Clip to Designer**.

   Go to the blank dashboard, which is called **New dashboard** by default. Save the dashboard as **Lens Clip**.

5. Drag the three clipped lenses – which are now on the right-hand side of your dashboard designer as queries – to the design canvas.

6. Play with the lenses by resizing them until you're happy with the result.

7. **Save** the lens.

8. Click on **Preview** to view your dashboard or choose the **Present** view.

The result might look something like this:

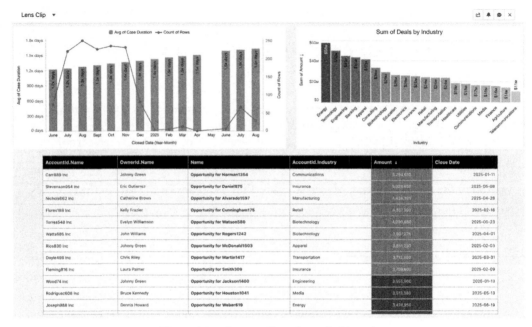

Figure 6.27 – Lenses clipped to a dashboard

As we mentioned previously, we will look at designing and building dashboards in more detail in *Chapter 8, Building Your First CRMA Dashboard.*

Before we close this chapter, I want to share a few tips and hints.

Tips and hints

Let me share a few tips and hints when it comes to working with lenses.

First, here are a few keyboard shortcuts:

- *S*: Save (no need to use the dialog box).
- *P*: Present (full screen) Mode.
- *Esc*: Exit Present Mode.
- *L*: Clip to dashboard designer.
- *Ctrl + E* (Windows)/*Cmd + E* (macOS): Open JSON Editor.

Second, you can do some cool stuff with subtotals, totals, and so on in tables and pivot tables using some clever SAQL.

Third, it is important to remember that when you modify field labels and colors in the **Fields** panel, the changes will be propagated through all the dashboards and lenses. Modify them carefully!

Fourth, the default number of rows in a values table can be changed using the **Query Limit** setting, or by using the SAQL limit statement.

Last, watch the query limit as it can have a serious impact on query results and make your numbers look incorrect since the default value is 2,000. This limit can also be edited or removed in SAQL.

Summary

As you have seen, lenses are the investigative journalists of CRMA. In this chapter, you learned what a lens is, how it is a flexible tool to investigate data, and how lenses are the building blocks of analytics dashboards in CRMA.

Now, you can create, edit, and clone lenses using the familiar lens UI. Finally, you understand how to build dashboards using lenses as building blocks.

The next chapter will teach you how to control who sees what in your lenses and dashboards by utilizing CRMA security tools.

Questions

Here are some questions for you to test your knowledge of this chapter's content:

- What does a lens enable you to do?
- What is the purpose of the Clip command for lenses?
- Name one use of a pivot table.
- How might you use a scatter plot chart? A combo chart? A flat gauge?
- How can you share a lens?
- What is the purpose of Query Mode?
- What are the three uses of a compare table?

7
Security in CRM Analytics

How do you decide who sees what in CRM Analytics? This is one of the least understood aspects of CRMA development, so in this chapter, you will learn how to secure your CRMA data. We will begin by providing an overview of CRMA security. We will then walk through each of the tools that CRMA makes available to determine who sees what data.

By the end of this chapter, you will understand the basics of CRMA security. Moving on, you will be able to deploy and manage CRMA access permissions. You will understand CRMA app-level security and be able to deploy and edit this as required. Furthermore, you will be competent in assessing and deploying Salesforce sharing inheritance. Finally, you will be confident in building and deploying security predicates.

In this chapter, we're going to cover the following main topics:

- What is CRMA security and how does it work?
- Managing CRMA access permissions
- Configuring CRMA app-level security
- Deploying Salesforce sharing inheritance
- Understanding the concept and usage of security predicates

Technical requirements

You will need the following to successfully execute the instructions in this chapter:

- The latest version of the Google Chrome browser (Chrome is the preferred browser when working with CRMA)

- A working email address

Ensure that you're logged into your CRMA development organization.

Let's jump right in and gain a high-level understanding of CRMA security.

What is CRMA security and how does it work?

Controlling access to information that is surfaced in CRM Analytics is critical in the broader context of data governance and security.

> **Important Note**
>
> Once a field is visible in CRMA, there is no way that you can prevent someone from seeing its data. Anyone who has access to the dataset has access to all fields, as opposed to Salesforce, where you have field-level security.

The CRMA administrator has four security tools at his or her disposal:

- **Salesforce Data Access**: The administrator can configure permissions on Salesforce fields and objects to implement field-level and object-level security, which means that access to Salesforce data can be controlled. For example, access to sensitive, personal information can be restricted at the ingestion level to prevent this data from being loaded into CRMA.

- **CRMA App-Level Security**: When you assign manager access to users, app owners, and administrators, they will be able to govern access to the assets within the app – lenses, datasets, and dashboards.

- **Salesforce Sharing Inheritance**: Sharing inheritance synchronizes with the sharing rules that are configured in Salesforce, subject to certain limitations. If used, it is prudent to also set a security predicate for situations when sharing settings cannot be honored.

- **Security Predicates**: Security predicates enable you to apply different types of access controls on datasets via a flexible and customizable row-level security capability.

Here is a visual to help you understand how this all works together:

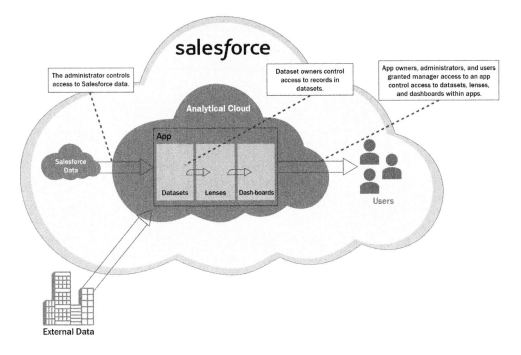

Figure 7.1 – CRMA security overview

The first CRMA security feature to be discussed is controlling permissions for **Salesforce data**.

Managing CRMA access permissions

To ingest data and use it as a part of row-level security, you must have access to Salesforce data. Based on the permissions of the two systems of CRMA/Salesforce users, CRM Analytics gains access to Salesforce data. These two systems of CRMA/Salesforce users are as follows:

- **Integration User**
- **Security User**

Here is **Integration User**, as viewed in **Setup** in Salesforce:

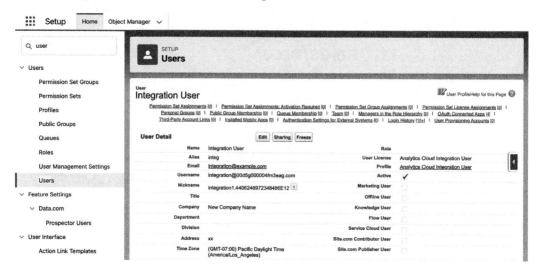

Figure 7.2 – Integration User. Note the user profile; that is, Analytics Cloud Integration User

CRMA uses the permissions of **Integration User** when a data preparation job runs so that it can ingest data from Salesforce objects and fields. Access to any fields and objects that contain sensitive data should be restricted because the **View All Data** access is with **Integration User**.

The job will fail if the dataflow tries to read data from a field or an object where view permission is not given to **Integration User**.

Based on the User object, if a dataset that has row-level security is queried, CRMA will utilize the permissions of **Security User** to read the User object and its fields. A few read permissions are required by **Security User** for each User object field that is included in a predicate.

You might be wondering, what is a predicate? When row-level security for a dataset is defined by a filter condition, this is known as a predicate. See the *What are security predicates and how do you use them?* section for more information. By default, **Security User** has read permissions on all the standard fields of the User object. If a custom field is utilized by a predicate, you need to ensure that **Security User** has read access for the field. An error will be triggered if you attempt to query a dataset using a predicate where **Security User** does not have read access to all relevant User object fields.

When setting up permissions for **Security User** or **Integration User**, do not modify the original profiles; changes should be always made to a cloned version of the user profile by you. To control access to Salesforce data, the permissions of **Integration User** on Salesforce fields and objects should be configured by you. To facilitate row-level security based on the custom fields of User object, the permissions of **Security User** need to be configured as well.

> **Important Note**
>
> Never delete **Integration User** or **Security User** because CRM Analytics requires these users to access Salesforce data.

In summary, when the data is ingested and used as row-level security, CRM Analytics must have read access to Salesforce data.

Therefore, you must be sure that the following has happened:

- Permissions of **Integration User** to govern the dataflow's access to Salesforce data have been set up.

- Permissions of **Security User** to facilitate row-level security based on the custom fields of the User object have been set up.

As a practical example, follow these steps in your CRMA development organization:

1. In Salesforce, not CRMA, go into **Setup**.
2. In **Quick Find**, search for **Permission Sets** and click on it.
3. Click **New** to create a new permission set.
4. Choose **Analytics Cloud Integration User** under **License**.
5. Set the name for the permission set to **Test** and click **Save**.
6. Assign app- and object-level permissions to the permission set by selecting **Object Settings** and **App Permissions**. Choose a variety of options for this exercise.
7. Configure **Apex Class Access**, **Visualforce Page Access**, and **Flow Access** permissions for the permission set. Choose a variety of options for this exercise.
8. This new permission set is now ready to be assigned to the CRMA **Integration User**.
9. Under **Salesforce Setup**, find and select **Profiles**.
10. Select the **Analytics Integration User** profile.
11. Click the **Clone** button to create a cloned copy of the profile.

12. Remove **View All Data** access by deselecting the checkbox.

13. Save the profile as **Test**.

14. Under **Salesforce Setup**, select **Users**.

15. Select **Integration User** from the list (User, Integration).

16. Edit the user and change the profile of the user to the cloned profile, **Test**, that we created in *Step 11*.

17. Navigate to the **Permission Set Assignments** section for **Integration User**.

18. Assign the newly created permission set in *Step 6*, **Test**, to **Integration User**. This enables the CRMA integration user to have access to Salesforce objects and other components.

The next tool to be examined is app-level security.

Configuring CRMA app-level security

As you might remember from what we learned in *Chapter 2, Developing Your First OOTB Analytics App in CRMA*, a CRM Analytics app is similar to a folder, enabling users to organize their data projects and control the access of datasets, lenses, and dashboards, as well as how they're shared. This functionality of CRMA apps makes them a useful security tool to restrict or grant access to assets as required.

By default, all CRMA users begin with Viewer access to **Shared App**. An administrator may modify this setting to open or restrict access. An out-of-the-box app, **My Private App**, can be accessed by every user, which is suitable for personal works in progress. The contents of a user's **My Private App** are not visible to administrators, but lenses and dashboards can be shared with users.

Also, by default, all new apps are set to private. Manager access is with the administrators and app owner; therefore, they can extend **VIEWER**, **EDITOR**, or **MANAGER** access to other roles, groups, or users. The following table shows a quick summary of what actions the users can perform with various levels of access:

	A	B	C	D
	ACTION	VIEWER	EDITOR	MANAGER
1				
2	View dashboards, lenses, and datasets in the app	×	×	×
3	See who has access to the app	×	×	×
4	Save contents of the app to another app that the user has Editor or Manager access to	×	×	×
5	Save changes to existing dashboards, lenses, and datasets in the app (saving dashboards requires the appropriate 5 permission set license and permission)		×	×
6	Change the app's sharing settings			×
7	Rename the app			×
8	Update asset visibility in an app		×	×
9	Delete the app			×

Figure 7.3 – What can users do with VIEWER, EDITOR, and MANAGER access?

To grant access to a CRMA user, you simply need to click on the **Share** button at the top right-hand corner of the page when viewing the app. This brings up the following dialog box, where you can grant access as required and then **Save**:

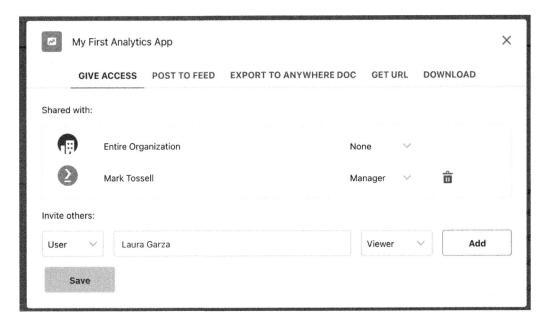

Figure 7.4 – Granting access to an analytics app using the Share button

> **Tips**
>
> First, if the dataset is in a different app than a dashboard or a lens, a CRMA user must be able to access both apps if he or she will view a lens or dashboard.
>
> Second, deactivated users lose *share* and *delete* access to all apps they manage. Therefore, to make sure this does not happen, before deactivating the user, assign **Manager** access to at least one active user.

As a practical example, follow these steps to share a new private dashboard with a single user:

1. First, create a new app called **Private App**.
2. Now, create a new blank dashboard and save it to **My Private App** as **Private dashboard**.
3. To give access to an active user, Julie Chavez, open the **Share** dialog box and add Julie as a user with **Viewer** permission under **Invite others**.
4. Click on **Add**.
5. Click on **Save**.

The completed sharing dialog box should look like this:

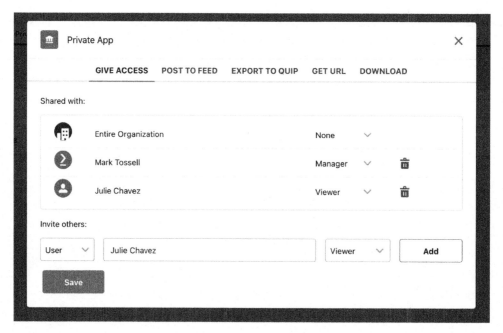

Figure 7.5 – The completed sharing dialog box with Julie added as with Viewer permission

Now, let's examine Salesforce sharing inheritance.

Deploying Salesforce sharing inheritance

If you want the sharing setup for your datasets to replicate the ones that are applied for your objects by Salesforce, then you can do this by deploying sharing inheritance.

Sharing inheritance reduces or eliminates the need for complex security predicates in many cases. On the flip side, applying sharing inheritance results in an increase in the time required to process data and create/update datasets – completing data syncs, recipe jobs, and more. Keep in mind that the more complicated the sharing settings are, the more impact there is on data processing time. Keep in mind that the time taken for data processing will have a higher impact if the sharing settings are more complicated.

The Salesforce admin most likely uses a combination of sharing settings to provide users with access to Salesforce data about their roles, including sharing based on the following:

- Manual sharing rules
- Role hierarchy
- Role
- Group
- Apex-managed sharing
- Team-based sharing

You may enable sharing inheritance to use the Salesforce sharing settings in CRM Analytics, but only for a limited selection of supported objects. When creating or editing datasets, be sure to specify the objects to inherit sharing from. The supported objects are as follows:

- Account
- Case
- Contact
- Lead
- Opportunity

To enable sharing inheritance, you need to switch on sharing inheritance. Next, select the objects that are to be used as sharing sources. Note that sharing inheritance is turned on by default in new Salesforce environments.

After you turn on sharing inheritance, it is best practice to run the Sharing Inheritance Coverage Assessment report on an object, then the users for that object, to investigate how well sharing inheritance will work for you. Under **Analytics**, from the **Salesforce Setup** menu, select **Sharing Inheritance Coverage Assessment**.

> **Note**
>
> It is a best practice to test sharing inheritance in a sandbox environment before deploying it to production. This lets you test use cases against your environment's security model and data to be confident that sharing inheritance will work as desired.

To turn on sharing inheritance, follow these steps:

1. In the **Setup Quick Find** box, enter **Analytics** and click **Settings**.
2. Choose **Inherit sharing from under Salesforce** and click **Save**.

If **Data Sync** is enabled, you must turn on sharing inheritance for every object that you will use as a sharing source. Follow these steps to do so:

1. In CRM Analytics Studio, click on **Data Manager**.
2. In **Data Manager**, click on **Connect**.
3. Click on the **dropdown list** on the right end of the row to find the object you want to enable.
4. Click on **Row Level Sharing**.
5. Turn **Sharing inheritance on**.
6. Click on the **Save** button.

Sharing inheritance does have some limitations. For example, one challenge is the amount of space that is consumed by the sharing rules in a CRMA instance.

Other limitations and considerations for Salesforce sharing inheritance are as follows:

- It can only be applied if all supported object records have less than 400 sharing descriptors each.
- It can impede the performance of queries, dataflows, and data prep recipes.

For detailed, up-to-date technical information and specifications, go to https:// help.salesforce.com/s/articleView?id=sf.bi_security_datasets_ sharing_about.htm&type=5.

Now, let's examine the most powerful and flexible tool at your disposal: security predicates.

Understanding the concept and usage of security predicates

Data visibility in CRMA can be controlled using security predicates. As we mentioned earlier, row-level security for a dataset that is defined by a filter condition is called a predicate. Predicates can control data visibility based on these scenarios:

- **Role Hierarchy**: In the Salesforce org, predicates can filter the data based on the user's role, but only if they are logged in. A user can only view the records that are owned by them or by the people below them in the role hierarchy in Salesforce.

- **Manager Hierarchy**: In the User object, predicates can filter the data based on the `Manager` field in the User object. Therefore, the logged-in user may view the records that are owned by them, and by any user that reports under them in the manager hierarchy.

- **Logged-in User's Country**: The data can also be filtered based on the logged-in user's country, by the predicates. A user from one country can access the records that are owned by the users from the same country.

- **Opportunity Team and Accounts Team**: If data visibility needs to be governed depending on the logged-in users being part of the Opportunity Team and Accounts Team of the record owner, then predicates can be used for this as well.

- **User Territory**: Predicates can implement row-level security based upon User Territory.

- **A Combination of Various Requirements**: Defines a predicate based on a combination of these scenarios.

When defining a security predicate expression, you must use a valid syntax:

```
<dataset column> <operator> <value>
```

Here is an example:

```
'UserId' == "$User.Id"
```

Let's look at each of the components in the preceding example:

- `UserId`: This is the name of the API of the dataset column.
- `==`: This is the operator.
- `$User.Id`: This is the Salesforce User ID for the logged-in user.

Make sure to note the following points regarding predicate expressions:

- They are case-sensitive.
- They cannot contain more than 5,000 characters.
- Before and after the logical operators, between the operator and the value, and between the column and the operator, at least be one space must be present.
- Single quotes must be used to enclose `dataset column`, such as `OwnerId`.
- The values for the expression can be field values from the User object in Salesforce.
- String, number, and multi-value picklist fields are supported by the User object.
- Values can be strings or numbers.
- You must possess read access to the relevant User object fields to define a predicate for a dataset.

For example, the following is not a valid expression:

```
'Revenue'>100
```

It must contain spaces, as shown here:

```
'Revenue' > 100
```

Here are four examples of security predicates for datasets:

- `Static Filter: 'Product.Family' == "Phones"`
- `Record Ownership: 'Opportunity.OwnerId' == "$User.Id"`
- `Role Hierarchy: 'Opportunity.OwnerId' == "$User.Id" ||`
  `'Opportunity.User_Role_Id_Path' == "$User.UserRoleId"`
- `Custom: 'Opportunity.OwnerId' == "$User.Id" ||`
  `'Opportunity.User_Role_Id_Path' == "$User.UserRoleId" ||`
  `'Opportunity.View_All_Settings' == "$User.View_All__c`

Consider these requirements for each value type:

Value Type	Requirements	Predicate Expression Examples
string literal	Enclose in double quotes and escape the double quotes.	• `'Owner' == "Amber"` • `'Stage Name' == "Closed Won"`
number literal	Can be a float or long datatype. Do not enclose in quotes.	• `'Expected Revenue' >= 2000.00` • `'NetLoss' < -10000`
field value	When referencing a field from the User object, use the $User.[field] syntax. Use the API name for the field. You can specify standard or custom fields of type string, number, or multivalue picklist. When you define a predicate for a dataset, you must have read access on all User object fields used to create the predicate expression.	• `'Owner.Role' == "$User.UserRoleId"` • `'GroupID' == "$User.UserGroupId_c"` ⓘ Note: Supported User object field value types are string, number, and multivalue picklist.

Figure 7.6 – Values in a predicate expression

If a user tries to query the dataset that a non-valid predicate is applied to, an error will appear for the user.

Now, go into Analytics Studio in your CRMA development organization and follow these steps:

1. Open **My First Analytics App** and view your list of datasets.

2. Edit the **Opportunities** dataset by clicking on the drop-down arrow on the right-hand side of the list.

3. Delete the existing security predicate (as seen in the code snippet following this bulleted list) by clicking on the pencil icon (as shown in the preceding table) and deleting the predicate code.

4. **Security predicate** should now be **None**.

5. Edit the predicate and add **New opportunity dataset predicate**.

6. Create a lens for the **Opportunities** dataset and check that the new predicate works as you expect. You may need to log out and then log back in for the predicates to take effect.

7. Undo your work by editing the dataset and replacing the new predicate with the previous one.

The pencil icon that you need to click to edit the predicate is highlighted with a bold arrow in the following screenshot:

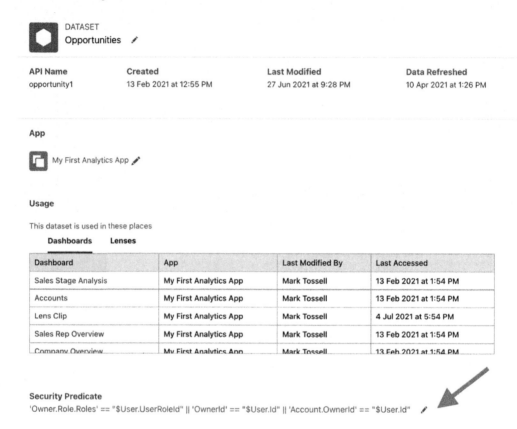

Figure 7.7 – Opportunities dataset showing the existing security predicate

Here is the existing opportunity dataset predicate:

```
'Owner.Role.Roles' == "$User.UserRoleId" || 'OwnerId' ==
"$User.Id" || 'Account.OwnerId' == "$User.Id"
```

This predicate ensures that opportunity data is only available for viewing where it is permitted based upon the role hierarchy, opportunity ownership, and account ownership.

Here is the new opportunity dataset predicate:

```
'OwnerId' == "$User.Id" || 'Account.OwnerId' == "$User.Id"
```

This predicate has removed access based upon the role hierarchy.

Now, go back and replace the new predicate with the original one.

For a highly detailed reference on predicates, see the *CRM Analytics Security Implementation Guide* here:

```
https://resources.docs.salesforce.com/232/latest/en-us/sfdc/
pdf/bi_admin_guide_security.pdf
```

Summary

The following diagram provides a useful summary of how security works in CRM Analytics:

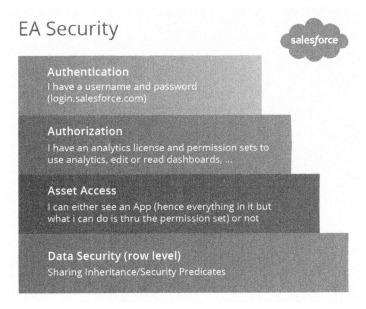

Figure 7.8 – CRMA security review

As you have seen, you have a variety of options for implementing security in CRM Analytics. In this chapter, you learned about these security tools and how to deploy them.

What have you learned? First, you grasped the basics of security in CRMA. Next, you learned how to govern CRMA access permissions. Third, you learned how to use app-level security to control access to CRMA analytics app assets. Next, you became competent in configuring and enabling Salesforce sharing inheritance. Lastly, you learned how to build and deploy security predicates for more complex, detailed data governance use cases.

In the next chapter, you will learn to build your very first CRMA dashboard.

Questions

Here are some questions to test your knowledge of this chapter:

- What is the purpose of app-level security in CRMA?

- How can you control CRMA security from Salesforce objects and field access?

- When a dataflow job runs, CRMA uses the permissions of _____ user to extract data from Salesforce objects and fields.

- What are three limitations of Salesforce sharing inheritance?

- What are three use case scenarios for security predicates?

- A security predicate expression must not exceed how many characters?

- Is this is a valid predicate expression? Why, or why not?

  `"Revenue">100`

- A security predicate expression is case-sensitive – true or false?

Section 3: How to Build Awesome Analytics Dashboards in CRMA

In this section, you will learn how to design, build, test, and deploy powerful and useful dynamic analytics dashboards within CRMA.

This section comprises the following chapters:

8
Building Your First CRMA Dashboard

It's time to put your new understanding to use and build your first **CRM Analytics (CRMA)** dashboard. By the end of this chapter, you will be able to create a dashboard from scratch, navigate through the dashboard editor, add and edit widgets, add pages, slice and dice data, and share your findings with others.

We will cover the following main topics in this chapter:

- Getting to know your dashboard editor
- Creating a dashboard and placing widgets
- The devil is in the details
- Understanding the top-down design with pages
- A user's guide to a CRMA dashboard

Technical requirements

You will need the following to successfully execute the instructions in this chapter:

- The latest version of the Google Chrome browser (Chrome is the preferred browser when working with CRMA)

- A working email address

Be sure to be logged in to your CRMA dev org.

Time to jump in and build your first CRMA dashboard!

Getting to know your dashboard editor

In this section, you will get hands-on and learn how to use the dashboard editor in CRMA.

From your Analytics Studio home page, click on **Create** and select **Dashboard**, then click on **Create Blank Dashboard**. You will come to the dashboard editor canvas, which looks like this:

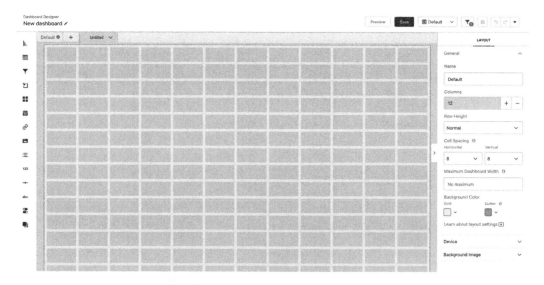

Figure 8.1 – The initial dashboard editor canvas

Before proceeding with the next steps, save your dashboard as **My First Dashboard** in **My First Analytics App**.

Now, configure the dashboard settings by clicking on the **Default** gear icon. I typically use these default settings:

- **Name**: `Default`
- **Columns**: `50`
- **Row Height**: `Fine`
- **Cell Spacing**: `8` (horizontal) and `0` (vertical)
- **Maximum Dashboard Width**: `1500`
- **Background Color**: Leave as-is for now

There are 14 tools available on the left-hand side of the canvas, as detailed next; these will be explained as you add them to your dashboard:

- **Chart**
- **Table**
- **Filter**
- **Container**
- **Component**
- **Date**
- **Link**
- **Image**
- **List**
- **Number**
- **Range**
- **Text**
- **Toggle**
- **Navigation**

When you click on the drop-down arrow at the top right of the editor, you have these options:

- **Clone in New Tab**: Creates a clone of the current dashboard in a new tab.
- **Dashboard Properties**: General options and widget default properties.

- **Pick Initial Values**: Set the default filter and facet values for the dashboard; these will apply every time the dashboard is opened.

- **Conversations**: Lets you query your data using conversational, everyday language. This needs to be enabled and the correct permissions assigned for the user to see and use this functionality.

- **Connect Data Sources**: Join data sources using a common field.

- **Delete**: Permanently delete the dashboard.

It's now time to flesh out your dashboard.

Creating a dashboard and placing widgets

The best way to show you how to build a dashboard and help you become familiar with the dashboard editor is to walk you through a simple dashboard build.

Creating a sales dashboard

We will create a sales dashboard based upon the **Opportunities** dataset in **My First Analytics App**. Follow these steps:

1. Create a fresh query by clicking on the **Create Query** button on the right-hand side of the canvas.

2. Select the **Opportunities** dataset in **My First Analytics App**. This brings you to a view that is familiar to you as being almost identical to a lens.

3. At the top left, where you see a pencil icon, rename the query **Pipeline by Close Date**.

4. Change the measure (**Bar Length**) to **Sum of Amount**.

5. Add a grouping (**Bar**) for **Close Date (Year-Month)**.

6. On the far right, click on the **Charts** icon and change the chart type to **Time Bar** in the **DATES & TIMES** category.

7. Add a filter for **Closed** equal to the value of **False** (as in, open opportunities).

8. Click **Done**, which will close the window.

    The query now appears in the query list on the right, under the **Opportunities** dataset.

9. Drag the query onto the canvas. This creates a chart widget.

10. Enlarge the widget by dragging the handles.

11. Click **Save** to save your dashboard.

Please note that the result you achieved from the preceding steps can also be achieved by dragging the chart widget onto the canvas from the left-hand side menu.

The dashboard should now look like this:

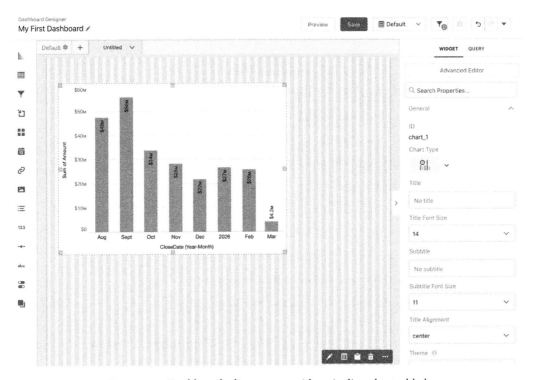

Figure 8.2 – Dashboard editor canvas with a pipeline chart added

Placing widgets on the sales dashboard

When you select the widget, you now have several widget options available at the bottom right-hand side of the canvas, as follows:

- **Edit Query and Widget**: Opens the widget for editing.

- **Advanced Editor**: Opens **Advanced Interaction Editor**. This will be covered in *Chapter 9, Advanced Dashboard Design and Build*.

- **Copy widget to clipboard**: Copies the widget so that it can be pasted into this dashboard or any open dashboard.

- **Delete Widget**: Deletes a widget from the dashboard without deleting the query.

- **Duplicate Widget**: Copies the widget with a query and adds it to the dashboard.

- **View Query Properties**: Opens the query property window on the right-hand side.
- **Clone Query**: Clones the query and opens it for editing.
- **Remove Query**: Removes the query from the widget and retains its format without removing the widget from the dashboard.

You are now going to edit the pipeline widget by following these steps:

1. On the far right, click on the **Formatting** (paintbrush) icon.
2. In the **Title** field, add a title for the widget: `Pipeline by Close Date`.
3. Change the **Title Font Size** setting to `18`.
4. In the **Subtitle** field, add a subtitle: `All open deals`.
5. Change the **Subtitle Font Size** setting to `14`.
6. Change **Title Alignment** to `left`.
7. Change the **Theme** field to `Light`.
8. Under **Time Bar Chart**, uncheck the option for **Show values in chart bars**.
9. Under the *x* axis, add a custom title: **Close Date Month**.
10. Under the *y* axis (left), add a custom title: **Deal Size**.
11. Add a reference line under the *y* axis with a **Value** setting of `30000000` and a **Label** value of **Target**.
12. Under **Conditional Formatting**, click on **Apply Conditional Formatting To** and select **Sum of Amount**. Leave the default gradient setting.
13. Under **Widget Style**, add a border as you see fit.
14. Add a text widget to give the dashboard a title, **Sales Insights**, and change the font and color as you see fit. Go into **Preview** mode.

The result of the preceding steps should look like this:

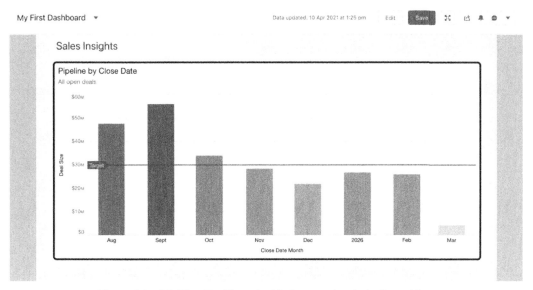

Figure 8.3 – My First Dashboard with the completed pipeline widget

Before you go any further, make some subtle changes to improve the dashboard aesthetics, as follows:

1. Click on **Edit** to edit the dashboard.
2. Click on the **Default** gear icon to open the dashboard settings.
3. Under **Background Color**, change **Grid** to `White`.
4. Select **Dashboard Properties** from the drop-down list at the top right of the dashboard editor.
5. Change the default widget background color to transparent by clicking on **Background Color**, selecting **Custom**, and dragging the transparency bar all the way to the left.
6. Add a default widget border with a transparent color, and a width and radius of 8.
7. Click **Save** to save the dashboard.

You are now going to add a second widget to the dashboard by beginning with the existing pipeline widget. The pipeline widget is the main chart, often referred to as a *hero chart*, and it needs supporting charts and metrics. Follow these steps to add a second widget to the dashboard:

1. Select the pipeline widget and click on **Copy Widget**.
2. Paste the duplicate widget onto the dashboard canvas.
3. Select the new widget and go to the **Widget** panel on the right-hand side.
4. Remove the widget border by deselecting the border icon.
5. Remove the target reference line by clicking on the **x** next to the reference line in the format panel.
6. Change the chart type to **Bar** by clicking on the **Chart Type** button and choosing a bar chart.
7. Click on **Edit Query and Widget** for the new widget.
8. Change the bar grouping to **Stage**.
9. Sort the **Sum of Amount** field in **Descending** order.
10. Remove the legend by deselecting the **Show legend** checkbox.
11. Remove the title on the *y* axis.
12. Remove the axis and title on the *x* axis (top).
13. Check **Show values in chart bars**.
14. Change the widget title to `Pipeline by Stage` and reduce the font size to `16`.
15. Remove the subtitle.
16. Rename the query `Pipeline by Stage`.
17. Click on **Update**.
18. Move and resize (shrink) the widget, as it supports the first pipeline chart.
19. Remove the default border from the dashboard title text widget by deselecting the border icon.
20. Click on **Save**.

The dashboard should now look like this:

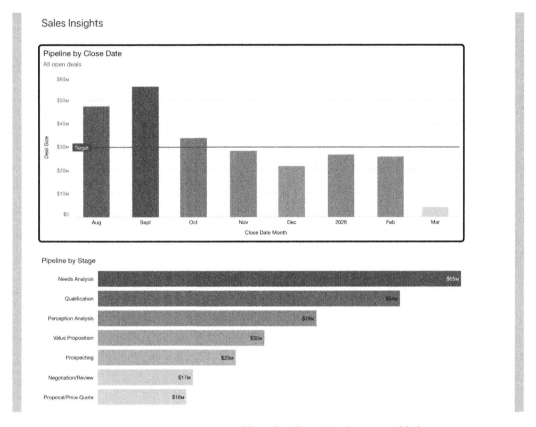

Figure 8.4 – My First Dashboard with Pipeline by Stage added

Adding a highlights panel to the sales dashboard

Now, it's time to add a highlights panel to your dashboard. This is useful to draw attention to key metrics and the dashboard filters. To do so, you can follow these steps:

1. Select the two chart widgets together by holding *Cmd* or *Ctrl* while clicking on each of them, then drag down a few rows to make room for the highlights panel.

2. Drag a **Container** widget onto the canvas.

3. Resize/enlarge the container, move the title text widget into the container, then make sure the container fills the space above the hero chart.

4. Create a new sales query by clicking on **Create Query** and selecting the **Opportunities** dataset.

5. We want to track the total number of deals won, so go ahead and add a filter for **Won** = **True**.

6. Change the query title to **# of Deals Won**.

7. Click on **Done**.

8. Drag a **Number** widget into the highlights panel container and enlarge it.

9. Drag the new query (**# of Deals Won**) onto the widget. You should now see a number with the title **Count of Rows**.

10. Select the **Number** widget and change the title to **# of Deals Won**.

11. Under **Text Style,** edit the colors and sizes for number and title so that the number stands out.

12. Clone this **Number** widget by using the **Duplicate Widget** button.

13. Drag the new widget into the highlights panel.

14. Edit the second **Number** widget and change the measure (**Bar Length**) to **Sum of Amount**. This now captures the value of deals won.

15. Rename the widget query **Value of Deals Won**.

16. Click on **Update**.

17. Format to match the first number widget.

18. Check the **Shorten Number** option.

19. To make the highlights panel stand out, select the container and change the background color to a dark blue.

20. Edit the title and number widgets to suit so that they stand out.

21. Go to your dashboard settings under **Default** and change **Cell Spacing** to 0.

22. Change **Maximum Dashboard Width** to 1400.

23. Click **Save**.

The dashboard with the highlights panel added should look like this:

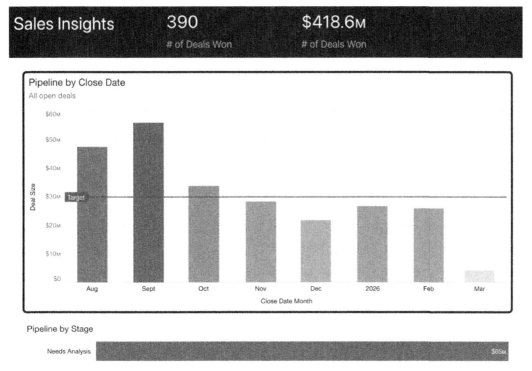

Figure 8.5 – Dashboard with the highlights panel added: close up

Adding filters to the sales dashboard

Now, you will add global filters and a toggle by following these steps:

1. Drag a **Filter** widget into the container.

2. Select the new widget and click on **Filter**.

3. Choose the **Opportunities** dataset, select the **Industry** field, and click on **Create**. You have now created a global filter for the dashboard that enables a user to drill in by industry.

4. As this will become a small panel of global filters, click on the **All Global Filters** radio button on the right-hand side of the canvas (**Widget** panel).

5. Click on **Manage Global Filters** to bring up the **Dashboard Global Filters** panel.

6. Where you see the **Opportunities** dataset, click on the + button to add another filter from this dataset, and choose **Billing Country**.

7. Add a third filter for **Opportunity Type**. It does not yet appear on the dashboard because the **Filters Per Row** option is set to only 2.

8. Come out of the **Manage Global Filters** edit screen and click on the widget, then increase **Filters Per Row** to 3.

9. Edit the filter titles by clicking on the pencil icon while in the **Dashboard Global Filters** panel. The values should be **Country**, **Industry**, and **Type**.

10. Drag the handles on the **Filter** widget and increase its size, leaving room for one widget on the right.

11. Edit the format of the **Filter** widget to suit your personal preference. You will find an example in *Figure 8.6.*

12. You're going to need more room to fit the **Toggle** widget in, so resize and move the highlights panel widgets to make space.

13. Drag a **Toggle** widget onto the container, to the right of the new **Filter** widget.

14. Click on **Toggle** and select **Account Type**.

15. Change **Measure Field** to -- **none** --.

16. Change the **Toggle** widget border to **White**, width 2, radius 4.

17. Increase the **Text Size** setting to 16.

18. Change the **Text Color** setting to a light blue.

19. Click on **Save** to save the dashboard.

Go into **Preview** mode and see what happens when you select various filters and use the toggle. It is very easy to drill into your dashboard using these features, as well as faceting by clicking on dimensions in charts. Your dashboard should now look like this:

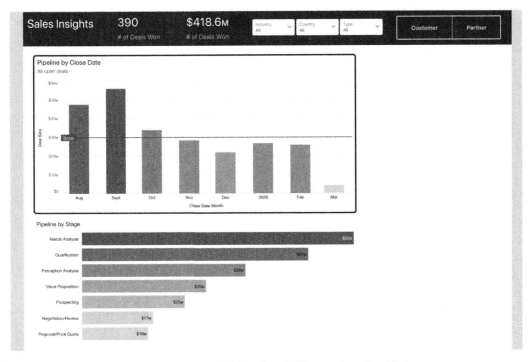

Figure 8.6 – Sales dashboard with filters and toggle added

Adding Image, Date, List, and Range widgets to the sales dashboard

You will now add **Image**, **Date**, **List**, and **Range** widgets by following these steps:

1. Add a logo to your dashboard by dragging an **Image** widget onto the canvas and clicking on **Image**.

2. Upload a suitable image, such as a fake business logo.

3. Remove the widget border.

4. Move the dashboard title to the bottom of the container and modify the font size as required.

5. Shrink the **Image** widget and place it above the dashboard title. Change **Image Scale** to **Fit Height**.

6. Drag a **Date** widget onto the canvas, under the toggle, then click on **Date**, and choose **Close Date**.

7. Change the **Title** field to **Close Date**.

8. Resize the **Date** widget to half the width of the space, make it taller, and move to the right edge of the canvas.

9. Drag a **List** widget onto the canvas, click on **List**, and select **Segment**.

10. Resize the **List** widget to match the **Date** widget.

11. Change the **Title** field to **Segment**.

12. Click on the **QUERY** tab on the right and change **Selection Type** to **Multiple Selection**.

13. Drag a **Range** widget onto the canvas, under the two widgets just added.

14. Stretch the **Range** widget to fill the available space.

15. Click on **Range** and choose **Amount**.

16. Click on **Save** to save the dashboard.

Add two more charts to your dashboard that break down **Pipeline by Industry** and **Top Ten Account Owners** (use **Query Limit** for this). Format as you see fit. Save the dashboard; it should look something like this:

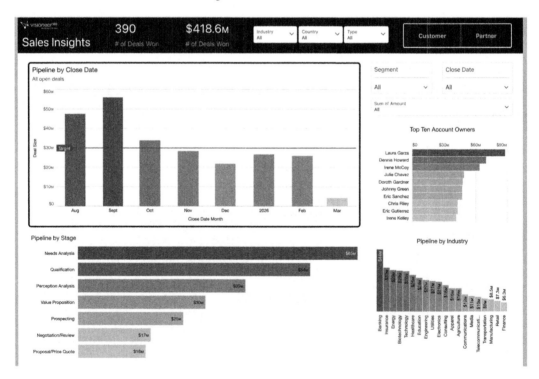

Figure 8.7 – Sales dashboard with the first page completed

Now that you have built your first complete dashboard page, you are going to learn more about the detailed options available to you.

The devil is in the details

In this section, you will learn about the detailed options available for editing your dashboard.

While in your new dashboard, check out the query panel and the options available there. You can see an overview of this in the following screenshot:

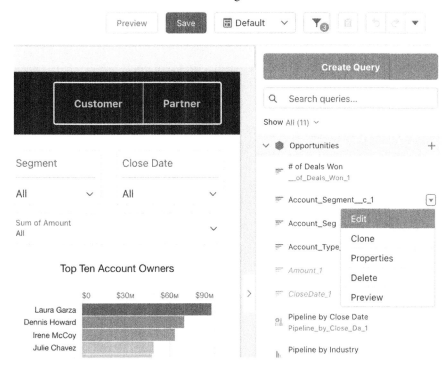

Figure 8.8 – Query panel and options

You have five actions available for each query from the panel, outlined as follows:

- **Edit**: Opens the query for editing and formatting.
- **Clone**: Creates a copy of the query and opens it in **Edit** mode.
- **Properties**: Gives access to query configuration options such as faceting, selection type, and initial selections. More detail will follow in this section.
- **Delete**: Deletes the query from the dashboard.
- **Preview**: Opens a preview window in a values table format.

Regarding the query properties, here is some more detail:

- **Display label**: The user-facing query label can be edited here.

- **Apply global filters**: Uncheck if you do not want the dashboard global filters to apply to this query and the widgets that it drives.

- **Faceting**: You have four options here—**All**, **Include**, **Exclude**, and **None**. The default value of **All** means that selecting values on other widgets will apply those faceting values to this query and the widgets that it drives, as in standard dashboard behavior. This default behavior can be modified by selecting **Include** (choose which specific queries to include as faceting values for this query), **Exclude** (choose which specific queries to exclude as faceting values for this query), or **None** (no faceting will apply to this query).

- **Selection Type**: Choose which type of selection will apply when a user clicks on a widget selection: **None**, **Single Selection**, **Multiple Selection**, **Single Selection (required)**, and **Multiple Selection (required)**.

- **Broadcast selections as facets**: You can turn off the default faceting behavior by unchecking this, meaning that making selections on this query will not facet other queries.

- **Initial selections**: Shows the initial selections that have been configured for this dashboard.

These query actions and properties give you great flexibility in dashboard design. Now, let's look at the powerful functionality of dashboard pages.

Understanding the top-down design with pages

From a business user perspective, it is inconvenient to have to constantly move from dashboard to dashboard when investigating and analyzing data. Also, filters applied to one CRMA dashboard are not carried over to another dashboard. A versatile, top-down design for dashboards using CRMA pages overcomes these obstacles and provides a simple, flexible interface for slicing and dicing data.

The best way to understand the pages functionality is to apply it to a dashboard, so edit your **My First Dashboard** dashboard, and follow these steps:

1. Open the **user interface (UI)** for CRMA pages by clicking on the drop-down arrow next to **Untitled**, to the right of **Default**.

2. Click on **Rename** and rename the existing page **Sales**.

3. You could click on + to add a new blank page, but we want to carry across the highlights panel, so select the drop-down arrow and then select **Clone**. A new page appears, named **Clone of Sales**.

4. Rename the new page **Marketing**.

Here is the UI for CRMA pages:

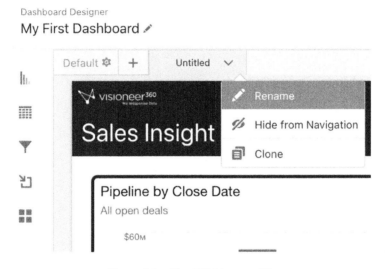

Figure 8.9 – The CRMA pages UI

Now, go ahead and build out the new page, as follows:

1. Delete every widget except for the highlights panel; you can select multiple widgets by holding down *Cmd* (Mac) or *Ctrl* (Windows) while selecting each with a mouse click. Don't worry—they won't be removed from the **Sales** page!

2. Remove widgets on the highlights panel except for the logo and title. You will be asked: **Delete widget and global filter?**. Click on **Delete Widget Only**, as you do not want to delete the global filters.

3. Click on the title text widget. Notice on the **Widget** panel on the right that there is a message: **This widget exists on multiple pages. Changes here apply to instances on other pages, unless you unlink it.**. This is important—if you modify this widget, it will modify all other copies of this widget.

4. Click on **Unlink**.

5. Change the title to **Marketing Insights**.

6. Resize the title text widget so that the text appears correctly.

7. Save your dashboard and close it.

Before we can flesh out the **Marketing** page, we first need to create a dataset called **Leads**, based upon the Salesforce **Lead** object. Using your knowledge from previous chapters, go ahead and do so. We want to keep things simple for now, so just use **Lead object data** and choose the following fields:

- **Annual Revenue**
- **City**
- **Company**
- **Converted**
- **Converted Date**
- **Country**
- **Created Date**
- **Email**
- **Employees**
- **Full Name**
- **Industry**
- **Lead Source**
- **Phone**
- **State/Province**
- **Status**

Go ahead and click **Create Dataset**. Review the monitor in **Data Manager** and proceed once the new **Leads** dataset has been created. First, you need to add a page navigator widget so that you can move easily between pages when in **Preview** mode. To do so, follow these steps:

1. Drag the **Navigation** widget onto your **Marketing** page.
2. Remove the border on the **Navigation** widget.
3. Resize this widget by making it one cell higher.
4. Move the **Navigation** widget up so that it butts against the highlights panel container.
5. Format the **Navigation** widget so that it will stand out on the page but not conflict with other widgets. See *Figure 8.10* for an example.

6. Go to the **Sales** page and move all widgets (not including the highlights panel) down as required (use the arrow button on your keyboard while multiple widgets are selected to do so). This will make room for the **Navigation** widget.

7. Under the **Move/Add** action at the bottom of the canvas, while the **Navigation** widget is selected, click on **Add to Page** and choose **Sales**.

8. The **Navigation** widget should now show on the **Sales** page. If need be, move it into place, moving other widgets as required.

The dashboard with the **Navigation** widget in place should look like this:

Figure 8.10 – Your dashboard with the Navigation widget in place

Now, it's time to build out the new page with marketing data. Follow these steps:

1. Edit the dashboard and select the **Marketing** page.

2. Create a new query based upon the **Leads** dataset.

3. Group the count of rows by **Lead Source**.

4. Rename the query **Leads by Source** and add this as a title.

5. Choose a **Donut** chart for the query.

6. Click on **Done**.

7. You will now notice that the **Query** panel now lists queries under **Leads** as well as **Opportunities**.

8. Drag this new **Leads** query onto the canvas.

9. Resize and format the **Chart** widget to suit your preference. In my example, seen in the following screenshot, I chose to create a pie chart with a **Center Size** value of 0% and show the pie chart value as **Percentage**.

10. Create and add a widget for **Leads by Status**—use an Origami chart and put the legend at the top center.

11. Create and add a widget for **Leads Count by State and Status**—use a stacked column chart.

12. Create and add a widget for **Heat Map of Source and Status**.

13. Format and edit to suit your preference.

14. Click **Save** to save the dashboard.

15. Add a **List** widget for **Lead Source** to the highlights panel. Change **Selection Type** to **Multiple Selection**.

16. Add a **List** widget for **Industry** to the highlights panel.

17. Add a **Number** widget for **Total Leads** to the highlights panel.

18. Add a **Number** widget for **Open Leads** to the highlights panel (filter by **Status** is not equal to **Closed**).

19. Click **Save** to save the dashboard.

Your marketing page should look something like this:

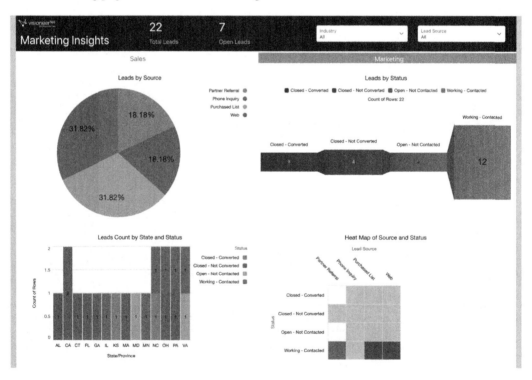

Figure 8.11 – The completed marketing analytics page

Now, we want to connect our data sources so that a filter by **Lead Source** will apply across both pages. Without connecting data sources, the filter will only work on each individual page, as each page was created with queries from one dataset (**Opportunities** or **Leads**). Follow these steps to connect the data sources:

1. Using the drop-down list at the top right of the dashboard editor, click on **Connect Data Sources**. A dialog box will appear.

2. Click on **New Connection**.

3. Name the connection **Leads and Opportunities by Source**.

4. Click on **Choose Data Source 1**.

5. Under **Select Data Source**, choose **Opportunities**.

6. Under **Select a field**, choose **Lead Source**.

7. Click on **Choose Data Source 2**.

8. Under **Select Data Source**, choose **Leads**.

9. Under **Select a field**, choose **Lead Source**.

10. Click on **Save**.

The dialog box prior to saving the connection should look like this:

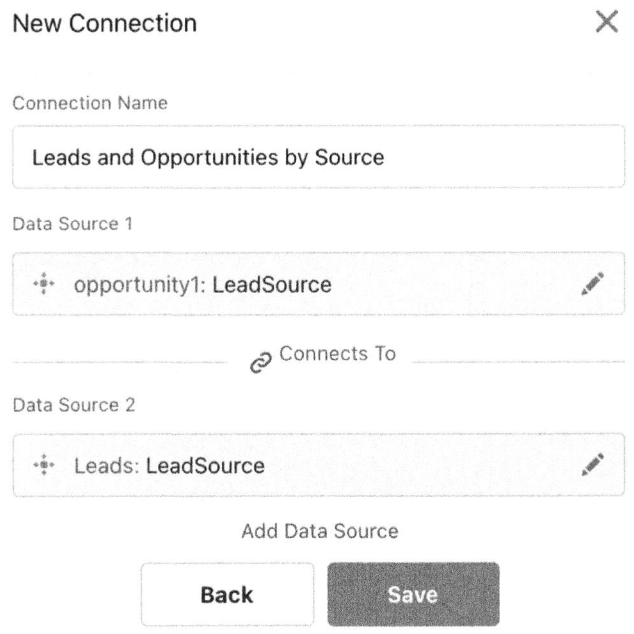

New Connection   ✕

Connection Name

Leads and Opportunities by Source

Data Source 1

⟐ opportunity1: **LeadSource**   ✎

⟿ Connects To

Data Source 2

⟐ Leads: **LeadSource**   ✎

Add Data Source

Back   Save

Figure 8.12 – Completed data connection dialog box

Now, it's time to test out the connection.

While on the **Marketing** page, click on the **List** widget for **Lead Source** and select **Web**. The page will now filter by the selected value. Now, move to the **Sales** page, and you will see that the sales data has also been filtered by the web source of leads and deals.

Now that you've successfully created your first CRMA dashboard from scratch, including the versatility of pages, it's time to learn how to use and share a dashboard.

A user's guide to a CRMA dashboard

You will now open your new dashboard in **Preview** mode and approach it as a business user, learning how to slice and dice your data in CRMA. Before we explore the data, remove the static target on the hero chart, **Pipeline by Close Date**, as this will hinder our exploration. We will look at dynamic reference lines in *Chapter 9, Advanced Dashboard Design and Build*. Also, make sure all chart widgets have **Selection Type** set to **Multiple Selection**.

The following steps will help you to explore and share your dashboard:

1. Open the **My First Dashboard** dashboard and enter **Present** mode.

2. Filter by **Segment** by choosing **MM** and **GB** in the **List** widget.

3. Drill in by deal size by selecting **50,000 – 500,000** under **Sum of Amount**.

4. We're interested in new deals only for this analysis, so exclude **Existing Business** under the **Type** global filter (using **Does Not Equal**).

5. Facet the dashboard by going to the **Pipeline by Stage** chart and selecting these two bars: **Negotiation/Review** and **Perception Analysis**.

6. Save this dashboard view. Next to the dashboard title, click on the down arrow next to **Modified**, and select **Save View**. Name it **Sales drill down** and click on **Create**.

7. Click on **Save** to save the dashboard.

Your dashboard should now look like the one shown in the following screenshot; note that the results for **# of Deals Won** in the highlights panel show **No Results Found** because of the stages that you selected:

Figure 8.13 – Your dashboard in Sales drill-down view after drilling into the data

You are now going to share this dashboard view with the help of the following steps:

1. Click on the **Share** button at the top right of your screen.

2. There are several ways for sharing this dashboard view, but for now, you want to share the link with a colleague who has access to this app and include a screenshot for reference. First, you will click on **GET URL**, then copy the **Uniform Resource Locator** (**URL**) and add it to an email.

3. Next, click on **DOWNLOAD** and download the dashboard view as an image. Add the image to your email.

4. Your colleague can now quickly review the dashboard as an image and then click on the URL to view the data live in the CRMA dashboard. Note that their view will retain the filtering and faceting that you applied when slicing and dicing your data to arrive at the view.

Here is what you see when you want to share the URL for **My First Dashboard**:

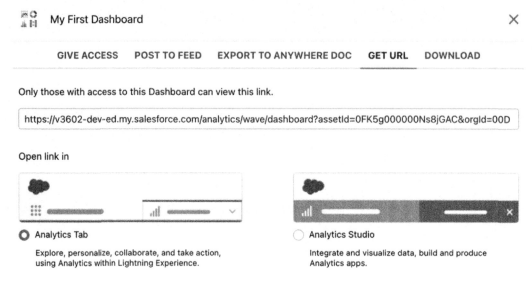

Figure 8.14 – Sharing the URL for My First Dashboard

This is what you see when you want to download **My First Dashboard** as an image:

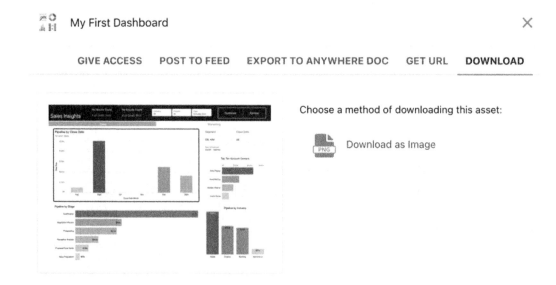

Figure 8.15 – Downloading My First Dashboard as an image

Let's proceed to create a lens from the dashboard, drill into the data, and share it with colleagues with the help of the following steps:

1. Go to the **Top Ten Account Owners** chart widget and click on the drop-down arrow at the top right of the widget.

2. Click on **Explore**.

3. Click on the **FILTERS** tab. Notice that the exploration lens retailed the four filters applied at the dashboard level for **Opportunity Type**, **Amount**, **Segment**, and **Stage**.

4. Click on the bar with the highest value, **Kelly Frazier**.

5. Click on the drill-down button with the magnifying glass icon.

6. Under **Drill Into This By**, search for **Opportunity Name** and select it.

7. You should now see two open deals for Kelly Frazier. This is the information you wanted, so now, click on **Save**.

8. Save this lens as **Kelly's deals for discussion** under **My Private App**.

9. Now, share this lens with Kelly by copying the URL under **GET URL** and sharing via Slack or Teams.

The lens should look like this:

Figure 8.16 – Kelly's deals for discussion

Now that you know how to slice and dice your CRMA dashboard and share the results with a colleague, let's review what you learned in this chapter.

Summary

As you have seen in this chapter, CRMA is a versatile and user-friendly platform for building dashboards, analyzing data, and sharing findings.

What exactly have you learned? First, you are now able to identify and use the tools available in the CRMA dashboard editor. Also, you can create widgets and add them to a dashboard. Third, you can edit and format widgets to meet your requirements. Plus, you are confident in adding and managing CRMA pages. Lastly, you should be competent in using a dashboard and sharing findings with others.

The next chapter will teach you how to build advanced features into your CRMA dashboard.

Questions

Here is a list of questions to test your knowledge:

- If you want a colleague to access a particular view of a dashboard and drill into the data, how would you share it with them?

- What is the purpose of the **Copy widget to clipboard** command?

- What is the recommended number of default columns for a dashboard?

- When you move from one dashboard to another, do any filters applied to the first page remain in place?

- How could you use the **Container** widget in a dashboard?

- What is meant by a top-down dashboard design, and how is it facilitated by CRMA pages?

- The **Clone Query** command clones the query and opens it for _____.

9

Advanced Dashboard Design and Build

Now that you have built your first dashboard, it's time to move beyond the basics. In this chapter, you will learn about advanced dashboard design and build. When you've completed this chapter, you will know how to enhance designs with **CRM Analytics (CRMA)** pages, use **Salesforce Analytics Query Language (SAQL)** to create more complex queries, and build interactions and bindings using code or clicks.

What will you learn to do in this chapter? We'll be looking at the following topics:

- Creative use of page animations
- Beginning with code – an introduction to SAQL
- Tying things together with bindings
- Working with the Advanced Editor

Technical requirements

You will need the following to successfully execute the instructions in this chapter:

- The latest version of the Google Chrome browser (Chrome is the preferred browser when working with CRMA)

- A working email address

Be sure to be logged in to your CRMA dev org.

Let's begin with when and how to use page animations in CRMA.

Creative use of page animations

The CRMA pages functionality gives you the capability to create clever dashboards that use animation to enhance dashboard functionality and useability.

From your Analytics Studio home page, open the **My First Dashboard** dashboard you created in *Chapter 8, Building Your First CRMA Dashboard*. Follow these steps to create a dashboard where you will work with multiple pages:

1. Clone it to create a new dashboard, **My Advanced Dashboard**.

2. Open this new dashboard in **Edit** mode.

3. Clone the **Sales** page and rename this new page **Sales Clean**.

4. Under the **Page Options** drop-down menu, select **Hide from Navigation**. Notice that this removes the page from the navigation widget.

5. Remove and rearrange widgets so that the page matches what you see in *Figure 9.1*. When prompted about removing the global filter widget, select **Delete Widget Only**.

6. Click **Save** to save the dashboard.

The result should look like this:

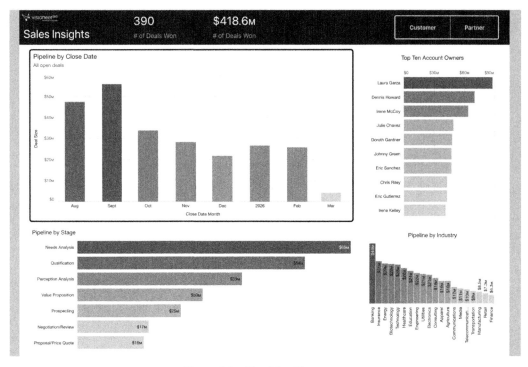

Figure 9.1 – The Sales Clean page

Now, you need to add a way to navigate between the new page and the original **Sales** page. This will be accomplished by using a link widget. Follow these steps:

1. Drag a **Link** widget to the highlights panel.
2. Remove the border from the widget.
3. Change the text color to a light pink or similar.
4. Increase the font size to 18.
5. Change the link text to **Back**.
6. Under **Link To**, select **Page in layout**.
7. Under **Page**, select **Sales**.
8. Click **Save** to save the dashboard.

This is what the finished link widget format will look like:

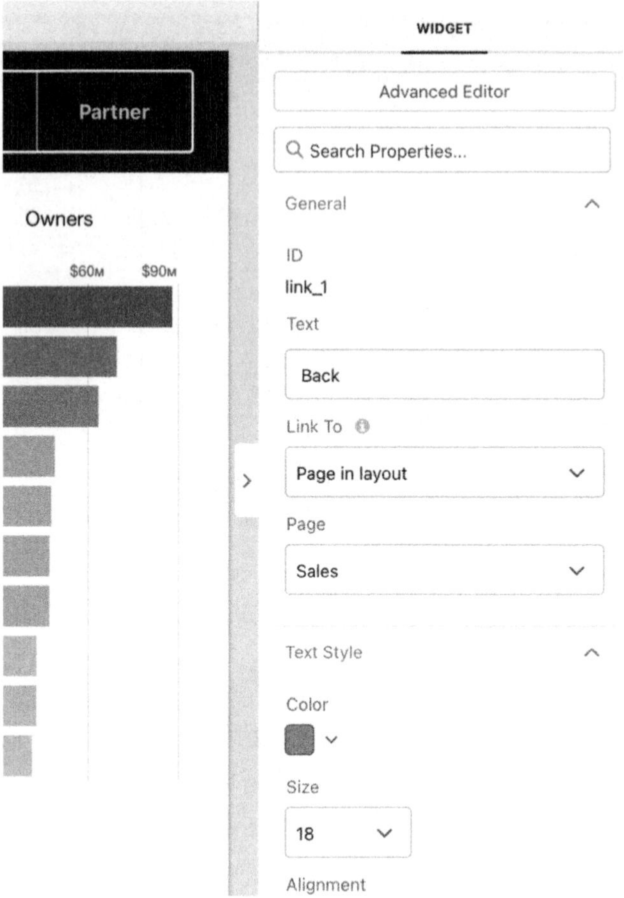

Figure 9.2 – The finished link widget format

Now that your minimalist page has a link back to the original **Sales** page, you need to give users a way to get to the minimalist page from the **Sales** page. Follow these steps:

1. Copy the link widget.

2. Navigate to the **Sales** page.

3. Paste the link widget; it should appear at the bottom of the page.

4. You now need to make room for the link widget. First, remove the title from the **Pipeline by Close Date** hero chart, and save the text to your clipboard.

5. Add a container widget at the bottom of the page and resize it to make room for the hero chart to be moved inside.

6. Add a border to match the hero chart.

7. Remove the border from the hero chart.

8. Drag the hero chart into the container, then resize it to make room for a title.

9. Drag a new text widget into the container.

10. Move the link widget into the container at the far right.

11. Change the text for the link widget to **No Filters** and make it link to the page in layout, **Sales Clean**.

12. Move the container to the top of the page under the page navigator.

13. Go into **Preview** mode and test the navigation.

14. Click **Save** to save your dashboard.

The **Sales** page with navigation added to the revised hero chart should look like this:

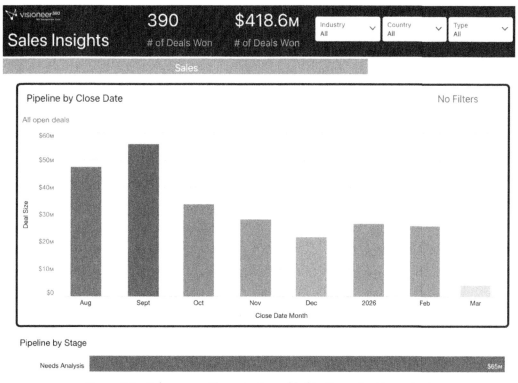

Figure 9.3 – Sales page with navigation added to the revised hero chart

Let's create a fresh dashboard to learn more about working pages and animation. Name this dashboard **Clever Pages** and change the settings as follows:

- **Columns**: 50
- **Row Height**: Fine

- **Cell Spacing**: 0
- **Maximum Dashboard Width**: 1200
- **Background Color**: Choose white for the gutter and pick a dark color for the grid.
- Under **Widget Default Properties**, make the background color transparent and add a transparent border.
- Click **Save** to save the dashboard.

To get started with your new dashboard, copy the highlights panel from **My Advanced Dashboard** and paste it into the **Clever Pages** dashboard. Edit the colors until you get something like this:

Figure 9.4 – Highlights panel on the Clever Pages dashboard

What you are now going to do is create a simple dashboard and learn how to use pages to zoom, expand, and contract. Create a home page by following the next steps (look ahead to *Figure 9.5* to make sure you're on the right track). Choose a dark theme for widgets:

1. Add a stacked column chart with the title **Open Pipeline by Close Date and Stage**.
2. Replace the title for this chart with a link widget that will later be used to navigate to the **Expansion** page.
3. Add a donut chart with the title **Open Deals by Stage %**; make the center size 0% to create a pie chart.
4. Add a heat map chart with the title **Deals Won by Industry and Lead Source**.
5. Add a combo chart with the title **Deals Won by Opportunity Owner**, showing count and value.
6. Click **Save** to save the dashboard.

This is what your new dashboard should look like:

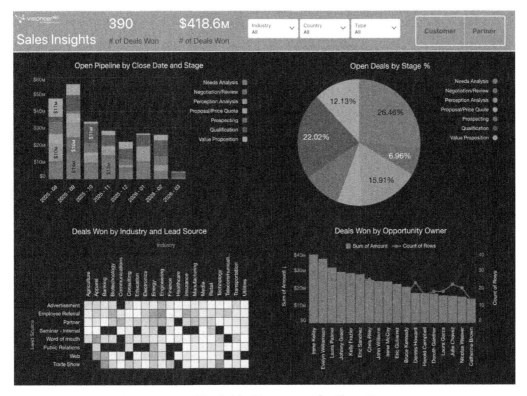

Figure 9.5 – The finished home page for Clever Pages

The next stage is to clone this page and use it to create an expansion page for the hero chart, using these steps:

1. Rename the existing page **Home**.

2. Clone this page and rename the new page **Expansion**.

3. Unlink the link widget that appears as the title **Open Pipeline by Close Date and Stage**.

4. Edit this link on the **Home** page to point to the **Expansion** page.

5. Go to the **Expansion** page and edit the layout so that the **Open Pipeline by Close Date and Stage** hero chart is highly prominent. You can remove the pie chart.

6. Resize the link widget acting as a title to make room for a second link widget on the right.

7. Point the title link widget to the **Home** page.

8. Add a second link widget on the right, above the hero chart, that points back to the **Home** page. The link text should be **Home**.

9. Click **Save** to save your dashboard.

The finished result should look like this:

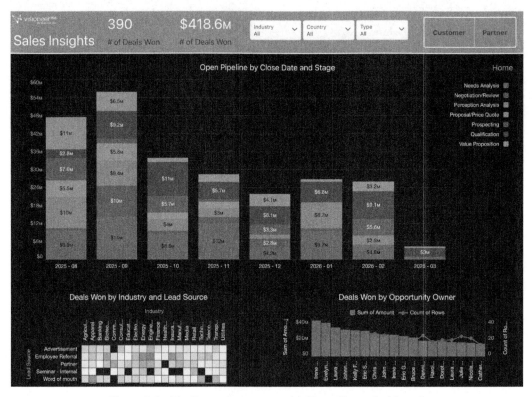

Figure 9.6 – The Expansion page on the Clever Pages dashboard

Test the navigation—from the **Home** page, clicking on the title of the hero chart will expand that chart and allow detailed analysis; clicking on the **Home** link takes you back, as does clicking on the hero chart title. Nice! This functionality is very useful in dashboard design. For example, it can be used to zoom in and out on charts for further analysis, reveal greater detail on a hero chart, or facilitate data segmentation.

Let's add a different type of animation with pages where drill-down can be enabled with just one click. Open the **Clever Pages** dashboard and follow these steps:

1. Clone the **Home** page and rename this new page **Industry and Lead Source**.

2. Remove the link widget with the text **Open Pipeline by Close Date and Stage**.

3. Remove all charts except **Deals Won by Industry and Lead Source**.

4. Move the heat map chart to the top left of the page.

5. Clone the heat map and edit the copy as **Pipeline by Industry and Lead Source**; change the filters to suit.

6. Add a stacked bar chart titled **Breakdown of Deals Won and Lost by Industry**.

7. Add a bar chart titled **Open Pipeline by Lead Source**.

8. Remove the global filters (widget only).

9. Add list widgets for **Lead Source and Industry** to the highlights panel.

10. Remove the toggle widget in the highlights panel.

11. Add a link to the highlights panel with the text **Go Back**, pointing to the **Home** page.

12. Go to the **Home** page and unlink the **Deals Won by Industry and Lead Source** chart.

13. Replace the title of this chart with a link that has the same text and points to the **Industry and Lead Source** page.

14. Unlink the page title in the highlights panel and change the text to **Sales Breakdown**.

15. Test the navigation. Clicking on the title for **Deals Won by Industry and Lead Source** now takes you to a page that slices and dices your sales data by industry and lead source. Cool!

16. Click **Save** to save your dashboard.

The result will look like this:

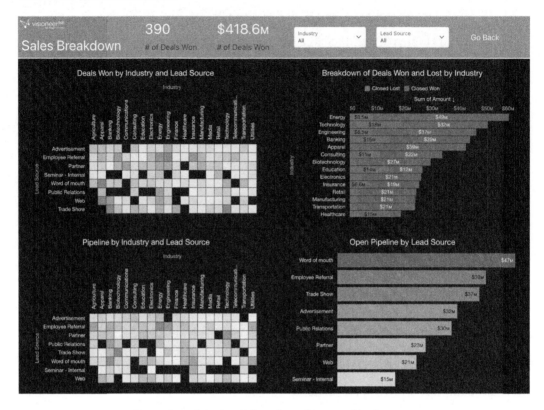

Figure 9.7 – Sales breakdown by industry and lead source

Another way of using page animation to enhance the **user experience (UX)** is to use pages to show or hide a detail panel. Open your **Clever Pages** dashboard and follow these steps:

1. Go to the **Expansion** page and clone it.

2. Rename the page **Expansion Detail**.

3. Remove the heat map chart.

4. Move the combo chart to the left and make it fit the width of the hero chart.

5. Add a container widget that runs from top to bottom; see *Figure 9.8*.

6. Change the container widget background color to match the highlights panel.

7. Unlink the link widget that says **Home** and change its color to white. Move this to the top right of the container.

8. Add another link widget to the left of the **Home** link widget. **Text** should be **Back**; **Link To** will be **Page in layout** and **Page** is **Expansion**.

9. Go to the **Expansion** page and unlink the **Open Pipeline by Close Date and Stage** link widget.

10. Edit this widget so that it now links to the **Expansion Detail** page.

11. Go back to the **Expansion Detail** page and add a timeline chart titled **Trend of Deals Won**.

12. Add a bar chart titled **Pipeline by Stage**.

13. Add a donut chart titled **Pipeline by Product Family**.

14. Click **Save** to save your dashboard.

The **Expansion Detail** page should look like this:

Figure 9.8 – The Expansion Detail page

If you test the page navigation by clicking on the hero chart title, you see that the pages enable drill-down, as follows:

- **Home** page
- **Focus on Open Pipeline by Close Date and Stage**
- **Details for Open Pipeline by Close Date and Stage**
- **Back to Focus on Open Pipeline by Close Date and Stage**
- **Back to Home page**

As our last example of intelligent design with CRMA pages, let's look at embedding a navigation link on an image. Follow these steps:

1. Edit the **Clever Pages** dashboard.
2. Go to the **Expansion Detail** page.
3. Reduce the width of the text widget that says **Open Pipeline by Close Date and Stage** while keeping it centered above the chart widget.
4. Add a container widget to the page, shrink it in size, and move it to the left of the text widget that you just resized.
5. Download a transparent image from the internet.
6. Add this image to the new container as a background image.
7. Click **Save** to save your dashboard.

This is what your progress should look like so far:

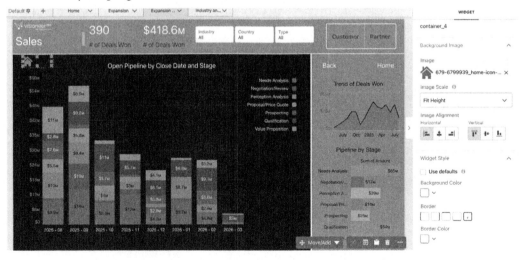

Figure 9.9 – Formatting the container with a background image

Time to add a link to your container! Follow these steps:

1. Add a link to your page and shrink it so that it will fit inside your new container.

2. Move the link onto the container with the **Home** icon.

3. Remove all text from the link.

4. Make sure that the link widget has a transparent background.

5. Set the link to navigate to the **Home** page.

6. Click **Save** to save your dashboard.

Test your dashboard—the home icon will now take you back to the **Home** page.

Let's now have a look at an introduction to SAQL—your first foray into code in CRMA!

Beginning with code – an introduction to SAQL

This section will introduce you to coding in CRMA using SAQL.

Definitions

We'll now look at detailed definitions regarding what SAQL is and when it can be used.

What is SAQL?

SAQL is a runtime query language that enables ad hoc analysis of datasets. A SAQL script consists of a sequence of statements that are made up of keywords (such as filter, group, and order), **identifiers (IDs)**, literals, or special characters. It is **JavaScript Object Notation (JSON)**-based and **Apache Pig Latin (PIGQL)**-familiar. A SAQL query loads an input dataset, operates on it, and outputs the results.

Here is a SAQL example:

```
q = load "My_Dataset";
q = group q by 'Division_Name';
q = foreach q generate 'Division_Name' as 'Division_Name',
sum('Amount')/sum('Quantity') as 'sum_Amt/Qty'; q = order q by
'sum_Amt/Qty' desc;
```

What you see in the preceding snippet are basic SAQL elements, as follows:

- Load statement to load data
- Stream ID—in this case, `"q"`
- Statements using various SAQL functions and keywords

When do you use SAQL?

You may use SAQL when you need to do custom calculations, advanced data manipulations on the fly, co-grouping (joining) data from different datasets, and top/bottom lists, in conjunction with binding for dynamic values on charts, and so on.

Which syntax is used for SAQL?

Here is some basic SAQL syntax:

- Keywords and functions are written in lowercase and they are case-sensitive.
- **Application programming interface (API)** names being called from the dataset should be enclosed in single quotes, like this: `'Division_Name'`.
- API names are case-sensitive.
- Strings must be enclosed in double quotes, such as `"Open"`.

Where do you edit SAQL?

Every step of a lens is SAQL-based so that it can be edited and/or custom SAQL can be added. These can be viewed in JSON editor mode or copied to a JSON editor of your choice.

Follow these steps to see how to view and edit SAQL:

1. Create a new lens from the **Opportunities** dataset.
2. Add filters to the lens as you wish.
3. Add groupings to the lens as you wish.
4. Select two measures.
5. Change to query mode by clicking on the **Query Mode** button at the top right of the chart in your lens.

This is what my example lens looks like in chart mode:

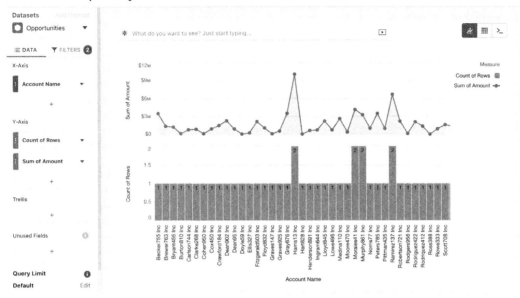

Figure 9.10 – A sample opportunity lens in chart mode

My example SAQL looks like this in query mode:

```
1 q = load "opportunity1";
2 q = filter q by (!('StageName' in ["Closed Lost", "Closed Won"]) || 'StageName' is null);
3 q = filter q by 'Account.Industry' in ["Banking", "Biotechnology", "Communications", "Education",
  "Electronics"];
4 q = group q by 'Account.Name';
5 q = foreach q generate 'Account.Name' as 'Account.Name', count() as 'count', sum('Amount') as
  'sum_Amount';
6 q = order q by 'Account.Name' asc;
7 q = limit q 2000;
```

Account Name ↑	Count of Rows	Sum of Amount
Becker755 Inc	1	$3,526,355
Brewer763 Inc	1	$1,422,600
Bryant456 Inc	1	$1,269,390
Burton810 Inc	1	$136,800
Carlson744 Inc	1	$788,800

Figure 9.11 – A sample opportunity lens with SAQL revealed in query mode

This is what the code looks like:

```
q = load "opportunity1";
q = filter q by (!('StageName' in ["Closed Lost", "Closed
Won"]) || 'StageName' is null);
q = filter q by 'Account.Industry' in ["Banking",
"Biotechnology", "Communications", "Education", "Electronics"];
q = group q by 'Account.Name';
q = foreach q generate 'Account.Name' as 'Account.Name',
count() as 'count', sum('Amount') as 'sum_Amount';
q = order q by 'Account.Name' asc;
q = limit q 2000;
```

The best way to learn how SAQL works is to get your hands dirty, so let's dive into some example use cases.

Example use cases

Here are some example use cases where SAQL is helpful.

Union use case

Follow these steps to create and edit a Union SAQL query:

1. Create a lens from the **Opportunities** dataset with no grouping, using **Sum of Amount** as the measure.

2. Switch to **Compare Table** mode.

3. Filter **Sum of Amount** as follows:

    - **Opportunity Type = New Business**

    - **Account Type = Customer**

    - **Industry [1] Agriculture, Apparel**

4. Clone the column and filter by selecting **Existing Business** under **Opportunity Type**.

5. Edit the column names as follows:

    - New Business

    - Existing Business

6. **Save** the lens as **Union Use Case**.

Your progress so far will look like this:

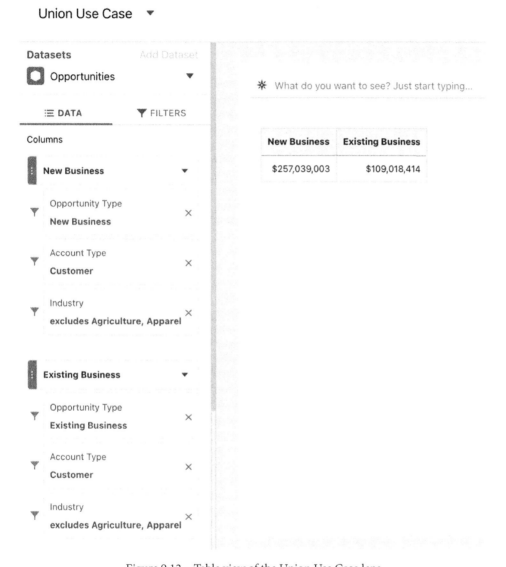

Figure 9.12 – Table view of the Union Use Case lens

7. Change the lens to a Funnel chart and notice that it cannot be used correctly; it shows one value at a time only. Switch to **Query Mode** to view and edit the SAQL content.

This is your starting point with the SAQL content:

```
q = load "opportunity1";

q_A = filter q by 'Type' == "New Business" && 'Account.Type'
== "Customer" && (!('Account.Industry' in ["Agriculture",
"Apparel"]) || 'Account.Industry' is null);

q_B = filter q by 'Type' == "Existing Business" && 'Account.
Type' == "Customer" && (!('Account.Industry' in ["Agriculture",
"Apparel"]) || 'Account.Industry' is null);

result = group q_A by all full, q_B by all;

result = foreach result generate sum(q_A.'Amount') as 'A',
sum(q_B.'Amount') as 'B';

result = limit result 2000;
```

Notice that you have three data streams in your query: q_A, q_B, and `result`.

8. Update your code to remove the query limit and union your two columns, as follows:

```
q = load "opportunity1";

q_A = filter q by 'Type' == "New Business" && 'Account.Type'
== "Customer" && (!('Account.Industry' in ["Agriculture",
"Apparel"]) || 'Account.Industry' is null);

q_B = filter q by 'Type' == "Existing Business" && 'Account.
Type' == "Customer" && (!('Account.Industry' in ["Agriculture",
"Apparel"]) || 'Account.Industry' is null);

result = group q_A by all full, q_B by all;

result = foreach result generate sum(q_A.'Amount') as 'A',
sum(q_B.'Amount') as 'B';

final1 = foreach result generate "New Business" as
'Description', sum('A') as 'Sum';

final2 = foreach result generate "Existing Business" as
'Description', sum('B') as 'Sum';

final = union final1,final2;
```

The union function combines multiple result sets into one result set. You need the same structure and field names in result sets. You do have a choice to either use a different dataset or the same dataset when it comes to creating result datasets.

When you click **Run Query**, you will see a table, as follows:

Learn how to write and edit SAQL queries ▶

Query

```
 1 q = load "opportunity1";
 2 q_A = filter q by 'Type' == "New Business" && 'Account.Type' == "Customer" && (!
   ('Account.Industry' in ["Agriculture", "Apparel"]) || 'Account.Industry' is null);
 3 q_B = filter q by 'Type' == "Existing Business" && 'Account.Type' == "Customer" && (!
   ('Account.Industry' in ["Agriculture", "Apparel"]) || 'Account.Industry' is null);
 4 result = group q_A by all full, q_B by all;
 5 result = foreach result generate sum(q_A.'Amount') as 'A', sum(q_B.'Amount') as 'B';
 6 result = limit result 2000;
 7
 8 final1 = foreach result generate "New Business" as 'Description', sum('A') as 'Sum';
 9 final2 = foreach result generate "Existing Business" as 'Description', sum('B') as
   'Sum';
10 final = union final1,final2;
```

#	Description	Sum
1	New Business	257,039,003
2	Existing Business	109,018,414

Figure 9.13 – Table results from the Union function

You can now use a funnel or other chart type to visualize the sum broken up into two components: new and existing business.

Another use case for the Union function is to analyze the same metric showing a rolling 3 months, as follows:

```
q3 = load "opportunity";
q3 = filter q3 by date('CloseDate_Year', 'CloseDate_Month',
'CloseDate_Day') in ["3 months ago".."3 months ago"]; q3 =
group q3 by ('CloseDate_Year', 'CloseDate_Month');
q3 = foreach q3 generate 'CloseDate_Year' as 'CloseDate_Year',
'CloseDate_Month' as 'CloseDate_Month', sum('Amount') as 'sum_
Amount';
q2 = load "opportunity";
q2 = filter q2 by date('CloseDate_Year', 'CloseDate_Month',
'CloseDate_Day') in ["2 months ago".."2 months ago"]; q2 =
group q2 by ('CloseDate_Year', 'CloseDate_Month');
```

```
q2 = foreach q2 generate 'CloseDate_Year' as 'CloseDate_Year',
'CloseDate_Month' as 'CloseDate_Month', sum('Amount') as 'sum_
Amount';
```

```
q1 = load "opportunity";
```

```
q1 = filter q1 by date('CloseDate_Year', 'CloseDate_Month',
'CloseDate_Day') in ["1 months ago".."1 months ago"]; q1 =
group q1 by ('CloseDate_Year', 'CloseDate_Month');
```

```
q1 = foreach q1 generate 'CloseDate_Year' as 'CloseDate_Year',
'CloseDate_Month' as 'CloseDate_Month', sum('Amount') as 'sum_
Amount';
```

```
final = union q3, q2, q1;
```

Creating buckets using the case statement

Follow these steps to try this use case for yourself:

1. Create a new lens from the **Opportunities** dataset.
2. Group by **Opportunity Name** and measure **Sum of Amount**.
3. Filter by **Won deals**.
4. Change to **Query Mode**.
5. Remove the `limit` statement.
6. Click **Save** to save your lens.

Now that you have your basic SAQL prepared, add the following case statement:

```
result = foreach q generate 'Name' as 'Name', 'sum_Amount' as
'Amount', (case when 'sum_Amount' > 2000000 then "Big" when
'sum_Amount' > 500000 then "Medium"  else "Small" end) as
'Size';
```

The finished SAQL code should look like this:

```
q = load "opportunity1";
```

```
q = filter q by 'IsWon' == "true";
```

```
q = group q by 'Name';
```

```
q = foreach q generate 'Name' as 'Name', sum('Amount') as 'sum_
Amount';
```

```
q = order q by 'Name' asc;
```

```
result = foreach q generate 'Name' as 'Name', 'sum_Amount' as
'Amount', (case when 'sum_Amount' > 2000000 then "Big" when
'sum_Amount' > 500000 then "Medium"  else "Small" end) as
'Size';
```

When you click **Run Query**, you should see this:

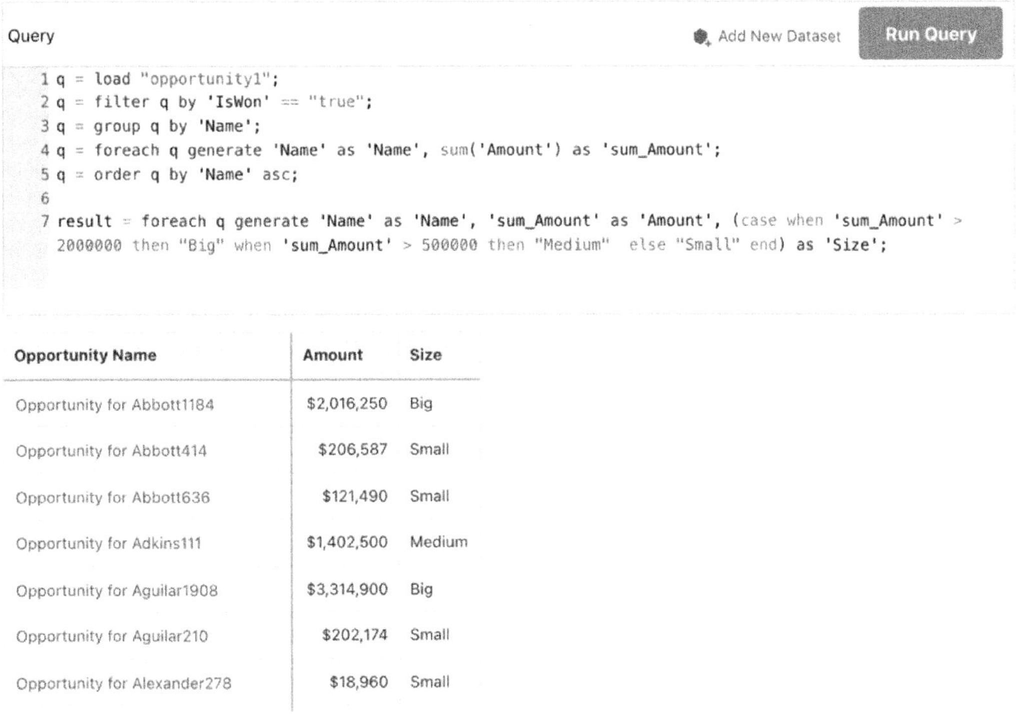

```
Query                                      Add New Dataset   Run Query
1 q = load "opportunity1";
2 q = filter q by 'IsWon' == "true";
3 q = group q by 'Name';
4 q = foreach q generate 'Name' as 'Name', sum('Amount') as 'sum_Amount';
5 q = order q by 'Name' asc;
6
7 result = foreach q generate 'Name' as 'Name', 'sum_Amount' as 'Amount', (case when 'sum_Amount' >
  2000000 then "Big" when 'sum_Amount' > 500000 then "Medium"  else "Small" end) as 'Size';
```

Opportunity Name	Amount	Size
Opportunity for Abbott1184	$2,016,250	Big
Opportunity for Abbott414	$206,587	Small
Opportunity for Abbott636	$121,490	Small
Opportunity for Adkins111	$1,402,500	Medium
Opportunity for Aguilar1908	$3,314,900	Big
Opportunity for Aguilar210	$202,174	Small
Opportunity for Alexander278	$18,960	Small

Figure 9.14 – Bucketed results created using the Case function

> Tip
>
> If you're looking to dive deep into SAQL, I can recommend these resources:
>
> https://developer.salesforce.com/docs/atlas.en-us.
> bi_dev_guide_saql.meta/bi_dev_guide_saql/bi_saql_
> reference.htm
>
> https://www.salesforceblogger.com/all-about-saql/

We are now going to learn how to create dashboard bindings using both JSON and the **user interface (UI)**.

Tying things together with bindings

What are bindings in CRMA? Bindings are used to pass values between steps and widgets—that is, parameterizing values for dynamic values and selections. Example use cases include the following:

- Dynamic reference lines
- Dynamic groupings
- Dynamic measures
- Dynamic sort
- Dynamic chart types

There are two types of bindings to consider. First, selection binding is used to update a query based on the selection in another query, such as choosing a date range via a toggle widget. Second, results binding is used to update a query based on the results of another query, such as using a calculated value from a case statement to bucket your data.

CRMA is slowly moving away from requiring code to create bindings, but many use cases still require development work in the JSON, as you will see in the following section.

Bindings in JSON

We're now going to talk about JSON. You may be familiar with JSON, but perhaps not in the context of CRMA. The following diagram shows how JSON and the CRMA dashboard fit together:

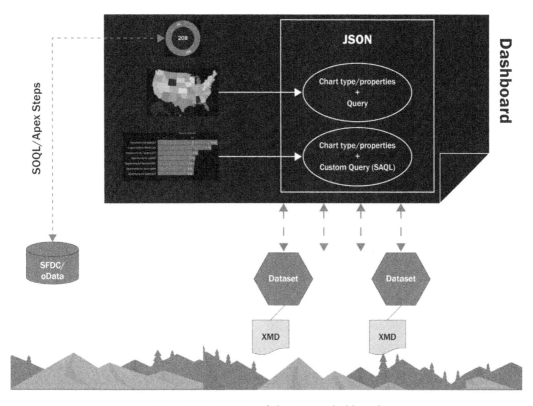

Figure 9.15 – JSON and the CRMA dashboard

When in the dashboard editor, press *Cmd + E* (or *Ctrl + E*) to show the JSON behind the dashboard. JSON is just the language in which the instructions are written. The JSON contains all the widgets/charts descriptions and the queries to run against the datasets. Each chart is actually several lines of JSON describing the types and properties and the query to run. A special case is when one of these queries is custom-written directly, using SAQL.

What is JSON? Put simply, it is descriptive instructions in a file made of a bunch of *keys* and *values* enclosed in brackets { }. The values can be text, numeric, Boolean, or arrays of text/numeric; you can have multiple brackets of such information. Here is a simple breakdown of JSON:

```
{
  "Name" : "Homer Simpson",
  "Age" : 39,
  "Children" : [ "Lisa", "Bart", "Maggie" ]
},
{
  "Name" : "Bart Simpson",
  "Age" : 10,
  "Children" : [ ]
}
```

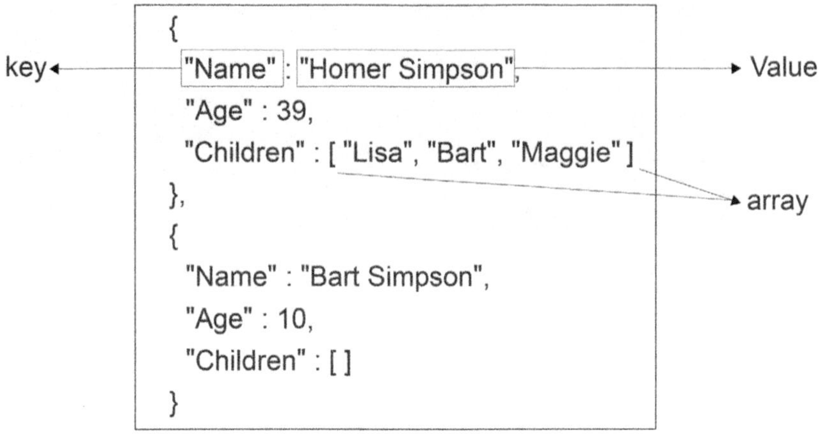

Figure 9.16 – A simple breakdown of JSON

Here is an abridged example of JSON from **My First Dashboard**:

```
"steps": {
    "Leads_by_Status_1": {
        "broadcastFacet": true,
        "datasets": [
            {
                "id": "0Fb5g000000U115CAC",
                "label": "Leads",
                "name": "Leads",
                "url": "/services/data/v52.0/wave/
datasets/0Fb5g000000U115CAC"
            }
        ],
        "isGlobal": false,
        "label": "Leads by Status",
        "query": {
            "measures": [
                [
```

```
                    "count",
                    "*"
                ]
            ],
            "groups": [
                "Status"
            ]
        },
        "receiveFacetSource": {
            "mode": "all",
            "steps": []
        },
        "selectMode": "multi",
        "type": "aggregateflex",
        "useGlobal": true,
        "visualizationParameters": {
            "parameters": {
                "autoFitMode": "keepLabels",
                "showValues": true,
                "bins": {
                    "breakpoints": {
                        "high": 100,
                        "low": 0
                    },
                    "bands": {
                        "high": {
                            "color": "#008000",
                            "label": ""
                        },
                        "low": {
                            "color": "#B22222",
                            "label": ""
                        },
                        "medium": {
                            "color": "#ffa500",
                            "label": ""
```

```
                }
              }
            },
            "legend": {
                "descOrder": false,
                "showHeader": true,
                "show": true,
                "customSize": "auto",
                "position": "right-top",
                "inside": false
            },
            "axisMode": "multi",
            "tooltip": {
                "showBinLabel": true,
                "measures": "",
                "showNullValues": true,
                "showPercentage": true,
                "showDimensions": true,
                "showMeasures": true,
                "customizeTooltip": false,
                "dimensions": ""
            },
            "visualizationType": "hbar",
            "title": {
                "fontSize": 16,
                "subtitleFontSize": 11,
                "label": "Leads by Status",
                "align": "center",
                "subtitleLabel": ""
            },
            "binValues": false,
            "trellis": {
                "flipLabels": false,
                "showGridLines": true,
                "size": [
                    100,
```

```
                    100
                ],
                "enable": false,
                "type": "x",
                "chartsPerLine": 4
            },
            "columnMap": {
                "trellis": [],
                "dimensionAxis": [
                    "Status"
                ],
                "plots": [
                    "count"
                ]
            },
            "showActionMenu": true,
            "measureAxis2": {
                "sqrtScale": false,
                "showTitle": true,
                "showAxis": true,
                "title": "",
                "customDomain": {
                    "showDomain": false
                }
            },
            "measureAxis1": {
                "sqrtScale": false,
                "showTitle": true,
                "showAxis": true,
                "title": "",
                "customDomain": {
                    "showDomain": false
                }
            },
            "theme": "wave",
            "dimensionAxis": {
```

```
                        "showTitle": true,
                        "customSize": "auto",
                        "showAxis": true,
                        "title": "",
                        "icons": {
                            "useIcons": false,
                            "iconProps": {
                                "fit": "cover",
                                "column": "",
                                "type": "round"
                            }
                        }
                    },
                        "applyConditionalFormatting": true
                },
                "type": "chart",
                "options": {}
            }
        },
"Pipeline_by_Industry_1": {
            "broadcastFacet": true,
            "datasets": [
                {
                    "id": "0Fb5g000000TV2bCAG",
                    "label": "Opportunities",
                    "name": "opportunity1",
                    "url": "/services/data/v52.0/wave/
datasets/0Fb5g000000TV2bCAG"
                }
            ],
```

```
        "isGlobal": false,
        "label": "Pipeline by Industry",
        "query": {
            "measures": [
                [
                        "sum",
                        "Amount"
                ]
            ],
            "groups": [
                "Account.Industry"
            ],
            "filters": [
                [
                        "IsWon",
                        [
                                "false"
                        ],
                        "in"
                ]
            ],
            "order": [
                [
                        "sum_Amount",
                        {
                                "ascending": false
                        }
                ]
            ]
        },
```

If you look carefully at this example, you'll see that it contains instructions for building the dashboard. The following example shows basic widget/step JSON:

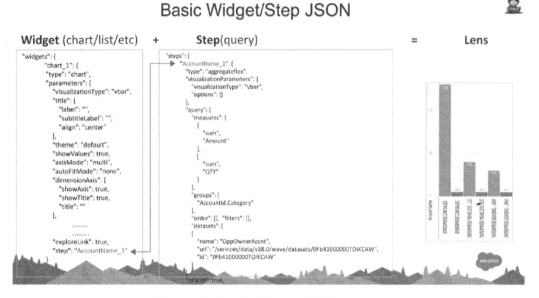

Figure 9.17 – Basic widget/step JSON example

Here, we have a simplified example of dashboard JSON:

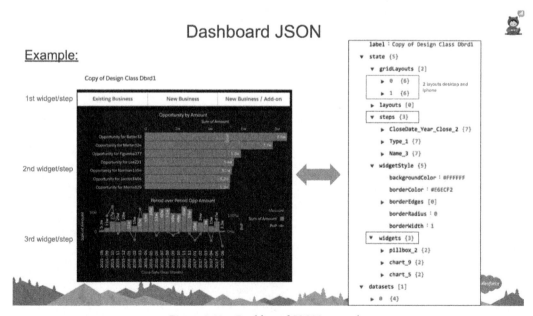

Figure 9.18 – Dashboard JSON example

Let's look at one simple example of a JSON binding—a dynamic grouping. This example comes from the publicly available *Learning Adventure* app, which I refer to at the end of this section. Follow these steps:

1. Create a new blank dashboard.

2. Create a toggle widget (`pillbox_1`) with a step (`Grouping_Toggle_1`) that specifies different groupings.

3. Create a bar chart (`chart_1`) with a step (`Dynamic_Query`) in a compact form that groups the total amount by the selected grouping in the toggle widget.

4. In the Spring 2018 release, a new `columnMap` chart property was introduced to build more powerful visualizations; however, `columnMap` is not necessary for this dynamic visualization. Replace this `columnMap {}` parameter with `columnMap: null`.

5. To dynamically set the grouping in the chart based on the selection in the toggle widget, open the dashboard JSON and bind the `groups` property in the `Dynamic_ Query` step—see the code snippet following this list of steps.

6. Click **Done** and you're ready to go.

Here is the JSON used to bind the `groups` property in the `Dynamic_Query` step:

```
"groups": "{{ cell(Grouping_Toggle_1.selection, 0, \"groups\").
asObject() }}"
```

What does this code mean? Let's break it down, as follows:

- `cell(Grouping_Toggle_1.selection, 0, \"groups\")` returns the selected grouping from the `Grouping_Toggle_1` step and gets the value from `cell (first row, "groups" column)` in the step selection. Index `0` is the first row, index `1` is the second row, and so on.

- `asObject()` formats the results as an array of strings, which is the expected format in dashboard JSON.

This is what the example looks like in the *Learning Adventure* app:

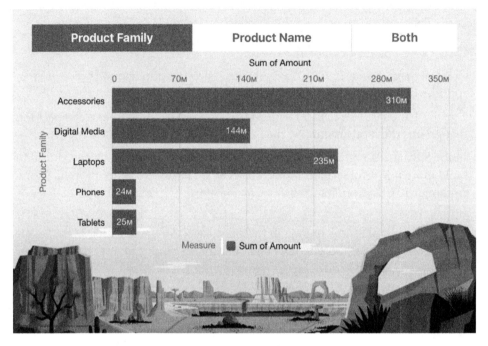

Figure 9.19 – Dynamic grouping example

There are many references out there that dive into details around JSON, bindings, and so on. As mentioned, I would recommend you create the *Learning Adventure* app from your CRMA dev org— it looks like this in Analytics Studio once you choose to create a templated app:

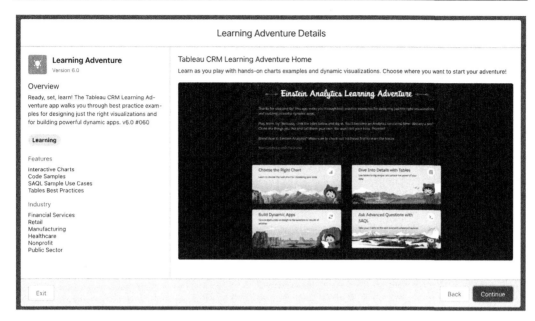

Figure 9.20 – The Learning Adventure app

You can also refer here to the *CRM Analytics Dashboard JSON Developer Guide*:

```
https://developer.salesforce.com/docs/atlas.en-us.bi_dev_
guide_json.meta/bi_dev_guide_json/bi_dbjson_intro.htm
```

Now, we are going to see how some bindings can be created from the UI, without code.

Bindings in the UI

There are several ways to create bindings without going into the dashboard JSON.
We will look at one example here, creating a dynamic reference line, then look at a second
example, where we'll learn about the **Advanced Editor**.

Follow these steps to create a dynamic reference line:

1. Open **My First Dashboard.**

2. Create a new chart that shows the average deal size (won) by industry.

3. Add this chart to the bottom of the **Sales** page.

4. Create a new query to calculate the average deal size (won) overall.

5. Under the Format pane for the new chart, under **Y-Axis** (on the left), select the arrow icon under **Value** and choose your average won deal size query for the dynamic reference line.

6. Similarly, add the average deal size to the label, and prefix with Average =.

7. Click **Save** to save your dashboard.

Adding the source query to the line value looks like this:

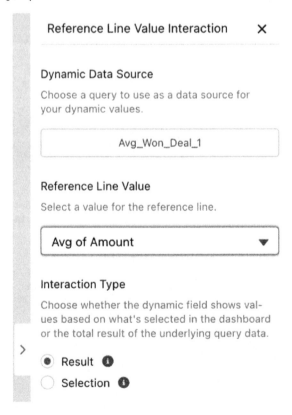

Figure 9.21 – Adding the source query to the line value

The format panel for the dynamic reference line should look like this when complete:

Figure 9.22 – The completed format panel for the dynamic reference line

The finished result should look like this:

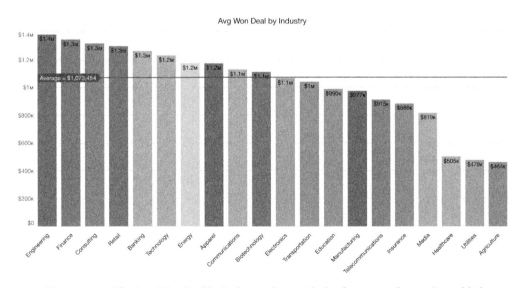

Figure 9.23 – The Avg Won Deal by Industry chart with the dynamic reference line added

Now, let's look at what the **Advanced Editor** is and how to use it.

Working with the Advanced Editor

Editing a widget using the **Advanced Editor** opens up a world of possibilities for clicks, not code. Let's see how this works in **My First Dashboard**. In **My First Dashboard**, click on the **Avg Won Deal by Industry** chart just created for the previous exercise on dynamic reference lines. Click on the **Advanced Editor** button and you'll see this:

Figure 9.24 – Avg Won Deal by Industry in the Advanced Editor

If you click on the **Query** tab, the code changes, but the rest of the window remains the same. How can you use the **Advanced Editor**? Other than for simple use cases such as changing the font size of a title to a custom value, or editing widget colors manually, the **Advanced Editor** can be used to create, edit, and preview dashboard bindings and interactions with clicks. To do so, you would follow these steps:

1. Click **Select query** under **Source Query** and choose from any query in the dashboard. Note that queries can be searched by name.

2. Under **Source Data**, click **Choose data**.

3. Under **Data Selection**, select **Row**, **Column**, or **Cell**.

4. Select the desired options under **Row Index** and **Column**.

5. Use the **Preview** button to see details of the query without leaving the **Interaction Editor**.

6. Click the left arrow.

7. For **Interaction Type**, choose **Result** or **Selection**.

8. Click **More Options** to set a default value or change the data serialization function.

9. If you wish, once you have built the interaction, you can edit it manually.

10. Copy your interaction.

11. Paste the interaction into the JSON or SAQL.

12. Click **Save**.

Now that you have learned how to build more advanced dashboard functionality, let's review what you have learned in this chapter.

Summary

You have now dipped your feet into the water of a more advanced CRMA design and build. I would encourage you to take what you have learned and put it to good use—practice using these advanced tools in your dev org and become proficient at using them.

What have you learned? First, you created and edited CRMA pages to help you to build more advanced dashboard functionality. Next, you were introduced to CRMA code by using SAQL. Third, you learned the basics of building dynamic dashboards using bindings. Last, you utilized the Advanced Editor to build interactions with clicks, not code.

The next chapter will teach you about when to code and when not to code.

Questions

Here are some questions to test your knowledge:

- Give three examples of use cases for using CRMA pages.

- When you move from page to page within a dashboard, do the applied filters remain, or are they cleared?

- When might you need SAQL?

- Keywords and functions are written in uppercase and they are not case-sensitive. True or false?

- Where do you edit SAQL?

- Which keyboard shortcut do you use to access dashboard JSON?

- Give three examples of use cases for bindings to make a dashboard more interactive and dynamic.

10
To Code or Not to Code?

One of the greatest challenges for **CRM Analytics (CRMA)** admins and developers is knowing when to code and when not to code. This causes a considerable amount of confusion. The purpose of this chapter is to guide you through how to determine when code is required by covering numerous practical examples.

Where code is required, examples of the sources will be given. However, please note that this book is not intended to be a detailed manual for CRM Analytics developers. Also, the code snippets given are, of necessity, often only small portions of the complete source code.

In this chapter, we will cover the following topics:

- When do you need code?
- You might not need to code if…
- Occasions of ambiguity

Technical requirements

You will need the following to successfully execute the instructions in this chapter:

- The latest version of the Google Chrome browser (Chrome is the preferred browser when working with CRMA)

- A working email address

Ensure that you're logged into your CRMA development organization.

Let's begin by understanding where you may need to use code in your CRMA application.

When do you need code?

The GUI of CRMA has come a very long way indeed since Wave was launched by Salesforce in 2014. Early users of the platform were forced to build everything in JSON, SAQL, and XMD as there was, essentially, no declarative option. Things are different now, with every new release of CRMA providing more point-and-click functionality.

However, there are applications of CRMA that do require code as you move into more advanced data transformation and dashboard building.

Here are six common applications in CRMA where you are required to deploy code:

- Security predicates
- Bindings in the JSON
- SAQL expressions
- Bulk actions (using Visualforce and the CRMA REST API)
- `timeseries` (modified)
- XMD – advanced formatting options

Let's begin with security predicates.

Security predicates

As you saw in *Chapter 7, Security in CRM Analytics*, a predicate is a filter condition that defines row-level security for a dataset. Security predicates range from extremely simple to highly complex, depending on the requirements. All require at least a little code.

For example, take a look at the following code:

```
'FFACompanyId' == "Unknown" || 'UserCompany.c2g__User__c' ==
"$User.Id"
```

Another example is as follows:

```
'Owner.Role.Roles' == "$User.UserRoleId" || 'OwnerId' ==
"$User.Id" || 'Account.OwnerId' == "$User.Id"
```

For detailed information and instructions about security predicates, see the following reference guide:

`https://resources.docs.salesforce.com/latest/latest/en-us/`
`sfdc/pdf/bi_admin_guide_security.pdf`

Next, you will learn how to use code to create bindings in the dashboard JSON.

Bindings in JSON

We will now examine several ways in which JSON can be used for dashboard bindings.

Dynamic charts

The user can select the visualization type dynamically by making a toggle selection on the dashboard. Here is an example of what this selection binding could look like:

```
{{coalesce(cell(static_1.selection, 0, \"visualizationType\"),
cell(static_1.result, 0, \"visualizationType\")).asString()}}
```

In the dashboard JSON, it might look like this:

```
        },
                        "axisMode": "multi",
                        "tooltip": {
                                "showBinLabel": true,
                                "measures": "",
                                "showPercentage": true,
                                "showDimensions": true,
                                "showMeasures": true,
                                "customizeTooltip": false,
                                "dimensions": ""
                        },
```

```
                        "visualizationType":
"{{coalesce(cell(static_1.selection, 0, \"visualizationType\"),
 cell(static_1.result, 0, \"visualizationType\")).asString()}}",
                        "binValues": false,
                        "title": {
                            "fontSize": 14,
                            "subtitleFontSize": 11,
                            "label": "",
                            "align": "center",
                            "subtitleLabel": ""
```

Custom selection bindings

Simple selection bindings can be created and edited in the GUI with a basic understanding of code, but more complex use cases require the use of JSON.

Here is an example of a date period toggle filter:

```
"static_1": {
    "broadcastFacet": true,
    "groups": [],
    "numbers": [],
    "selectMode": "singlerequired",
    "strings": [],
    "type": "staticflex",
    "values": [
        {
            "display": "MTD",
            "value": "month"
        },
        {
            "display": "QTD",
            "value": "quarter"
        },
        {
            "display": "YTD",
            "value": "year"
        }
```

```
    ],
    "start": {
        "display": [
            "MTD"
        ]
    }


    "Customers_spending_1_1": {
        "type": "saql",
        "query": "q = load \"bankingData\";\nq = filter
q by date('Date_Year', 'Date_Month', 'Date_Day') in
[\"current {{cell(static_1.selection,0,\"value\").
asString()}}\"..\"current day\"];\nq = group q by all;\nq =
foreach q generate unique('comb.CustomerID') as 'unique_comb.
CustomerID';\nq = limit q 2000;",
        "selectMode": "single",
        "broadcastFacet": true,
        "receiveFacet": true,
        "useGlobal": true,
        "numbers": [],
        "groups": [],
        "strings": [],
        "visualizationParameters":
```

Nested bindings

Here is an example where we want to calculate a measure based on nested selection binding, where a selection binding references another selection binding:

```
"query": {
                    "measures": [
                        "{{cell(step_1.selection,0,cell(step_2.
selection,0,\"value\")).asObject()}}"
                    ],
                    "groups": [
                        "Account.Industry"
                    ]
                },
```

For detailed insights and instructions regarding bindings, please reference the following developer guide:

`https://resources.docs.salesforce.com/latest/latest/en-us/sfdc/pdf/bi_dev_guide_bindings.pdf`

Now, we will look at some use cases where it is necessary to code in SAQL.

SAQL expressions

SAQL is used where queries require additional complexity or customizability beyond what can be delivered in the GUI.

Union

Combining various data streams and manipulating in one query requires the use of SAQL.

Here is an example of calculating spending as a percentage of a target (in JSON format):

```
"steps": {
            "Spending_as___of_Tar_1": {
                "broadcastFacet": true,
                "groups": [],
                "label": "Spending as % of Target",
                "numbers": [],
                "query": "spend = load \"bankingData\";\
nspend = group spend by ('Date_Year', 'Date_Month');\
nspend = filter spend by date('Date_Year', 'Date_Month',
'Date_Day') in [\"30 days ago\"..\"current day\"];\nspend =
foreach spend generate 'Date_Year' + \"~~~\" + 'Date_Month'
as 'Date_Year~~~Date_Month', sum('Amount') as 'sum_Amount',0
as 'sum_Target';\n\ntarget = load \"Industry_Targets\";\
ntarget = group target by ('Date_Year', 'Date_Month');\
ntarget = filter target by date('Date_Year', 'Date_Month',
'Date_Day') in [\"30 days ago\"..\"current day\"];\ntarget =
foreach target generate 'Date_Year' + \"~~~\" + 'Date_Month'
as 'Date_Year~~~Date_Month', sum('Target') as 'sum_Target', 0
as 'sum_Amount';\n\nboth = union spend, target;\nboth = group
both by all;\nboth = foreach both generate sum('sum_Target')
as 'Target', sum('sum_Amount') as 'Spend';\nboth = foreach both
generate sum('Target') as 'Target', sum('Spend') as 'Spend',
100*(trunc(('Spend'/'Target'),3)) as '% of Target';\n",
```

Here is another example where a union is used to combine information for Last Year Generated and This Year Converted into one table:

```
q = load "OppOwnerAccnt";

q_A = filter q by  ('AccountId.Type' == "Partner" or 'Type' ==
"New Business")  && date('CloseDate_Year', 'CloseDate_Month',
'CloseDate_Day') in ["1 year ago".."1 year ago"] ;

q_B = filter q by ('AccountId.Type' == "Partner" or 'Type' ==
"New Business") && date('CloseDate_Year', 'CloseDate_Month',
'CloseDate_Day') in ["current year".."current year"] ;

result = group q_A by all full, q_B by all;

result = foreach result generate sum(q_A.'Amount') as 'A',
sum(q_B.'Amount') as 'B';

final1 = foreach result generate "Last Year Generated" as
'Description', sum('A') as 'Sum';

final2 = foreach result generate "This Year Converted" as
'Description', sum('B') as 'Sum';

final = union final1,final2;
```

Groupings, summaries, subtotals, averages, and more

Adding custom, complex groupings, summaries, subtotals, averages, and more often requires the use of SAQL.

Here is one example where the user wants to identify the top 5% of accounts:

```
q = load "Wave_Sample_Opportunities";
q = group q by 'Account_Name';
q = foreach q generate 'Account_Name',
sum('Amount') as 'sum_Revenue',
rank() over ([..] partition by all order by sum('Amount')) as
'Position', sum(1) over ([..] partition by all) as 'count';
q = foreach q generate 'Account_Name',
'sum_Revenue', ( case
when 'Position' >= (floor(((95*'count') + 1)/100)) then "Top 5
%"
else "Rest" end ) as 'Bracket';
q = filter q by 'Bracket' != "Rest";
q = group q by ('Account_Name', 'Bracket');
```

```
q = foreach q generate 'Bracket' as 'Bracket', 'Account_Name'
as 'Account Name', max('sum_Revenue') as 'sum_Revenue';
```

```
q = order q by 'sum_Revenue' desc;
```

Another example is where you want to calculate the average deal size and use this to create dynamic reference lines:

```
"query": "q = load \"Opportunity_MT\";\nq = filter q by
'Type' == \"New WM Client\";\nq = filter q by 'StageName'
== \"Revenue Received\";\nq = group q by ('CloseDate_Year',
'CloseDate_Quarter', 'AccountId.Name');\nq = foreach q generate
'CloseDate_Year' + \"~~~\" + 'CloseDate_Quarter' as 'CloseDate_
Year~~~CloseDate_Quarter', 'AccountId.Name' as 'Household',
sum('Amount') as 'Amount';\nq = group q by ('CloseDate_
Year~~~CloseDate_Quarter');\nq = foreach q generate 'CloseDate_
Year~~~CloseDate_Quarter' as 'CloseDate_Year~~~CloseDate_
Quarter', trunc(avg('Amount'),0) as 'Average';\nq = group q by
all;\nq = foreach q generate trunc(avg('Average'),-2) as 'Avg
Amount';",
```

```
"referenceLines": [
                                        {
                                            "color": "#9271E8",
                                            "label": "Target =
{{cell(gaugeRef6_1.result,0,\"target\").asString()}}",
                                            "value": "{{cell(gaugeRef6_1.
result,0,\"target\").asString()}}"
                                        },
                                        {
                                            "color": "rgb(0, 161, 224)",
                                            "label": "Avg = {{cell(Avg_of_
Avg_Deals_Siz_1.result, 0,\"Avg Amount\").asObject()}}",
                                            "value": "{{cell(Avg_of_Avg_
Deals_Siz_1.result, 0,\"Avg Amount\").asObject()}}"
                                        }
                                    ],
```

Using images as icons

Images can be used as icons to add to the aesthetics and make it more intuitive to drill down into user data, as shown in the following screenshot:

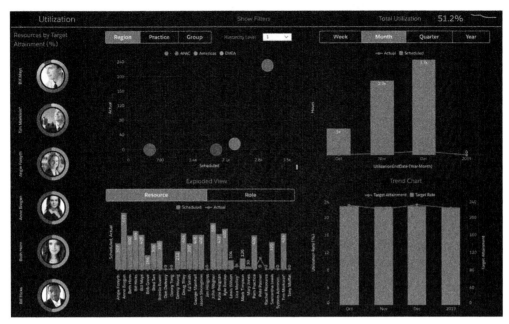

Figure 10.1 – Using images as icons

Here is some sample SAQL for where images were added as icons:

```
q = load "Utilization";
```

```
q = filter q by date('UtilizationEndDate_Year',
'UtilizationEndDate_Month', 'UtilizationEndDate_Day') in ["180
days ago".."current day"];
```

```
q = group q by 'ResourceName';
```

```
q = foreach q generate 'ResourceName' as 'ResourceName',
first('ResourceSalesforceUserPhotoUrl') as
'ResourceSalesforceUserPhotoUrl', sum('ValueBillableHours')
as 'sum_ValueBillableHours', sum('ValueCreditedHours') as
'sum_ValueCreditedHours', sum('ValueCalendarHours') as
'sum_ValueCalendarHours', sum('ValueExcludedHours') as 'sum_
ValueExcludedHours', sum('ValueUtilizationTargetHours') as
'sum_ValueUtilizationTargetHours';
```

```
q = foreach q generate 'ResourceName',
'ResourceSalesforceUserPhotoUrl', (case when ('sum_
ValueCalendarHours' - 'sum_ValueExcludedHours') == 0 then (case
when ('sum_ValueBillableHours' + 'sum_ValueCreditedHours') > 0
then 100 else 0 end) else (('sum_ValueBillableHours' + 'sum_
ValueCreditedHours') * 100 / ('sum_ValueCalendarHours' - 'sum_
ValueExcludedHours')) end) as 'TotalUtilizationRate', 'sum_
ValueCalendarHours', 'sum_ValueUtilizationTargetHours';
```

```
q = foreach q generate 'ResourceName',
'ResourceSalesforceUserPhotoUrl', coalesce('sum_
ValueUtilizationTargetHours' * 100 / 'sum_ValueCalendarHours',
0) as 'UtilizationTargetRate', 'TotalUtilizationRate';
```

```
q = foreach q generate 'ResourceName',
'ResourceSalesforceUserPhotoUrl', (case when
'UtilizationTargetRate' == 0 then (case when
'TotalUtilizationRate' > 0 then 100 else 0 end) else
('TotalUtilizationRate' * 100 / 'UtilizationTargetRate') end)
as 'Target Attainment';
```

```
q = order q by 'Target Attainment' desc;
```

```
q = limit q 10;
```

Grouping by more than six products

You can only group by up to six groups in the GUI. Consider the following screenshot:

Figure 10.2 – Opportunity pipeline with the maximum of six groupings

To add a seventh grouping, you need to modify the SAQL, like this:

```
q = load "opportunity1";
```

```
q = filter q by 'OpenClosedWonLost' == "Open";
```

```
q = group q by ('Account.Industry', 'Account.
Name', 'StageName', 'Account.Owner.Name', 'Pushed',
'ForecastCategoryName','Account.Segment__c');
```

```
q = foreach q generate 'Account.Industry' as 'Account.
Industry', 'Account.Name' as 'Account.Name', 'StageName'
as 'StageName', 'Account.Owner.Name' as 'Account.Owner.
```

```
Name', 'Pushed' as 'Pushed', 'ForecastCategoryName' as
'ForecastCategoryName', sum('Amount') as 'sum_Amount';
```

```
q = order q by ('Account.Industry' asc, 'Account.Name' asc,
'StageName' asc, 'Account.Owner.Name' asc, 'Pushed' asc,
'ForecastCategoryName' asc);
```

Buckets (complex)

Simple buckets can be created in the recipe builder; more complex use cases require code.
The following example was used to create custom-formatted reference lines:

```
"steps": {
            "Clone_of_myKPI_1": {
                "broadcastFacet": true,
                "groups": [],
                "label": "Clone of myKPI",
                "numbers": [],
                "query": "q = load \"opportunity\";\nq = group
q by 'Account.Industry';\nq = foreach q generate 'Account.
Industry' as 'Account.Industry', sum('Amount') as 'sum_
Amount';\nq = group q by all;\nq = foreach q generate \"Median
by Industry \" + case when median(sum_Amount) >= 1000000
then number_to_string(trunc(median(sum_Amount),-6)/1000000,
\"$#,###\") + \"M\" when median(sum_Amount) >= 1000 then
number_to_string(trunc(median(sum_Amount),-3)/1000, \"$###\")
+ \"K\" else number_to_string(trunc(median(sum_Amount)),
\"$###\") end as 'Median';\n\n",

"measureAxis1": {
                    "sqrtScale": false,
                    "showTitle": true,
                    "showAxis": true,
                    "referenceLines": [
                        {
                            "color": "#FF6419",
                            "label": "{{cell(myKPI_2.
result,0,\"Average\").asString()}}",
                            "value": "{{cell(myKPI_1.
result,0,\"avg_Amount\").asObject()}}"
                        },
```

```
                              {
                                "color": "#DED800",
                                "label": "{{cell(Clone_of_
myKPI_1.result,0,\"Median\").asString()}}",
                                "value": "{{cell(myKPI_1.
result,0,\"median_Amount\").asObject()}}"
                              }
                            ],
                            "title": "",
                            "customDomain": {
                              "showDomain": false
```

For detailed insights and instructions regarding SAQL, please reference the following developer guide:

```
https://developer.salesforce.com/docs/atlas.en-us.bi_dev_
guide_saql.meta/bi_dev_guide_saql/bi_saql_reference.htm
```

Now, we will look at how code is required for bulk actions in CRMA.

Bulk actions (using Visualforce and the CRMA REST API)

There is a considerable amount of effort required to build and deploy custom bulk actions in CRMA. For a starting place, reference this blog post by my colleague, **Gayathri Shivakumar**:

```
https://visioneer360.com.au/bulk-actions-the-secret-sauce-of-
einstein-analytics/
```

For example, you need to create a Batch Apex to update Contact records:

```
global class BatchContactActionUpdate implements Database.
Batchable <SObject> {
//Start Method
global BatchContactActionUpdate( set<Id> ContactRecId){
            this.ContactRecId = ContactRecId;
    }
global Database.QueryLocator start(Database.BatchableContext
BC) {
        return Database.getQueryLocator('Select Id From Contact
Where Id In :ContactRecId');
    }
```

```
       global void execute(Database.BatchableContext BC,
List<Contact> scope) {
           << code to update Contact Records>>
       }
//Finish Method
global void finish(Database.BatchableContext bc) {
    << Code to send email notificatin on batch completion>>
}
}
```

timeseries (modified)

The `timeseries` function, when used in a compare table, will get you started with timeseries predictive insights, but you will need to use SAQL to modify it further:

```
Here is an example where the standard timeseries function was
modified using SAQL:
q = load "Opportunity_MT";
q = filter q by 'StageName' == "Closed Won";
q = filter q by date('CloseDate_Year', 'CloseDate_Month',
'CloseDate_Day') in ["6 years ago".."current day"];
q = group q by ('CloseDate_Year', 'CloseDate_Month');
q = foreach q generate 'CloseDate_Year', 'CloseDate_Month',
sum('Amount') as 'sum_Amount';
q = fill q by (dateCols=('CloseDate_Year', 'CloseDate_Month',
"Y-M"));
q = timeseries q generate 'sum_Amount' as 'Forecasted_sum_
Amount' with (length=6, dateCols=('CloseDate_Year', 'CloseDate_
Month', "Y-M"),ignoreLast=true,predictionInterval=80);
q = foreach q generate 'CloseDate_Year' + "~~~" + 'CloseDate_
Month' as 'CloseDate_Year~~~CloseDate_Month', coalesce('sum_
Amount', 'Forecasted_sum_Amount') as 'Amount';
q = order q by 'CloseDate_Year~~~CloseDate_Month' asc;
```

For example, the `coalesce` function was used to merge the historical and predictive values, and various options were modified, such as setting `ignoreLast` and setting `predictionInterval` to `80`.

Next, let's look at using XMD.

XMD – advanced formatting options

XMD is not required anywhere near as often as it once was, now that the CRMA GUI gives us much more control over formatting and customizations. The **Edit Dataset** page allows you to customize record actions, and **Dataset Fields** enables you to customize things such as field labels and dimension value colors.

However, there are still times where advanced formatting options require the use of XMD. You can customize the following using XMD:

- Modify display labels for fields and values.
- Hide fields.
- Format measures.
- Multiply measures by a set amount.
- Customize row count measure labels.
- Modify dimension value colors in charts.
- Add actions to dimensions.
- Change the default fields in a values table.
- Format query results where multiple datasets are used.
- Custom format measures.
- Add suffixes and prefixes to measures.
- Define the first day of the week for the calendar year.

The following code shows how to format the `Amount` field to be in the currency format of `$9,999.99`:

```
{
    "dataset": {},
    "dates": [],
    "derivedDimensions": [],
    "derivedMeasures": [],
    "dimensions": [
        {
            "conditionalFormatting": {},
            "customActions": [],
            "field": "Region",
            "label": "Sales Region",
```

```
        "members": [],
        "recordDisplayFields": [],
        "salesforceActions": []
    }
  ],
  "measures": [
    {
      "conditionalFormatting": {},
      "field": "Amount",
      "format": {
        "customFormat": "[\"$#,##0.00\",1]"
      },
      "label": "Initial Amount"
    }
  ],
  "organizations": [],
  "showDetailsDefaultFields": []
}
```

For detailed insights and instructions regarding using XMD, please reference this developer guide:

```
https://developer.salesforce.com/docs/atlas.en-us.bi_dev_
guide_xmd.meta/bi_dev_guide_xmd/bi_xmd_intro.htm
```

You might not need to code if...

As Salesforce continues to develop CRMA, more advanced querying and customizations can be performed in the GUI, requiring less work to be performed using code. This aligns with the Salesforce mantra of *clicks and not code*.

The following are use cases where code was once required, but now may not be:

- Data flow, data prep, and recipes:

  Code is not required for data flows (JSON) or recipes except for complex use cases.

  For a detailed reference about dashboard JSON, see this developer guide:

  ```
  https://developer.salesforce.com/docs/atlas.en-us.bi_dev_
  guide_json.meta/bi_dev_guide_json/bi_dbjson_intro.htm.
  ```

- Dynamic reference lines (simple):

  This can now be performed in the dashboard editor.

- Simple application bindings:

  Simple bindings can be constructed using **Advanced Editor** in the dashboard editor.

- Adding datasets to a lens:

  Additional datasets can now be added to a lens via the GUI using the Add Dataset function. This will look as follows:

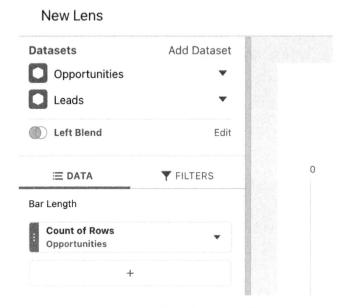

Figure 10.3 – Adding datasets to a lens

What about times where it is not clear whether you need to code?

Occasions of ambiguity

The more familiar you become with building lenses and dashboards using the CRMA GUI, the more you will understand where code is required. A best practice is to use the GUI whenever possible, and only resort to code where it cannot be avoided. Also, be sure to stay up to date with the new CRMA releases since the GUI becomes more capable with every release.

I want to share one final example of where I used code – in this case, customizing the JSON data flow to reset and refresh dates every time the data flow was run:

```
"relativeDates2": {
    "action": "computeExpression",
    "parameters": {
      "source": "substituteNewDate",
      "mergeWithSource": true,
      "computedFields": [
        {
            "defaultValue": "0",
            "precision": 18,
            "name": "dateAsEpochSec2",
            "saqlExpression": "case when 'Date_of_cancellation'
is null then null else Date_of_cancellation_sec_epoch end",
            "scale": 0,
            "label": "dateAsEpochSec2",
            "type": "Numeric"
        },
        {
            "defaultValue": "0",
            "precision": 18,
            "name": "dateDifference2",
            "saqlExpression": "case when 'Date_of_cancellation'
is null then null else dateAsEpochSec2 - 1522127025 end ",
            "scale": 0,
            "label": "dateDifference2",
            "type": "Numeric"
        },
        {
            "defaultValue": "0",
            "precision": 18,
            "name": "dateAsEpoch2",
            "saqlExpression": "case when 'Date_of_cancellation'
is null then null else dateDifference2 + date_to_epoch(now())
end ",
            "scale": 0,
```

```
        "label": "dateAsEpoch2",
        "type": "Numeric"
    },
    {
        "name": "newDate2",
        "saqlExpression": "case when 'Date_of_cancellation'
is null then null else toDate(dateAsEpoch2) end ",
        "format": "dd-MM-yyyy",
        "label": "newDate2",
        "type": "Date"
```

Now that you've learned about when to code or not to code, let's review this chapter.

Summary

The purpose of this chapter was to help you understand when code is required in a CRMA build and when it is not required.

What have you learned? First, you should now understand the various use cases where code is required to deliver your requirements. Next, functionality that once required code and is now available in the GUI is clear to you. Lastly, you have been shown an approach where the requirement for code is not clear.

In the next chapter, you will dive into the exciting world of dashboard design best practices.

Questions

Fill in the blanks – you learned about six applications where you are required to deploy code:

- Security _____
- Bindings in the _____
- SAQL _____
- Bulk actions (using _____and the CRMA REST API)
- _____ (modified)
- XMD – advanced _____options

11
Best Practices in Dashboard Design Using CRMA

Now that you can build a powerful dashboard in CRMA, how do you know *what* you ought to build? What are some common mistakes in dashboard design? What are the established principles of effective dashboard design? What are the best practices when designing, building, and deploying CRMA dashboards? This chapter explains this in detail to guide and inform great dashboard design.

We'll cover the following:

- Common mistakes in dashboard design
- Design philosophy for effective dashboard building
- Best practice in CRMA dashboard design

Technical requirements

You will need the following to successfully execute the instructions in this chapter:

- The latest version of the Google Chrome browser (Chrome is the preferred browser when working with CRMA)

- A working email address

Be sure to be logged in to your CRMA dev org.

Let's begin with understanding common mistakes in dashboard design.

Common mistakes in dashboard design

Here is a list of the most common mistakes that I see when it comes to dashboard design:

- Prioritizing form over function – making a dashboard *beautiful* but not useful, practical, and actionable.

- An absence of comparisons – not including targets, averages, benchmarks, and comparisons to provide business context to metrics.

- Overuse of color – adding a variety and abundance of color for the sake of it, and not with a clear purpose in mind.

- Too much of a good thing – adding too many charts and metrics to a page so that the user gets lost and confused.

- A lack of storytelling – the viewer is provided with metrics, charts, comparisons, and insights in abundance, but there is no clear storyline.

- Clutter – an absence of white space hinders the viewer's ability to decipher and interpret the visualizations presented to them.

- Ignorance of the desired business outcomes – building dashboards for the sake of building dashboards without clear business priorities and deliverables in mind.

- Use of inappropriate and incorrect visualizations – who wants to try and interpret a donut chart with 17 segments?

- Confusing and unintuitive design – the dashboard does not follow any kind of intuitive flow.

- Incomplete data – only providing information that tells half the story leaves users frustrated and uninformed.

- Use of inappropriate colors – some colors have meaning, like red and green, and they can influence how you read the charts.

- Use of inappropriate number formats – showing the same KPIs in numbers and percentages can sometimes lead to misunderstandings.

- Each chart/widget should answer a unique and simple question – do not try to put all the information in one single chart.

- Forgetting the security aspect – aggregations in dashboards does not mean that users can access raw data in the datasets.

- No action framework – *every* dashboard should tell a story where, at the end, the user can take an action.

How many of these mistakes can you find in the following dashboard?

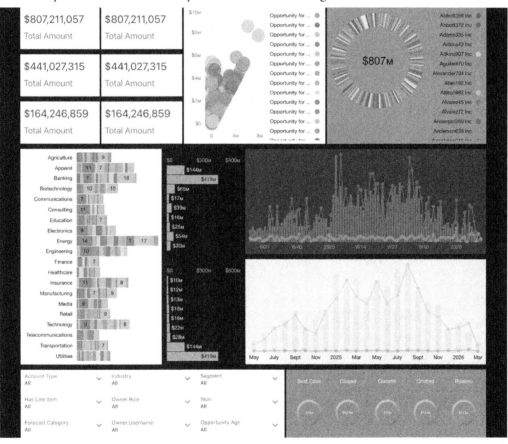

Figure 11.1 – An example of poor dashboard design

Now that we have identified what *not* to do, let's learn about a good design approach.

Design philosophy for effective dashboard building

I see an awful lot of dashboards in my line of work – most of them are poorly designed. Why do I say that? How do I know that to be true? What makes a *good* dashboard design?

Here are some principles of effective dashboard design.

A good dashboard provides actionable insights

It's all about taking the user from *data* to *insight* to *action*. A dashboard that leaves off the last step is incomplete and ineffective. Let me share three examples.

The first example is the risks insights page from our **Professional Services Automation (PSA)** dashboard built on top of FinancialForce. You can see from the following screenshot that the risk impact and likelihood matrix (heat map) allows you to quickly drill into the project data, and then those insights can be actioned from the record view:

Figure 11.2 – An actionable risks insights page for professional services automation

The second example comes from our donor segmentation analytics built for non-profit institutions. The following dashboard allows you to drill into the donor segment and choose the appropriate cohort for an appeal:

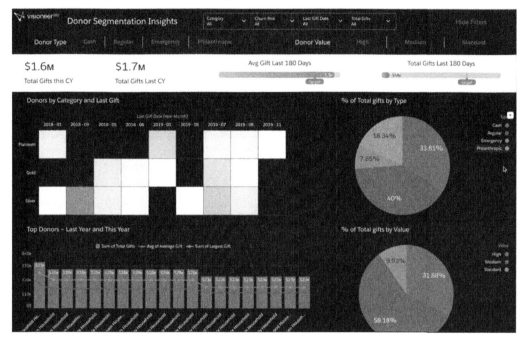

Figure 11.3 – The donor segmentation dashboard

Once the correct cohort has been selected, you can action the insights by adding donor records directly to a Salesforce campaign, as seen here:

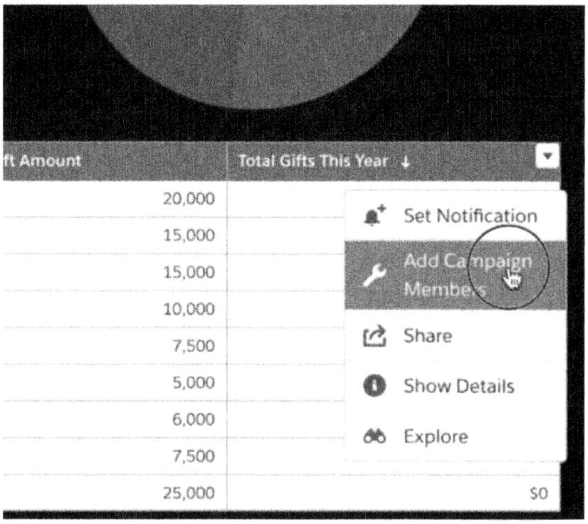

Figure 11.4 – The donor segmentation record action

The final example of going from data to insight to action is the student success insights dashboard. In this case, once the desired group of at-risk students is selected from the dashboard visualizations, intervention cases can be created in Salesforce and assigned to the appropriate student advisors directly from the dashboard record table, as seen in the following screenshot:

| | | | | Student Count | | |
| | | | | | 129 | |

Select the appropriate pre-determined risk factors on the left, and your "at risk" student list will update accordingly.

Name	GPA	Pace ↑	ProgEnrol.Major_Name__c	Program Length	Current Credits	Service Cases ▾
	0	0	Cybersecurity	6		🔔 Set Notification
	0	0	Cybersecurity	6		💬 Annotate
	0	0	Cybersecurity	6		🔧 Create Cases
	0	0	Cybersecurity	6		↪ Share
	0	0	Cybersecurity	6		① Show Details
	0	0	Cybersecurity	6		🔍 Explore
	0	0	Cybersecurity	6	0	1
	0	0	Cybersecurity	6	0	1
	0	0	Cybersecurity	6	0	4
	0	0	Cybersecurity	6	0	0

Figure 11.5 – The students at risk action list

Now, we will consider the importance of business understanding in dashboard design.

A good dashboard reflects and portrays business understanding

A well-designed dashboard must reflect clear business understanding, not just data literacy and technical skill. Business users will not use or benefit from a dashboard that betrays a poor understanding of the business context. You must start with the business in mind and stay focused on the business throughout the design and build process.

Data analytics + Business understanding = Business insights

Let me give you three examples of this.

The first example is a claims insights dashboard built for an insurance broker who needed highly bespoke analytics that reflected very particular business needs. This dashboard transformed the way the claims team worked and served their customers, as it was well aligned with the business context and desired deliverables, as shown in the following screenshot:

Figure 11.6 – Claims insights driven by deep business understanding

A wealth management (financial planning) business use case provides the second dashboard example of the importance of business acumen in analytics design. The following figure shows how this very simple approach solved the top-priority business problem of customers defaulting on compliance, as customers at risk were proactively identified and assigned to advisers for remedial action:

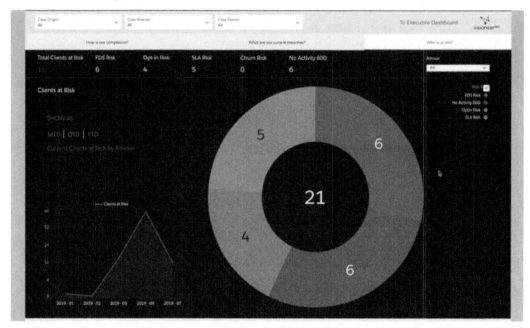

Figure 11.7 – Proactive compliance insights founded on business acumen

A final example of insights being driven by business requirements is this summary dashboard, where the make-up of the tiles displayed on the screen was totally dependent upon a keen understanding of business priorities and analytics needs:

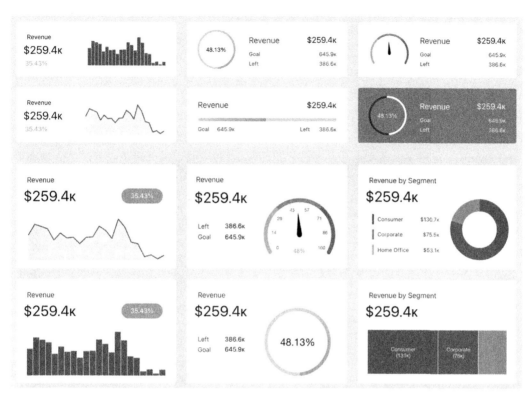

Figure 11.8 – Summary tiles provide an overview driven by business requirements

The next point to consider in great dashboard design is the criticality of telling a story.

A good dashboard tells a story with data

Well-designed analytics tell a story with data. They will narrate a story simply, clearly, and concisely, resulting in a clear and actionable business strategy. If a user reviews your dashboard and is unable to understand and action a data story being told, then it is high time to redesign your dashboard!

One example of data storytelling is seen in the following dashboard, where a summary of business performance is communicated clearly with great conciseness and simplicity:

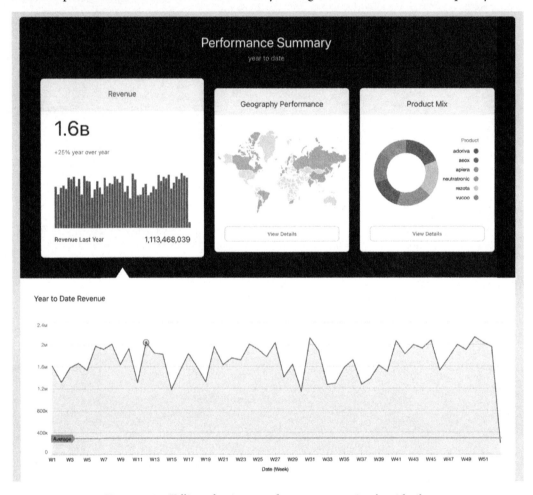

Figure 11.9 – Telling a business performance story simply with tiles

Another example of storytelling with data is this manufacturing analytics dashboard, where the user is given a clear insight into the materials inventory, lead time, and their impact upon production:

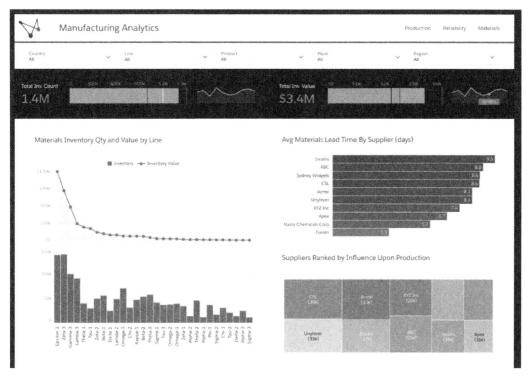

Figure 11.10 – Telling a manufacturing story with data

One last example of how to make your dashboard tell a story is this fundraising performance analytics dashboard, where the key metrics for donors, giving, and performance are presented at the top, complemented by supporting insights:

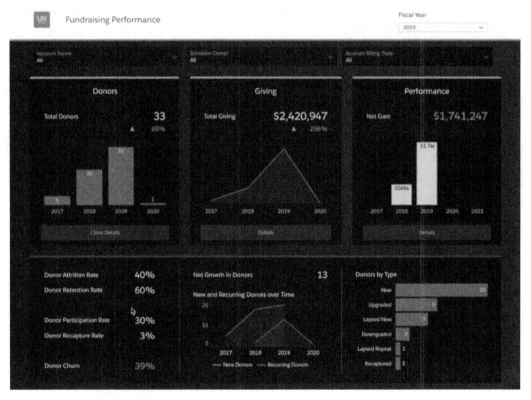

Figure 11.11 – Fundraising performance analytics – clear data flow and storytelling

Now that you understand the importance of storytelling with data, you need to appreciate the power of a simple dashboard.

A good dashboard is simple

A good analytics dashboard design will tell a story with data, without the user becoming overwhelmed and confused with too much information. Therefore, in your designs, eliminate or minimize the following:

- Clutter
- Noise
- Superfluous information

- Unnecessary use of color

- Distracting graphics

- Anything that does not have a clear purpose for being on the page!

Ideally, dashboard content should fit on just one screen.

Here is an example of the beauty and power of simplicity in dashboard design – an uncluttered and insightful PSA dashboard that tells a story without adding anything that isn't helpful or necessary:

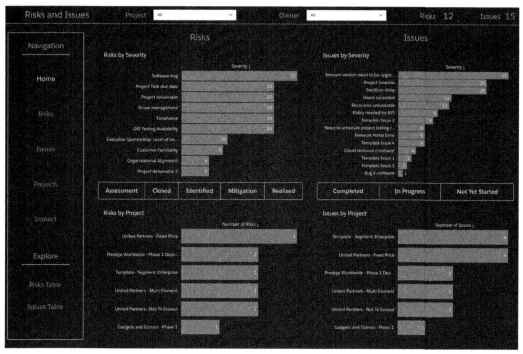

Figure 11.12 – A simple and intuitive PSA analytics home page

Notice that this design shuns the use of any *fancy* visuals, relying simply upon the humble bar chart. A dashboard does not need to *impress* – but it does need to *inform*!

The next example of simplicity in design is an equity insights dashboard built for a property development business. Note in the following screenshot that this design keeps things very simple and makes good use of white space to prevent clutter and complexity:

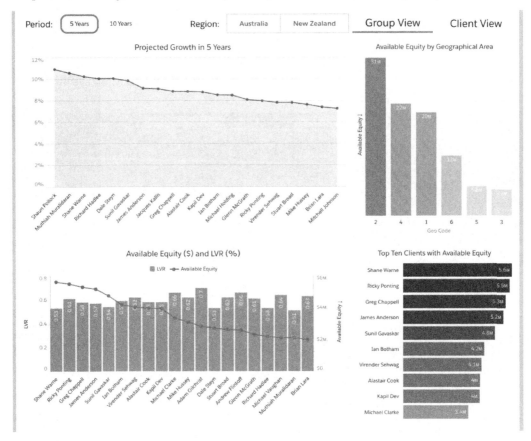

Figure 11.13 – Simple equity analytics – making use of white space!

Finally, consider this example of simplicity enhancing dashboard useability. The user home page contains an embedded CRMA dashboard with just three charts, providing the user with quick insights at the time of login. If they want to know more, note the **OPEN** link in the top-right corner:

Figure 11.14 – Clear visualization of summary analytics on a home page

When the **OPEN** link is clicked, the user is taken to a simple summary home page that provides headline metrics and links to detail pages:

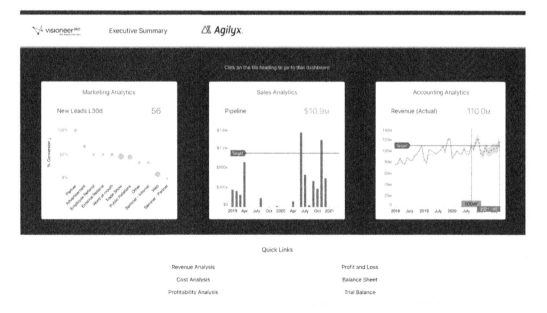

Figure 11.15 – Simple visuals telling a story for executives

Note several things about this minimalist design:

- The user has **Quick Links** to take them to common places of interest.

- We made judicious use of white space to deliver a very simple layout.

- The three charts were chosen because each one represents the key metric for each area of the business.

- The heading for each tile is a CRMA link that takes the user to a detail page.

- There is nothing superfluous that might distract the user from the data story.

- A user can inspect this dashboard in under 30 seconds and decide whether they want to dive deeper or move on.

Now, you will see the importance of ease of use in dashboard design.

A good dashboard is intuitive and easy to use

Great analytics design requires little or no instruction or training for use. It is truly intuitive – easy to understand or operate without explicit instruction. When a user sees an intuitive dashboard for the first time, they will know exactly what to do.

In the following example of intuitive sales analytics, the user simply clicks on the bars of the side charts to drill into their data and see the map reflect their choices:

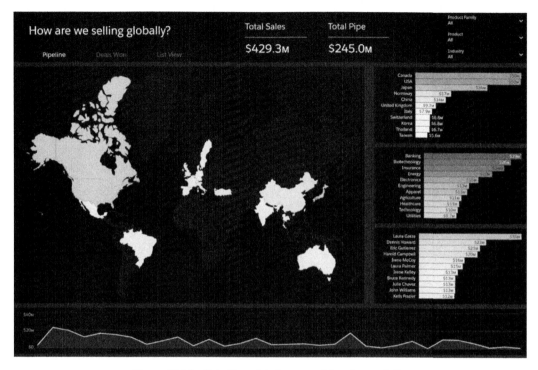

Figure 11.16 – Intuitive global geographic sales analytics

In the next example of intuitive design, we see that the user can simply click on the arrow at the bottom of any summary bubble to see more information about that metric and bring up a detail panel on the right:

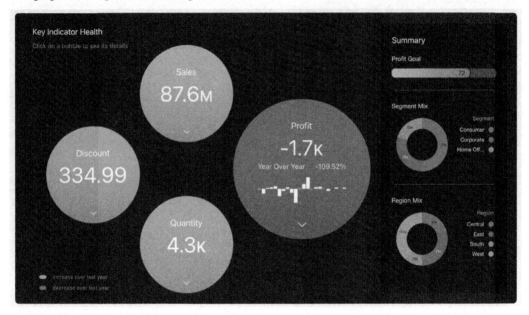

Figure 11.17 – Summary and drill-down on one page

How can you make your dashboard intuitive? Here are some ideas:

- Keep things as simple as possible.

- Use descriptive and clear titles and labels.

- Use color to aid in communication, not detract from it.

- Include instructive subtitles where required (as seen in *Figure 11.17*).

- Make the dashboard interactive and clickable.

- Follow an intuitive, sensible flow of data – this makes the user experience easy and instinctive. Bad flow causes confusion and frustration.

Now, we need to look at the importance of visual communication.

A good dashboard clearly communicates information visually

Effective analytics will employ visual understanding and tools to aid in data visualization and communication. This includes the prudent use of the following:

- Colors
- Shapes
- Borders
- Contrast
- Proximity
- Context

I recommend that you study and leverage the Gestalt principles to understand how people see and understand data, including the following:

- The law of closure
- The law of common region
- The law of proximity
- The law of similarity
- The law of symmetry

For more information on the Gestalt principles, consult this resource:

```
https://www.interaction-design.org/literature/topics/gestalt-
principles
```

In the following example of visual communication, I designed a very simple high-contrast dashboard to provide insight into general trending and facilitate drilling down to a record level for action:

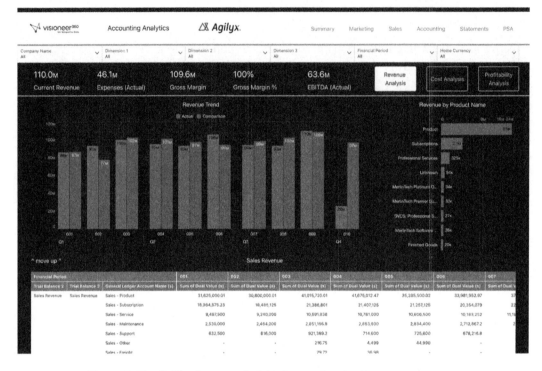

Figure 11.18 – Bold colors on a dark background – standing out on purpose

This dashboard is conspicuous by what is *not* present, as are many effective designs. As Antoine de Saint-Exupéry said, *"You know you've achieved perfection, not when you have nothing more to add, but when you have nothing to take away."*

A great dashboard will be designed with the intended audience in mind, as you will now see.

A good dashboard considers the audience

A good designer will get into their audience's headspace. A deep and complete understanding of your business users and how they will digest and action your dashboards is a *critical* step in the design process. Consider the following:

- How will the dashboard be utilized for next-step actions?

- What information does the reader require to be successful in their day-to-day work?

- What level of detail does the consumer really need?

- What actions will the business user take, and how will those actions be made?

- How will you highlight exceptions or insights that require follow-up?

- What user assumptions and preferences could affect your design choices?

- In the context of the business, what do colors mean and how are they likely to be interpreted visually?

- What icons, logos, and so on are familiar in the business environment?

- Remember to use color-blind-friendly color schemes.

The following dashboard is a good example of an effective design that utilizes a deep understanding of the intended audience, where the executive leader requires a high-level summary page that then links to detailed drill-down dashboard pages:

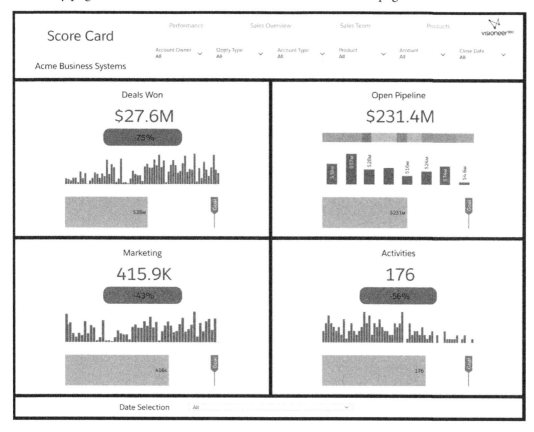

Figure 11.19 – A business score card, driven by audience understanding

In this case, each tile contains the following for the area of business considered:

- One key metric
- A comparison measurement that is color-coded to convey meaning
- One column chart to give content to the key metric
- One progress chart created with a bar and a target

Although the design appears simple, the level of business understanding required to create such a minimalist design effectively is considerable.

In the following dashboard example, the users are time-poor executives who want only high-level, critical information to be presented to them for a quick review, and then drill-down and action if required:

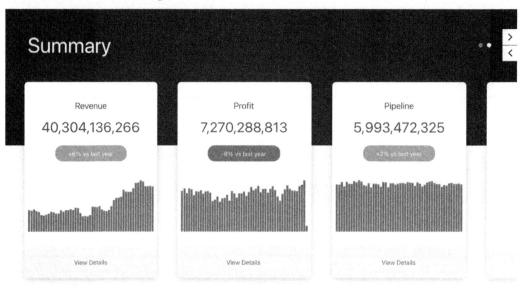

Figure 11.20 – Simple works for summary dashboards, with drill-down available as required

You will now see the importance of facilitating user engagement in your dashboard designs.

A good dashboard fosters user engagement

A dashboard that isn't used is wasted pixels on a screen – it is utterly worthless, no matter how beautiful or functional it may be. Therefore, your designs must foster user engagement and increase business adoption. Let me explain by way of examples.

The following example of marketing analytics showcases a design where the viewer is drawn into the dashboard and engaged in a data discussion, achieved through the use of simplicity, flow, and contrast:

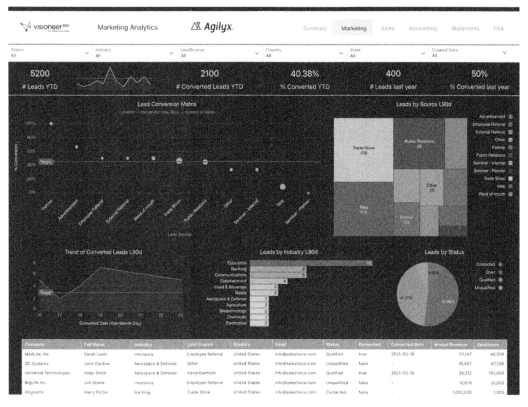

Figure 11.21 – Marketing analytics where the data analytics flow

When it comes to enabling user engagement, bold, contrasting colors are helpful. As seen in the following example, such a design makes information stand out and causes the user to take notice:

Figure 11.22 – Bold colors, a hero chart, and supporting metrics

Notice that your eyes are naturally drawn to the hero chart, the timeline on the bottom right, and then the accompanying numbers and visuals provide support and context.

In the next example, minimalism supports user engagement:

Figure 11.23 – Less is more with a Pareto chart for sales

Note a few things about this highly minimalist design:

- You have nothing to distract the user from the hero chart (the Pareto).

- The user's attention is naturally drawn to the Pareto chart, which itself is quick and easy to read.

- Drilling down into the hero chart is facilitated by the bar chart, **Sales by Product**, which has been sorted in descending order of amount on purpose.

- Once the user has identified the cohort of interest, they simply need to scroll down to see the individual records that can then be actioned in a variety of ways.

The next example of a dashboard that fosters engagement is one that utilizes a clear highlights panel at the top, supported by a row of global filters, and focuses on the one key hero chart, the **Last Touch and First Touch Matrix**:

Figure 11.24 – Simple and actionable marketing attribution analytics

Predictive analytics can be challenging to present in a way that is easy to understand and intuitive to action. Here is an example that does this well by using informative colors and two timeline charts to support the action table on the right:

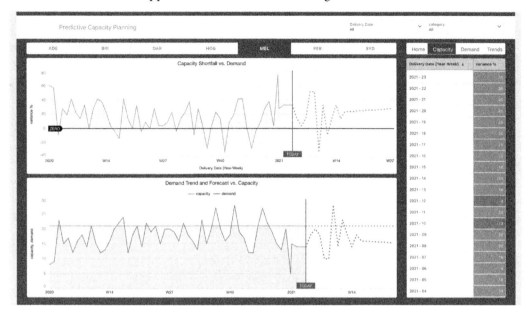

Figure 11.25 – Simple insights for predictive capacity planning

Another example of predictive insights done right is the following use of three time-series charts placed above a detailed accounting report. As you can see, the time-series charts summarize trends and the table provides the required level of detail for business users:

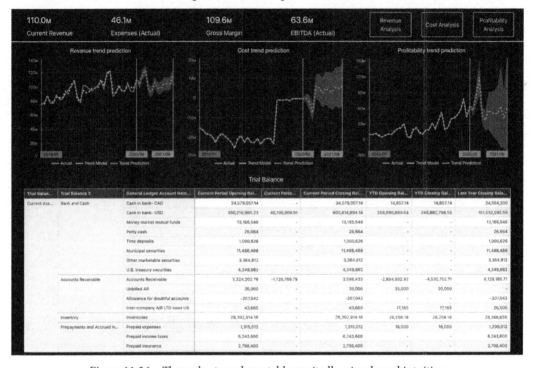

Figure 11.26 – Three charts and one table say it all – simple and intuitive

As a simple reference list, you can now review my list of 10 principles for guiding you in your design of data analytics.

The 10 principles of good dashboard design

Here are 10 principles to follow in your dashboard design and build:

- Choose your chart types carefully. It is critical that you fully understand the type of information you want to communicate and select the correct data visualization for the task at hand.

- Never seek to put all the available information on the same page; that is, do not build a one-size-fits-all dashboard by cramming all available data on one page.

- Utilize a small number of colors and shades. Use color by design and on purpose!

- Make the dashboard as easy to use as possible. If your design is too complex, users will become frustrated and give up on the dashboard.

- Employ wise layout choices. If a dashboard is well organized from a visual perspective, business users will be able to easily find the information they require. Therefore, I recommend that you begin with the big picture – key insights and call-outs must be quickly visible at a glance.

- Always provide context for your insights. Give your users comparison values.

- Keep things simple.

- Balance functionality with creativity – *effective* does not imply *boring*.

- Supply the user with the level of detail required, and no more. Otherwise, an overabundance of detailed information will prove to be a distraction.

- Understand how and where the dashboard will be used. For example, will the analytics be consumed on a phone, a tablet, or a PC? Consideration of such factors is important in good design.

One of my favorite examples of a simple, intuitive, and actionable dashboard is this sales forecasting tool, where users can quickly visualize the sales forecast and drill in by quarter, account, or stage, and then view action individual opportunities in the record table:

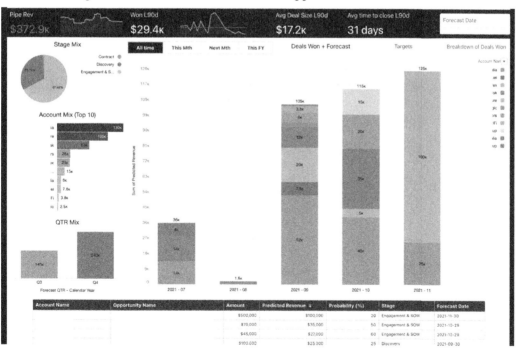

Figure 11.27 – A sales forecast story

For a succinct summary of dashboard design principles, see my blog, *Ten Commandments of Dashboard Building*:

```
https://marktossell.com/2019/06/22/the-ten-commandments-of-
dashboard-building/
```

References

These resources are great for help with dashboard design:

- *Storytelling with Data, Cole Nussbaumer Knaflic*
- *Information Dashboard Design, Stephen Few*

Now that you've learned about great dashboard design, let's have a look at the best practice when building dashboards in CRMA.

Best practice in CRMA dashboard design

In the context of building dashboards in CRMA, what constitutes best practice? First, let's consider how best to use CRMA pages.

Leverage the smart use of pages

CRMA pages give you an extraordinary amount of design flexibility. Rather than creating multiple dashboards and linking between them, thereby hindering performance and losing filters, it is often best to leverage the smart use of pages.

The best way to explain this is by way of an example. In the **Command Center** dashboard, multiple pages have been used to allow the user to drill down from a high-level, aggregated page to detail pages. The next screenshot shows the top-level page, or home page, which is the starting point for the business user:

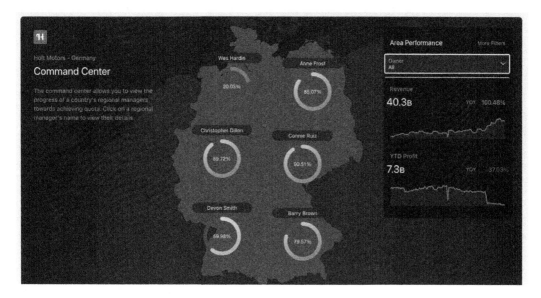

Figure 11.28 – The Command Center home page

In order to keep the home page as simple and as clean as possible, the dashboard filters are largely hidden from view, but they can be revealed with the click of the mouse, as shown in the following screenshot:

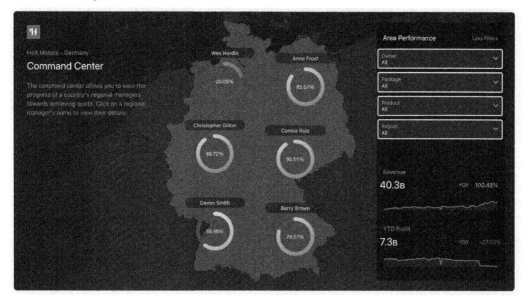

Figure 11.29 – The Command Center home page with filters revealed

The first level of drill-down for the business user is the team leader summary, where team metrics and trends are displayed. Note in the following screenshot that the home page is minimized and kept to one side in case the user wishes to return and select a different team and region:

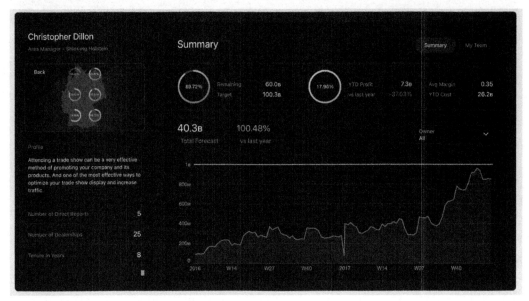

Figure 11.30 – Drill-down page one – team leader summary

The next drill-down layer is the team overview, as shown in *Figure 11.31*:

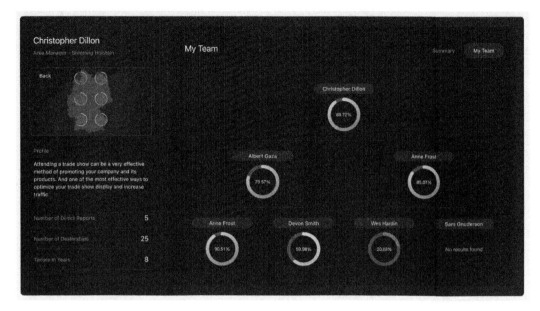

Figure 11.31 – Drill-down page two – team overview

Finally, the business user can click on the team member's name and see details of their individual performance, as seen in the next screenshot:

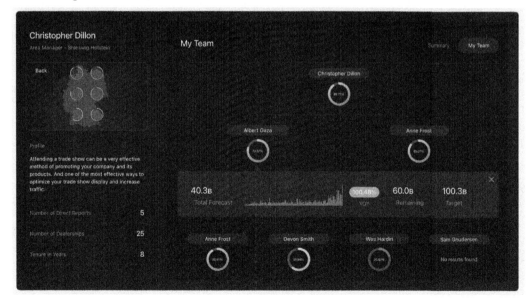

Figure 11.32 – Drill-down page three – team member details

This top-down design is powerful and intuitive. How was this page built with pages?

First, the home page contains links to both the expanded filter page and the pages for team leader summaries. Note that this example dashboard only contains pages for one team leader summary, as it is for demo purposes only; the complete dashboard would have many more pages. Here is the home page design, showing various pages at the top:

Figure 11.33 – The home page design

Next, we see the design for the home pages where the filters have been expanded:

Figure 11.34 – The home page design – with filters expanded

The powerful drill-down functionality is achieved by linking dashboard pages in order – a much better way of building than linking various dashboard pages. The next screenshot shows the first drill-down page with the team summary:

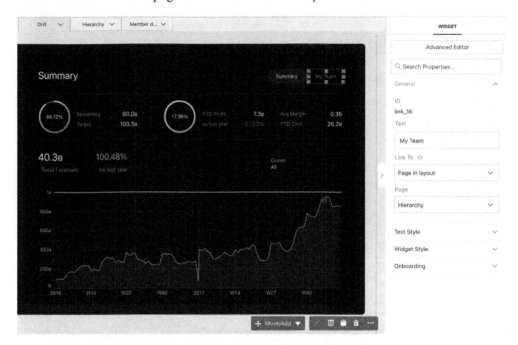

Figure 11.35 – The team summary page design showing the link to the hierarchy page

The team summary page then links to the hierarchy page, seen in the next screenshot:

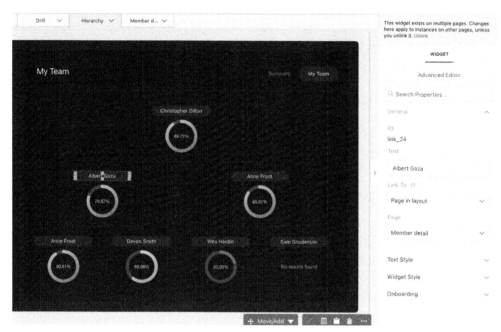

Figure 11.36 – The team overview page design showing the link to the member detail page

Lastly, the member detail page is linked to the team overview page. It also contains a link back to the home page, shown in the following screenshot:

Figure 11.37 – The team member page design showing the link back to the home page

Now, you will learn about the importance of maximizing your use of the GUI in dashboard design.

When possible, build with the GUI

One mistake I see quite regularly is where people with developer backgrounds – those who are confident building using code – build almost everything in CRMA using JSON and SAQL. The result is a clumsy, bulky build that is difficult for others to come in and edit. It is not robust or scalable.

As a general rule, it is best to work within the limits of the GUI, using clicks not code, until you hit a ceiling where you then supplement your build with SAQL and JSON as required.

Be judicious in your use of SAQL

This point follows on naturally from the previous one – limit your use of SAQL to where it is absolutely required. I will typically build a query in the dashboard editor (previously called a "step") with the UI, and then switch over to SAQL mode and finish my query. This also saves time and helps prevent syntax errors. Keep in mind several thoughts on this subject:

- Excessive SAQL queries in a dashboard will hinder performance.
- Lengthy, complex, and convoluted SAQL queries can be very difficult to troubleshoot, edit, or expand.
- Keep up to date with the latest CRMA release, as new releases generally add to the UI functionality and reduce your dependence upon code.
- To minimize your use of SAQL, it can be helpful in some cases to go back to the dataset and do your legwork there instead of in dashboard SAQL.

Following on the last bullet point, let's look at going back to your dataset/s.

Know when to go back to the dataset

As seen in the previous point, it can be helpful to go back to the dataset level to minimize the use of code; that is, aggregation and transformation can often best be performed in the dataset, as opposed to building code into the dashboard design itself. Examples of this approach include the following:

- Aggregating data
- Bucketing data

- Applying complex data transformations
- Joining datasets

Lastly, let's look at the use of dashboard components.

Leverage dashboard components where practical

Dashboard components can be a clever way to reduce effort and ensure consistency across your dashboard designs.

Follow along in your dev org as I walk you through an example of how to use components:

1. Open **My First Dashboard**.
2. Go into **Edit** mode.
3. Copy the dashboard by clicking on **Clone in New Tab**.
4. Save as a **Dashboard components** dashboard.
5. Create a new page and name it Playground.
6. Drag a component widget onto the new page.
7. Click on **Component** inside the widget.
8. Click on **Create new component**.
9. A new **Analytics Studio** tab will be created; this is where you will design the new component, ready to save and add to your dashboards.
10. Configure the component page to match your dashboard, with 50 columns, fine row height, and zero cell spacing.
11. From the **Dashboard components** dashboard, copy the highlights panel container and all of its widgets.
12. Change the widget backgrounds to transparent.
13. Save the component as **Highlights panel** in the **Shared App**.

The component will look like the following:

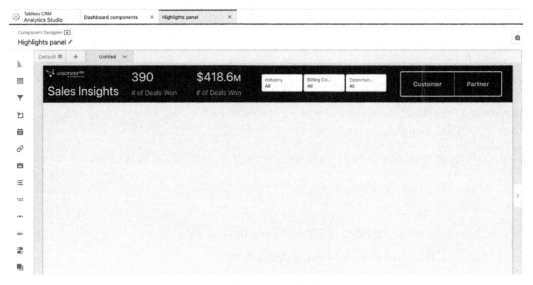

Figure 11.38 – The Highlights panel dashboard component

You can now go back to your **Dashboard components** dashboard and add the **Highlights panel** component, as the component will now appear in your list when you click on the blank component. The **Dashboard components** dashboard will now look as follows, with the component details shown on the right-hand side:

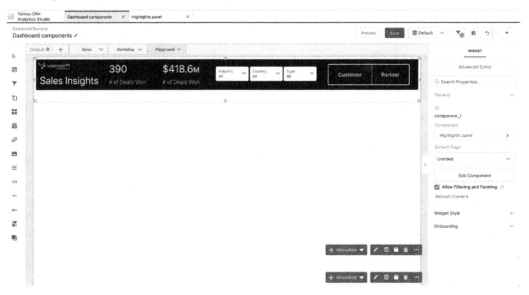

Figure 11.39 – The Dashboard components dashboard with the new component added

Dashboard components are a very powerful and versatile tool; they can even have multiple pages added so that a dashboard can have pages within pages!

Let's see what we have learned in this chapter before we move on to the next.

Summary

What did you learn in this chapter? First, you were instructed on common mistakes made in dashboard design. Next, you learned the principles of good dashboard design, along with many practical examples. Lastly, you were instructed in CRMA best practices, including the use of pages, the minimization of code, and the use of dashboard components.

In the next chapter, we will learn how to go from data to insight to action by embedding actioning CRMA dashboards.

Questions

Fill in the blanks:

- Choose your _____ types carefully.
- Never seek to put all the available _____ on the same page.
- Utilize a small number of _____ and _____.
- Make the dashboard as easy to _____ as possible.
- Employ wise _____ choices.
- Always provide _____ for your insights.
- Keep things _____.
- Balance functionality with _____ – *effective* does not imply *boring*.
- Supply the user with the level of _____ required, and no more.
- Understand _____ and _____ the dashboard will be used.

Section 4: From Data To Insight To Action

In this section, you will learn how best to help users get value from their CRMA dashboards by building in data-driven actions.

This section comprises the following chapter:

- *Chapter 12, Embedding and Actioning Your Insights*

12
Embedding and Actioning Your Insights

The *secret sauce* of CRMA compared to any other data analytics tool or platform is the ability to easily embed your dashboards in Salesforce and action insights directly from a chart or table. This increases user adoption and delivers great value from an investment in CRMA. In my opinion, the embedded and actionable functionalities of CRMA are its most neglected product features.

This chapter will teach you how to embed your analytics in the business workflow and make your insights actionable in the Salesforce CRM, enabling your organization to get the most out of CRMA.

We'll cover the following topics in this chapter:

- Creating and configuring record actions in CRMA
- Embedded dashboards

Technical requirements

You will need the following to successfully execute the instructions in this chapter:

- The latest version of the Google Chrome browser (Chrome is the preferred browser when working with CRMA)

- A working email address

Be sure to be logged into your CRMA dev org.

Let's begin with record actions.

Creating and configuring record actions in CRMA

Simply put, a record action enables you to *action a record*. This means that you do not need to jump from CRMA into Salesforce, export a report to Excel, or perform any other clumsy workaround to action your insights – you can action them directly from a CRMA dashboard.

Let's look at actioning Salesforce records using configured record actions.

Configured record actions

The best way to understand this is to walk through a hands-on exercise. We are going to configure a record action in the dashboard that you created earlier, **My First Dashboard**. Follow these steps:

1. Open **My First Dashboard** and go into **Edit** mode.
2. Create a values table from the **Opportunities** dataset. Be sure to include the **Opportunity Name** field.
3. Add the table to the bottom of your dashboard.
4. Click on **Save**.

Your dashboard will now look like this:

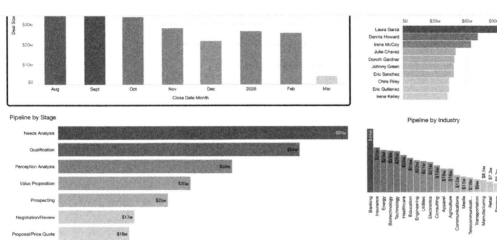

Figure 12.1 – My First Dashboard with the record table added

Now that you have added the table, it is time to configure the record actions that will enable the user to go easily from data to insight to action. Follow these steps:

1. In Analytics Studio, edit the **Opportunities** dataset.

2. At the top-right corner, click on the **Configure Actions** gear icon. Note that if actions have already been configured for a field on the object, you will see a checkmark beside it in the list.

3. Select the **Opportunity Name** field. You will see action configuration options on the right.

4. Configure the action to have a **Record ID Field** value of `Opportunity ID`.

5. Under **Display Fields**, select **Account Owner**. If multiple Salesforce records apply to the selected opportunity, this field provides information for choosing the correct record.

6. Check the box for **Open Salesforce record**.

7. Under **Open**, select Salesforce Record.

8. Under **Tooltip**, enter Open Opportunity record.

9. Check the box for **Perform Salesforce actions**.

10. Select **Choose actions**.

11. Select the **Log a call**, **New Case**, and **New task** actions.

12. Click on **Save**.

The completed dialog box should resemble the following screenshots. Here is the top half:

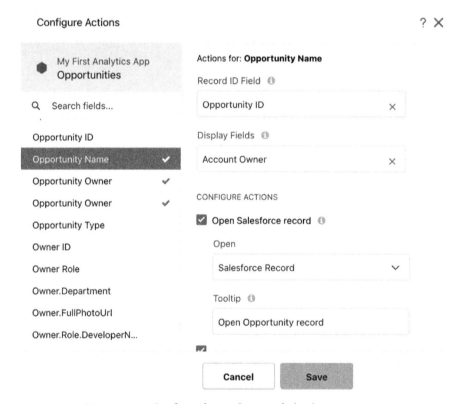

Figure 12.2 – Configured record action dialog box – part one

Here is the bottom half of the completed dialog box:

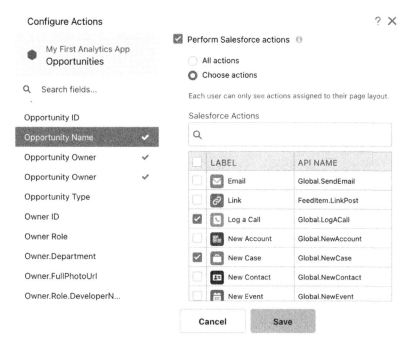

Figure 12.3 – Configured record action dialog box – part two

13. Close and reopen the **My First Dashboard** dashboard. Click on the drop-down arrow on the opportunity name for any record in the table. You should see these actions:

Opportunity record table

Opportunity Name	Opportunity Owner	Amount
Opportunity for Conner5	Laura Palmer	$32,400
Opportunity for McDonald13	Dennis Howard	$240,747
Opportunity for Jefferson17	Irene McCoy	$21,640
Opportunity for McLaughlin130	Open Record	$1,249,000
Opportunity for Chandler133		$754,640
Opportunity for Rice134		$243,450
Opportunity for Barnes141	Log a Call	$363,400
Opportunity for Edwards146	New Task	$4,212,140
Opportunity for Williams149		$2,305,550
Opportunity for Wagner150	New Case	$2,660,660
Opportunity for Lewis258	Laura Garza	$309,938
Opportunity for Barrett259	Doroth Gardner	$1,589,440
Opportunity for Dennis260	Bruce Kennedy	$2,868,400

Figure 12.4 – Configured record actions on the Opportunity Name field

Follow these steps to create and edit a follow-up task for a deal that requires attention:

1. Click on **New Task**.
2. Under **Subject**, select **Call**.
3. Enter a **Due Date** value.
4. Leave the **Name** field blank.
5. Note that the task is prefilled for the relevant opportunity under **Related To**.
6. Leave **Assigned To** and **Status** as they are.
7. Click on **Save**.
8. Click on **Open Record** for the opportunity and see how you are taken to the record in Salesforce.
9. Under the **Activity** tab for the opportunity in Salesforce, you will see the task that you just created. Click on it to be taken to the task record page.
10. Edit the task by changing the priority and adding comments.
11. Click on **Save**.

You did it! You created a task from a CRMA dashboard and edited that task in Salesforce with just a few clicks and *no* copying and pasting information!

Here is the task on the opportunity record:

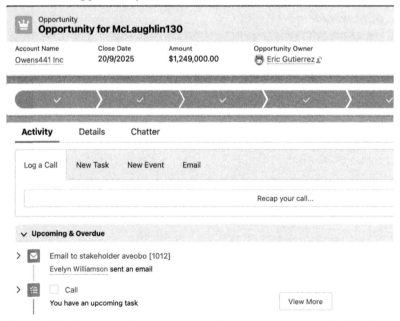

Figure 12.5 – The new task as it appears on the opportunity record in Salesforce

Here is the end result:

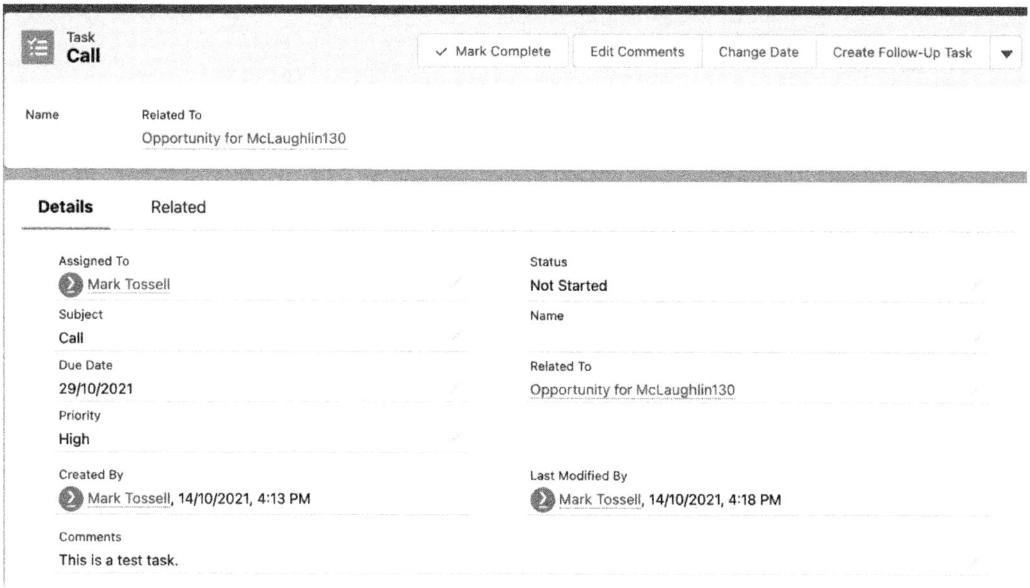

Figure 12.6 – The final task that was created and edited via CRMA

Keep in mind that record actions in CRMA support these objects and global actions:

- Create and update object records.
- Log a call.
- Custom actions to trigger Lightning components, flows, and Visualforce pages.
- Lightning components that use Lightning events are supported in embedded dashboards but are not supported in Analytics Studio.
- Standard Chatter actions, excluding *File*.

Global quick actions and canvas apps are not supported in CRMA configured record actions. CRMA does not support actions assigned to a page layout for the user object.

As you saw briefly in *Chapter 10, To Code, or Not to Code*, CRMA also offers the advanced functionality of bulk actions, where a group of records can be actioned in Salesforce with just a few clicks. However, as this is an advanced developer feature, it will not be covered in this book.

Let's now understand how to trigger an automation in Salesforce from CRMA.

Driving an automation in Salesforce from CRMA

There are many ways to kick off automations in Salesforce directly from CRMA without going into Salesforce. Here are three examples:

- Kick off a Lightning flow by creating a task that is configured in such a way as to trigger the flow.

- Create a case using a CRMA record action and set up an automation in Salesforce that uses the case (where the criteria is a predetermined case subject) to create and contain tasks that will bring that case to completion (a workflow example).

- Write information from CRMA back to a Salesforce record, where that updated field on the record triggers an automated process.

With the second example I gave, something as simple as a case subject of **Insurance Rollover** can trigger a Salesforce automation to create a case with related tasks and associated assignees, subjects, and due dates, as shown here:

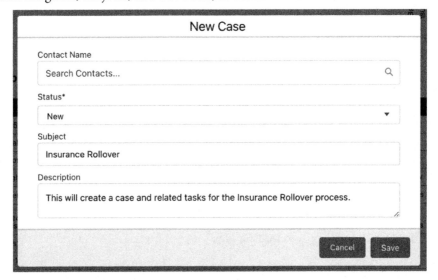

Figure 12.7 – Example of how a case created in CRMA can trigger a Salesforce automation

Now that you are capable with record actions, it is time to understand why and how to embed CRMA dashboards in Salesforce.

Embedded dashboards

The ability to easily embed a dashboard in Salesforce is one of the distinguishing features of CRMA. It sets CRMA apart from the crowd of BI tools out there. Let's see why it is important.

Why would you embed your dashboards?

One of the great struggles in the world of data analytics and business intelligence is *user adoption*. It is often the case that organizations spend hundreds of hours and many thousands of dollars on capturing, analyzing, and visualizing, only for the project to fail miserably because business users simply don't use and apply the insights.

One way to address poor user adoption is to embed the insights in front of the user in the CRM workflow, where they will inevitably view the dashboards as they work in their **Business As Usual** (**BAU**) environment. This is very different, and much more effective, than asking users to remember to review dashboards during their busy workdays, even if they are only a tab away in Salesforce. It really is a game changer for analytics adoption.

Here is an example that we created for one of our clients in the **Not-For-Profit** (**NFP**) space. In this use case, the NFP organization wanted insights about their donors added to the Salesforce home page and account record page. Once this was achieved, the usage of CRMA insights increased drastically, and users were able to action insights as a part of their daily BAU activity in Salesforce.

Here is the NFP home page with an embedded CRMA dashboard showcasing donor segmentation insights:

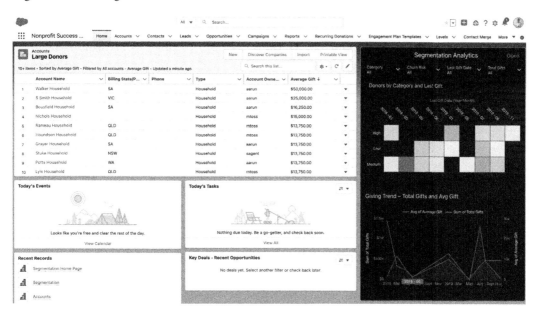

Figure 12. 8 – The NFP home page with an embedded CRMA dashboard on the right

Here is the account record with rich insights added from CRMA:

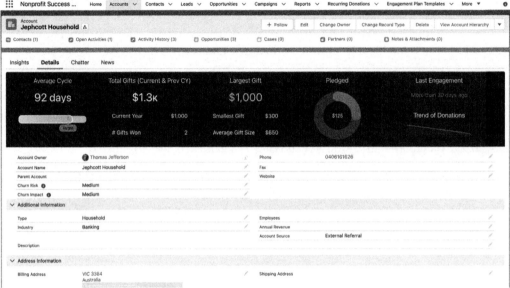

Figure 12.9 – The NFP account record page with an embedded CRMA dashboard

Is it difficult to embed CRMA dashboards in Salesforce? Do you need to be a developer? The answer to both questions is *no*. Let me show you how to embed your dashboards.

How do you embed your dashboards?

The best way to learn how to do embed dashboards is to do it, so follow these steps to embed a simple dashboard on the account record page in Salesforce:

1. Create a new blank dashboard and save it as `Mini Sales Insights` in **My First Analytics App**.

2. Create and add a chart for sales by close date month.

3. Create and add a chart for the pipeline by close date month.

4. Save your dashboard.

The end result should look like this:

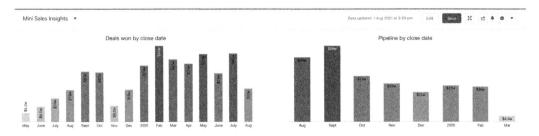

Figure 12.10 – The Mini Sales Insights dashboard

Now, let's go ahead and embed this dashboard on the account record page in Salesforce. Follow these steps:

1. Open any account record in Salesforce.

2. Click on the **Setup** gear icon at the top right of the page.

3. Click on **Edit Page**. You are now in the Lightning App Builder.

4. From the list of components on the left, select the **CRM Analytics Dashboard** component and drag it onto the canvas below the highlights panel.

5. Go into the component format panel on the right and make sure that **Dashboard** shows as **Mini Sales Insights**.

6. Adjust the **Height** value for the component so that the CRMA dashboard fits nicely on the page layout. For my example, this was a height of 400.

7. Leave the other options as they are.

8. The dashboard is ready, except that it will show information for all accounts, and we want it to show only information for the account record being displayed. To add a filter that will accomplish this, click on **Add Dashboard Filter**.

9. Select **Opportunities** under **Dataset**.

10. Select **Account ID** under **Dataset Field**.

11. Select **Equals** as **Operator**.

12. Select **Account > Id** under **Object Field**.

13. Click on **OK**.

14. Click on **Save**.

15. Activate the account record page and click on **Assign as Org Default**.

16. Go back to the account page in Salesforce (the left arrow in the top-left corner in the Lightning App Builder).

The format panel for the CRMA dashboard Lightning component should look like this:

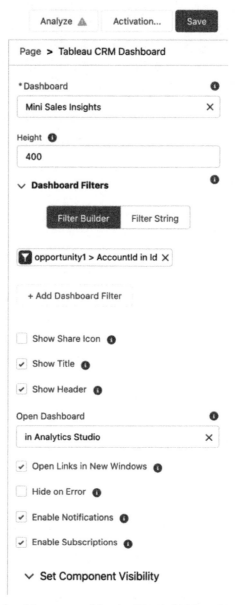

Figure 12.11 – Completed format panel for the CRMA dashboard Lightning component

It is also worth noting that the visibility of the CRMA component can be controlled from this format panel, where filters can be added, they control whether or not the embedded dashboard is visible to the logged-in user. These filters are based upon record fields or the device being used.

To best see the result, find and select an account that has some opportunity data, such as the following example:

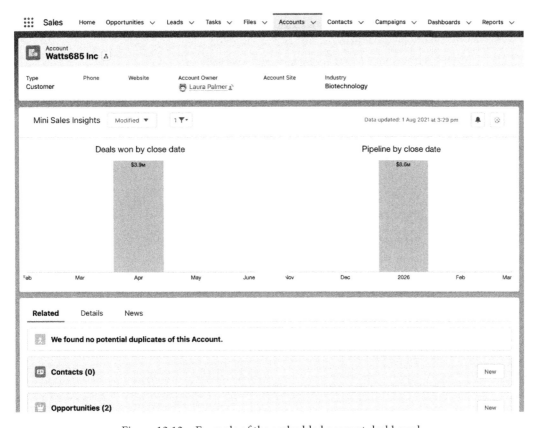

Figure 12.12 – Example of the embedded account dashboard

You can also follow a similar process to embed a CRMA dashboard on the Salesforce home page.

Let's review what we learned in this chapter.

Summary

What did you learn in this chapter? First, you learned how to create record actions for your CRMA dashboard. Then, you gained some insight into how to kick off automations in Salesforce from a CRMA dashboard. Third, I explained why embedded dashboards are a powerful aid to dashboard adoption. Finally, you learned how to embed a CRMA dashboard on a Salesforce record page.

I trust that this book has been a help to you, wherever you may be on your CRMA journey. I encourage you to dive into the platform and use it in real-world use cases, because the best way to learn is to solve problems, build assets, and deliver solutions. Make sure that you get involved in the vibrant CRMA online community, and avail yourself of the many great online resources available for CRMA.

Please feel free to reach out to me via LinkedIn with any feedback or questions about my book or CRMA in general. I would love to hear from you!

Questions

Answer the following questions to test your learning from this chapter:

- How do embedded dashboards aid user adoption of CRMA?

- Give three examples of configured record actions supported in CRMA.

- What is the purpose of the dashboard filter when embedding a CRMA dashboard via the Lightning App Builder?

- Give one example of how you can drive an automation in Salesforce from CRMA.

Questions and Answers

Chapter 1

- Define data analytics and what value it offers.

  Data analytics is gathering, understanding, sharing, and actioning data. It enables an organization to gain value from their data and obtain actionable business insights.

  Our goal is to go from data to insight to **action**.

- Name five features listed for CRMA.

  - Native, two-way integration with the Salesforce CRM platform

  - On-platform data extraction, combination, and transformation in the data manager

  - External connectivity to a variety of other platforms and cloud storage providers

  - Data visualization, analysis, and exploration

  - A data action framework to enable decision making based upon insights

- How does CRMA differ from Tableau?

  Tableau is used to analyze and visualize data from anywhere; CRMA provides a native Salesforce experience and optimizes Salesforce data.

- What are five practical use cases for CRMA?

  - Sales performance, such as actuals and forecast versus target

  - Lead conversion by lead source, region, and team member

  - ROI on marketing campaigns

  - Case management and service team performance

  - Global sales breakdown by region, territory, and country

- How does CRMA provide value to your organization or clients?

  This is an organization-specific answer.

- Does your organization excel at data analytics? If not, what is preventing it from doing so?

  This is an organization-specific answer.

Chapter 2

- What is a CRMA asset? Give one example.

  A CRMA asset is any one of four key items: dashboard, story, lens, or dataset.

- How can a CRMA app be shared?

  One of three ways:

  - Give access via CRMA.

  - Post to a Chatter feed.

  - Share via the app URL.

- What is a CRMA lens?

  A lens is a self-contained exploration of data; one query with a visualization or table.

- True or False – a CRMA app is restricted to standard, OOTB settings.

  False.

- What is the purpose of the "Favorites" link on the side menu of the CRMA home page?

  You can choose to favorite any CRMA asset, such as a dataset or lens, and add it to this list for ease of access.

- What do you do if the OOTB CRMA apps don't meet your requirements, even after you have customized them?

  CRMA is incredibly flexible and enables the custom development of assets.

- How do you turn on CRMA in a Salesforce environment?

  You can enable CRMA by going to **Setup | Analytics | Getting Started** and switching it on.

Chapter 3

- What is meant by data sync?

  Data sync refers to the process whereby data is staged for dataflows and recipes.

- Name five remote data connections available for CRMA.

  - External Salesforce org

  - NetSuite

  - Marketo

  - Google Analytics

  - Amazon Redshift

- What is the dataset builder used for – to create a dataset from Salesforce data, from external data, or both?

  To create a dataset from Salesforce data

- When working in the dataset builder, why is it important to make sure that you select any ID fields that will be required for adding object relationships?

  It is important to make sure that you select any ID fields that will be required to add object relationships to the dataset, otherwise the related objects will have no key to link to.

- What common error was given when editing dataset field attributes?

  Incorrectly classifying dimensions as measures

Chapter 4

- What is a data recipe, and when should you use it?

  A CRMA data recipe is used to join multiple datasets into one and to prepare, clean, and transform data with smart suggestions, column profiles, and powerful transformations. Recipes are perfect for Salesforce administrators or analysts with little to no data integration experience who want guidance on how to clean data, with the added benefit of previewing transformation results. Recipes are also a powerful tool for experienced data ninjas who want to create datasets using a no-code, visual interface.

- When would you need to append data in a recipe?

  Appending data is used when you need to add rows from one dataset, or multiple datasets, to another.

- What types of dataset joins are available in the recipe editor?

  Lookup, left join, right join, inner join, or full outer join

- Where can you find common calculations?

  Common calculations have their own function buttons in the Transform toolbar – these fill in the formula with the correct column and syntax for you.

- What is one real-world use case for the bucket transformation?

  Buckets are a useful tool when you want to create a heat map from two measures.

- Explain the Detect Sentiment transformation.

  It is used to determine the sentiment of text, whether positive, negative, or neutral, and adds those values to the specified column.

- Fill in the blanks:

  You must indicate the field that contains every **field** in the data hierarchy and also the field that contains the analogous **node** based on the hierarchy in order to compose the Flatten transformation. This will create one record for every hierarchy node, which is referred to as the **child** node.

  The Split transformation always creates **two** new columns.

Chapter 5

- What is the difference between a lookup join, an inner join, and a full join?

  The following list highlights the key differences between these joins:

  - The lookup source on the right is the User object, and the left data stream is the recipe dataset. Any user record that matches the user ID in the recipe dataset will return information relating to the user and augment it to the recipe dataset without adding any rows.

  - The inner join is used to create the intersection, or overlap, of two data sources, where only rows that match both data streams are included.

  - A full join is used when you want to include a record for every combination.

- Give one real-world example of how to use a full join.

  You want to combine products and product families and cater to every viable combination.

- Why would you need to connect data from external sources with Salesforce objects? Give one practical example.

You want to connect order data from an external ERP and join it with sales data in Salesforce so that you can compare pipelines, done deals, and actuals.

- Explain how to combine aggregation and grouping using two data streams in one recipe.

You can create a number of data streams in the Data Prep flow, perform aggregation and roll up in each stream as required, and then rejoin these streams and augment the granular data using a join node.

- The option for Multiple Row Formula must be selected to perform window functions – what are window functions? When might you use them?

Window functions are employed in a Data Prep recipe to perform calculations across rows, as opposed to across columns. One example use case is to calculate the change in opportunity amount over time using the lag function based upon a snapshot date.

- What is the flatten transformation, and what is a use case for this?

The flatten transformation flattens ranked data for a hierarchy into two columns. You can flatten data in preparation for use in security predicates.

Chapter 6

- What does a lens enable you to do?

The following list highlights the various things that can be done with a lens:

  - Explore the various characteristics of your dataset, including dimensions, measures, field labels, and names.

  - Slice and dice data using various measures, dimensions, filters, and formulas.

  - Create visualizations and tables that can be clipped to a dashboard.

  - Create visualizations and tables that can be shared with other users.

- What is the purpose of the Clip command for lenses?

If a dashboard is open in the dashboard editor, the lens is clipped, or exported, to the dashboard as a widget.

- Name one use of a pivot table.

Subtotaling and aggregating numeric data, and summarizing data by categories and subcategories.

- How might you use a scatter plot chart?

  Demonstration of the relationship between two variables. A combo chart? To visualize two measures on one timeline. A flat gauge? Showing progress to a target value.

- How can you share a lens?

  One of five ways:

  - Give access.

  - Post to a feed.

  - Export to Anywhere doc.

  - Get a URL.

  - Download.

- What is the purpose of Query mode?

  Query mode utilizes SAQL to query your data.

- What are three uses for a compare table?

  The three uses for a compare table are as follows:

  - Add calculations and filters to your table.

  - Perform arithmetic across the columns and rows.

  - Create labels by manipulating string values.

Chapter 7

- What is the purpose of app-level security in CRMA?

  It is used to govern access to the assets within the app – lenses, datasets, and dashboards.

- How can you control CRMA security from Salesforce object and field access?

  The administrator can configure permissions on Salesforce objects and fields to implement object-level and field-level security and therefore control access to Salesforce data. CRMA gains access to Salesforce data based upon the permissions of two system CRMA/Salesforce users: the Integration user and the Security user. Restricting access for these users via security profiles in Salesforce is how you can control CRMA security from Salesforce object and field access.

- When a dataflow job runs, CRMA uses the permissions of the **Integration** user to extract data from Salesforce objects and fields.

- What are three limitations of Salesforce sharing inheritance?

  The following list highlights the limitations:

  - It can be applied only if all supported object records have fewer than 400 sharing descriptors each.

  - It can impede the performance of queries, dataflows, and Data Prep recipes.

  - In order for an object to appear in the security-sharing source list, the primary key of the custom object must be a field in the dataset.

- What are three use case scenarios for security predicates?

  You can control data visibility via:

  - Role hierarchy

  - Manager hierarchy

  - User territory

- A security predicate expression must not exceed how many characters?

  5,000

- Is this a valid predicate expression? Why, or why not? "Revenue">100

  No; there must be at least one space between the dataset column and the operator, between the operator and the value, and before and after logical operators.

- A security predicate expression is case-sensitive – True or False?

  True

Chapter 8

- If you want a colleague to access a particular view of a dashboard and drill into the data, how would you share it with them?

  Use a sharing URL.

- What is the purpose of the "Copy widget to clipboard" command?

  It copies a widget, or several widgets, to the clipboard for pasting anywhere on a dashboard.

- What is the recommended number of default columns for a dashboard?

  50

- When you move from one dashboard page to another, do any filters applied to the first page remain in place?

  Yes

- How could you use the container widget in a dashboard?

  The container widget can be used to create a highlights panel that can be moved and resized as one item containing a group of widgets.

- What is meant by a top-down dashboard design, and how is it facilitated by CRMA pages?

  A versatile, top-down design for a dashboard using CRMA pages overcomes several obstacles and provides a simple, flexible interface for slicing and dicing data.

- The Clone Query command clones the query and opens it for **editing**.

Chapter 9

- Give three examples of use cases for using CRMA pages.

  Pages can be used to zoom in and out of charts for further analysis, reveal greater detail on a hero chart, or facilitate data segmentation.

- When you move from page to page within a dashboard, do the applied filters remain, or are they cleared?

  They remain.

- When might you need SAQL?

  You may use SAQL when you need to do custom calculations, advanced data manipulations on the fly, co-grouping (joining) data from different datasets, top/bottom lists, in conjunction with binding for dynamic values on charts, and so on.

- Keywords and functions are written in uppercase, and they are not case-sensitive. True or False?

  False

- Where do you edit SAQL?

  Every step of a lens is SAQL-based, so it can be edited and/or custom SAQL added. These can be viewed in JSON editor mode or copied to a JSON editor of your choice.

- What keyboard shortcut do you use to access the dashboard JSON?

  Command or Ctrl + E.

- Give three examples of use cases for bindings to make a dashboard more interactive and dynamic.

  - Dynamic reference lines

  - Dynamic groupings

  - Dynamic measures

Chapter 10

Fill in the blanks:

- Security **predicates**
- Bindings in the **JSON**
- SAQL **expressions**
- Bulk actions (using **Visualforce** and the CRMA REST API)
- **Timeseries** (modified)
- XMD – advanced **formatting** options

Chapter 11

Fill in the blanks:

- Choose your **chart** types carefully.
- Never seek to put all the available **information** on the same page.
- Utilize a small number of **colors** and **shades**.
- Make the dashboard as easy to **use** as possible.
- Employ wise **layout** choices.
- Always provide **context** for your insights.
- Keep things **simple**.
- Balance functionality with **creativity** – effective does not imply boring.
- Supply the user with the level of **detail** required and no more.
- Understand **how** and **where** the dashboard will be used.

338 Questions and Answers

Chapter 12

- How do embedded dashboards aid user adoption of CRMA?

  You embed the insights in front of the user in the CRM workflow, where they will inevitably view the dashboards as they work in their **business as usual** (**BAU**) environment.

- Give three examples of configured record actions supported in CRMA.

  - Create and update object records.

  - Log a call.

  - Custom actions to trigger Lightning components, flows, and Visualforce Pages.

- What is the purpose of the dashboard filter when embedding a CRMA dashboard via Lightning App Builder?

  When an embedded dashboard is ready in the layout, it will show information for all accounts, and you want it to show only information for the account record being displayed. Adding a dashboard filter will accomplish this.

- Give one example of how you can drive automation in Salesforce from CRMA.

  Kick off a Lightning flow by creating a task that is configured in such a way as to trigger the flow.

Other Books You May Enjoy

If you enjoyed this book, you may be interested in these other books by Packt:

Maximizing Tableau Server

Patrick Sarsfield, Brandi Locker

ISBN: 9781801071130

- Get well-versed in Tableau Server's interface to quickly and easily access essential content
- Explore the different types of content and navigate through the project hierarchy quickly
- Understand how to connect, publish, manage, and modify content on Tableau Server
- Discover how to share content and collaborate with others
- Automate tedious tasks by creating custom views, alerts, subscriptions, and data refresh schedules
- Build data visualizations using Web Edit
- Understand how to monitor disparate metrics on multiple dashboards

Extending Power BI with Python and R

Luca Zavarella

ISBN: 9781801078207

- Discover best practices for using Python and R in Power BI products
- Use Python and R to perform complex data manipulations in Power BI
- Apply data anonymization and data pseudonymization in Power BI
- Log data and load large datasets in Power BI using Python and R
- Enrich your Power BI dashboards using external APIs and machine learning models
- Extract insights from your data using linear optimization and other algorithms
- Handle outliers and missing values for multivariate and time-series data
- Create any visualization, as complex as you want, using R scripts

Packt is searching for authors like you

If you're interested in becoming an author for Packt, please visit authors.packtpub.com and apply today. We have worked with thousands of developers and tech professionals, just like you, to help them share their insight with the global tech community. You can make a general application, apply for a specific hot topic that we are recruiting an author for, or submit your own idea.

Share Your Thoughts

Now you've finished *Creating Actionable Insights Using CRM Analytics*, we'd love to hear your thoughts! Scan the QR code below to go straight to the Amazon review page for this book and share your feedback or leave a review on the site that you purchased it from.

https://packt.link/r/1-801-07439-9

Your review is important to us and the tech community and will help us make sure we're delivering excellent quality content.

Index

T

U

V

W

Printed in Great Britain
by Amazon

83931202R00210